THE TYRANNY OF LIBERALISM

The Tyranny of Liberalism

Understanding and Overcoming
Administered Freedom, Inquisitorial Tolerance,
and Equality by Command

James Kalb

Wilmington, Delaware

Kalb, James.

The tyranny of liberalism : understanding and overcoming administered freedom, inquisitorial tolerance, and equality by command / James Kalb.—1st ed.— Wilmington, Del. : ISI Books, c2008.

     p. ; cm.
     ISBN: 978-1-933859-74-3 (cloth) ; 978-1-933859-82-8 (pbk.)
     Includes bibliographical references and index.

     1. Liberalism. 2. Political science. 3. Rationalism. I. Title.

JC574 .K35 2008
320.51—dc22

2008928617
0811

ISI Books
Intercollegiate Studies Institute
Post Office Box 4431
Wilmington, DE 19807-0431
www.isibooks.org

Manufactured in the United States of America

UXORI DILECTISSIMAE

Contents

Introduction

THIS IS A BOOK ABOUT THE TYRANNY OF LIBERALISM: WHAT IT IS, HOW IT comes about, what its implications are, and what to do about it.

Such a theme is unusual enough to call for explanation. To many readers it will seem odd to hear of the "tyranny of liberalism." After all, they will say, liberalism has always stood against tyranny, and in any event is too moderate and diverse a tendency to have any very definite consequences, let alone tyrannical ones.

Still, man is rational, at least to the extent that how he thinks has consequences. To understand human society we must be able, among other things, to talk about particular ways of thinking and to identify their effects. This book is intended as an exercise in that activity. It will be successful if it identifies a reasonably coherent and enduring tendency of thought that can be called "liberalism," if it articulates liberalism's sources and tendencies, and if it draws a persuasive connection between those tendencies and basic trends in social life. We need not claim that basic tendencies of thought determine everything to claim that they exist and determine *some* important things.

To say there is a "tyranny of liberalism" is to say that a particular way of understanding political, social, and moral life, one that treats freedom, equality, and satisfaction of preferences as final standards, has become overwhelmingly dominant in serious public discussion and in the self-understanding of major institutions. That way of understanding life is closely associated with ways of thinking characteristic of the modern natural sciences, so much so that many persons take for granted that liberalism is simply equivalent to moral and political rationality. Indeed, liberalism is allied with interests and institutions that benefit from it and increasingly try to bring all social relations in line with its standards of rationality and justification.

The argument of the first half of this book is that such an approach to political, social, and moral life excludes too much. It takes an overly technological approach to social life and has no way to deal with the natural tendencies, particular connections, and higher goals that are an essential part of human existence. Liberal assumptions and ideas cause social authorities to lose touch with human reality, to supplant and suppress informal and traditional institutions such as the family, and eventually to overreach and become tyrannical, self-contradictory, and self-destructive. The common good, along with justice and liberty, demand a basically different approach. The second half of the book attempts to outline such an approach, one that makes much more room than liberalism now permits for tradition, religion, particularity, and transcendence. It includes a defense of the reasonableness of such things, and indeed of their necessity for a rational way of life.

Liberalism so surrounds us that it is hard to imagine an alternative. Even those who see difficulties with it almost never reject it fundamentally, but attempt to reinvent it in one way or another. Complaints that liberalism is not really free, equal, or democratic end not in its abandonment as misconceived and unworkable, but in proposals for some more authentic form of freedom, equality, and popular rule, and thus in a call for a more liberal liberalism. In contrast, traditionalist concerns about cultural degradation and deterioration of fine-grained social order are treated as secondary matters and handled by appeals to creativity, therapy, or ad hoc stopgaps.

Many readers are therefore likely to reject out of hand complaints about liberalism in general. In many cases their objections must be answered before the discussion can proceed in a way that makes sense to them. However, each will have his own objections, and they cannot all be dealt with first. In addition, those sympathetic to my point of view would be puzzled and bored by a presentation that starts off dealing with objections rather than giving a positive account of the matters under consideration. For the benefit of more sympathetic readers, I have laid out the discussion in the way that seems most natural to me, putting my positive account first and answering objections later. Those less sympathetic may want to change the order in which they read the book, and refer early on to sections dealing with objections they find crippling. In particular, those who want to know what specifically I mean by "liberalism" and why I treat it as a continuing and coherent active principle may want to refer to "What is Liberalism," "Transformations," and "Importance of Principles" in chapter 2 and "Ideas Have Consequences" in chapter 5. The latter chapter also deals with other objections—for example, claims that liberalism cannot be tyrannical because liberal government deals only with a narrow range of human concerns, or that to reject liberalism would be morally indecent.

Responses to objections can of course themselves meet with objections. In the case of a topic that has been discussed as voluminously as liberalism, the more important the point the more varied and complex the arguments are likely to have become. A comparatively short essay that covers a vast territory can hardly do more than lay out main lines of argument in the hope of initiating discussions that may be fruitful. Even that effort is likely to fall far short in the eyes of those who approach the matter with fundamentally different perspectives and commitments. Most readers of this book will (like myself) have been raised in a liberal society, surrounded by liberal influences, schooled in liberal ways of thinking, and affected by the political and social developments of recent decades. Each, then, has the basic knowledge needed to judge my descriptions and interpretations for himself. I hope that those who remain unsympathetic, while voicing whatever criticisms they think decisive, will consider whether my efforts advance discussion by clarifying and connecting a number of common objections to the understanding of political, social, and moral life now dominant. Naturally, I hope also to find sympathetic readers whose thoughts this book can clarify and systematize. It is for such readers that this book is first of all meant.

Part I
Decline and Fall

CHAPTER ONE

Liberal Tyranny

―――――――――――

"THE TYRANNY OF LIBERALISM" SEEMS A PARADOX. LIBERALS SAY THAT they favor freedom, reason, and the well-being of ordinary people. Many people consider them high-minded and fair to a fault, "too broadminded to take their own side in a quarrel," too soft to govern effectively. Even the word "liberal" suggests "liberty." How can such an outlook and the social order it promotes be tyrannical?

The answer is that wanting freedom is not the same as having it. Political single-mindedness leads to oppression, and a tyranny of freedom and equality is no less possible than one of virtue or religion. We cannot be forced to be free or made equal by command, but since the French Revolution the attempt has become all too common and the results have often been tyrannical.

Tyranny is not, of course, what liberals have intended. They want government to be based on equal freedom, which they see as the only possible goal of a just and rational public order. But the functioning of any form of political society is determined more by the logic of its principles than the intentions of its supporters. Liberals view themselves as idealistic and progressive, but such a self-image conceals dangers even if it is not wholly illusory. It leads liberals to ignore considerations, like human nature and fundamental social and religious traditions, that have normally been treated as limits on reform. Freedom and equality are abstract, open-ended, and ever-ramifying goals that can be taken to extremes. Liberals tend to view these goals as a simple matter of justice and rationality that prudential considerations may sometimes delay but no principle can legitimately override. In the absence of definite limiting principles, liberal demands become more and more far-reaching and the means used to advance them ever more comprehensive, detailed, and intrusive.

The incremental style of liberalism obscures the radicalism of what it eventually demands and enables it always to present itself as moderate. What is called progress—in effect, movement to the left—is thought normal in present-day society, so to stand in its way, let alone to try to reverse accepted changes, is thought radical and divisive. We have come to accept that what was inconceivable last week is mainstream today and altogether basic tomorrow. The result is that the past is increasingly discredited, deviancy is defined up or down, and it becomes incredible that, for instance, until 1969 high school gun-club members took their guns to school on New York City subways, and that in 1944 there were only forty-four homicides by gunshot in the entire city.[1]

Human life is harder to change than are proclaimed social standards. It is easier to denounce gender stereotypes than to make little boys and little girls the same. The triumph of liberalism in public discussion and the consequent disappearance of openly avowed nonliberal principles has led the outlook officially established to embody liberal views ever more completely and at the same time to diverge more and more from the permanent conditions of human life. The result has been a growing conflict between public standards and the normal human understandings that make commonsense judgments and good human relations possible.

The conflict between public standards and normal understandings has transformed and disordered such basic aspects of social life as politics, which depends on free and rational discussion; the family, which counts on a degree of harmony between public understandings and natural human tendencies; and scholarship, which relies on complex formal rules while attempting to explain reality. As a consequence, family life is chaotic and ill-tempered; young people are badly instructed and badly raised; politics are irrational, trivial, and mindlessly partisan; and scholarship is shoddy and disconnected from normal experience. Terms such as "zero tolerance" and "political correctness" reveal how an official outlook deeply at odds with normal ways of thinking has become oppressive while claiming to have reached an unprecedented level of fairness and rationality.

In a society that claims to be based on free speech and reason, intelligent discussion of many aspects of life has become all but impossible. Such a state of affairs is no passing fluke but a serious matter resulting from basic principles. It is the outcome of rationalizing and egalitarian trends that over time have become ever more self-conscious and all-embracing until they now make normal informal distinctions—for example, those between the sexes—seem intolerably arbitrary and unfair. Those trends have led to the politically correct managerial liberal regime that now dominates Western public life and makes demands that more and more people find unreasonable and even incomprehensible.[2]

What defines that regime is the effort to manage and rationalize social life in order to bring it in line with comprehensive standards aimed at implementing equal freedom. The result is a pattern of governance intended to promote equality and individual gratification and marked by entitlement programs, sexual and expressive freedoms, blurred distinctions between the public and the private, and the disappearance of self-government. To implement such a program of social transformation an extensive system of controls over social life has grown up, sometimes public and sometimes formally private, that appeals for its justification to expertise, equity, safety, security, and the need to modify social attitudes and relationships in order to eliminate discrimination and intolerance.

The last are never clearly defined, but in practice they turn out to include all attitudes and distinctions that affect the order of social life but cannot be brought fully in line with market or bureaucratic principles, and so from the standpoint of those principles are simply irrational. "Discrimination and intolerance" are thus held to include those attitudes, habits, and ties—sex roles, historical loyalties, authoritative cultural understandings, religious commitments and teachings—on which independent, informal, traditional, and nonmarket institutions and arrangements normally rely in order to function and endure.

Because such arrangements operate on principles that are regarded as irrational, and because they are difficult to supervise and control in the interest of rationality and equal freedom, they have no place in advanced liberal society and are edged out as the social order progresses. The normal functioning of the institutions of liberal society has precisely that effect. Social-welfare programs reduce the need for institutions and ties other than the state bureaucracy and various market and contractual arrangements, while "inclusiveness" abolishes the relation between the workings of society and any specific religious, cultural, or sexual standards. Only rational formal institutions remain functional and authoritative. What were once traditional social institutions with definite form, function, and authority become personal pursuits that each can make of what he wishes so long as all others remain free to participate or abstain as they will. Marriage and family are replaced by "relationships" and "living together"; religion becomes a freeform pursuit of individual fulfillment; and inherited culture becomes an optional consumer good, a matter of personal style or group assertiveness.

Such tendencies make it impossible to deal reasonably on their own terms with issues of identity, such as sex, kinship, ethnicity, and religion. Those distinctions play no role in the liberal understanding of rational social functioning, so they are understood as pure principles of irrational opposition and hatred: absolute, unbridgeable, and impossible to reconcile with a peaceful, just, and efficient social order. The consequence is that they must effectively be abolished—trivialized, conceptually dissolved, canceled through reverse discrimination, or kept from entering into thought at all.

Under the regime of liberalism, the way in which people have traditionally understood themselves and others now can have no bearing on their relations to each other, at least to the extent that those relations have substantive consequences. *Who* you are can have no connection to *how* things are with you, except to the extent that "who you are" refers to your relation to institutions liberalism accepts as authoritative. A man and woman have to be the same, but a Harvard and state-university graduate can be different. The result is the forcible imposition on everyone of a wholly abstract and radically depersonalized order that abolishes the connections and distinctions by which human beings have always lived in favor of more formal ones such as wealth, education, and bureaucratic position. Factually considered, that new order is unequal and unfree, but it is able to pass itself off as an indisputable application of neutral principles to which no sane and moral person could possibly object.

Advanced liberalism has become an immensely powerful social reality. Liberal standards for human rights and government procedures are widely viewed as universally obligatory, at least in principle, and no competitor has comparable general appeal as a way of organizing social life. The technically rational organization of the world to give each of us as much as possible of what he wants is quite generally accepted as the correct guiding ideal for politics and social morality. Pluralism, the fight against discrimination, and an ethic of "caring" are accepted as political, social, and moral imperatives. And administrative and therapeutic intervention in all aspects of social life is considered the self-evident means of vindicating them. Such views are especially strong in the societies that have been enduringly successful in modern times, and among the intelligent, well-educated, and well-placed, most of whom believe them a matter of simple justice and rationality and can conceive of no other legitimate outlook. Concerns about self-government, moral traditions, and inherited loyalties do not carry anything close to the same weight. To make a serious issue of such concerns is regarded as a sign of ignorance or psychological or moral defect.

In spite of serious chronic problems that no one knows how to attack—extraordinarily low natality, rising costs of social-welfare programs, growing immigrant populations that do not assimilate—basic change seems unthinkable. No matter how pressing the problem, only analyses and solutions compatible with liberal positions are allowed in the public square. Almost all serious discussion is carried on through academic and other institutions that are fully integrated with the ruling order, and in any case antidiscrimination rules make wholehearted subscription to principles such as inclusiveness the only way to avoid legal and public relations problems that would make institutional life impossible. Genuine political discussion disappears. What pass as battles between liberals and conservatives are almost always disputes between different stages or tendencies within liberalism itself.

So dominant is liberalism that it becomes invisible. Judges feel free to read it into the law without historical or textual warrant because it seems so obviously right. To oppose it in any basic way is to act incomprehensibly, in a way explicable, it is thought, only by reference to irrationality, ignorance, or evil. The whole of the nonliberal past is comprehensively blackened. Traditional ways are presented as the simple negation of unquestionable goods liberalism favors. Obvious declines in civility, morality, and cultural achievement are ignored, denied, or redefined as advances. Violence is said to be the fault of the persistence of sex roles, war of religion, theft of social inequality, suicide of stereotyping. Destruction of sex and historical community as ordering principles—and thus of settled family arrangements and cultural forms—is presented as a supremely desirable goal. The clear connection among the decline of traditional habits, standards, and social ties; the disintegration of institutions like the family; and other forms of personal and social disorder is ignored or treated as beside the point.

Many people find something deeply oppressive about the resulting situation, but no one really knows what to say about it. Some complain about those general restrictions, like political correctness, which make honest and productive discussion of public affairs impossible. Others have more concrete and personal objections. Parents are alarmed by the indoctrination of their children. Many people complain about affirmative action, massive and uncontrolled immigration, and the abolition of the family as a distinct social institution publicly recognized as fundamental and prior to the state. Still others have the uneasy sense that the world to which they are attached and which defines who they are is being taken from them.

Nonetheless, *these* victims and their complaints get no respect and little media coverage.[3] Their discontent remains inarticulate and obscure. People feel stifled, but cannot say just how. They make jokes or sarcastic comments, but when challenged have trouble explaining and defending themselves. The disappearance of common understandings that enable serious thought and action to be carried on by nonexperts and outside formal bureaucratic structures has made it hard even to think about the issues coherently. The result is a system of puzzled compliance. However ineffective the schools become, educators feel compelled to inculcate multicultural platitudes rather than to promote substantive learning. No matter how silly people find celebrations of "diversity," they become ever more frequent and surround themselves ever more insistently with happy talk.

Attempts to challenge the liberal hegemony occasionally emerge but always fail. No challenge seems possible when all social authorities that might compete with bureaucracy, money, and expertise have been discredited, co-opted, or radically weakened. When populist complaints make their half-articulate way into public life they are recognized as dangerous to the established order, debunked as ignorant and hateful, and quickly diverted or suppressed. Proponents of the standards now current always have the last word. Freedom, equality, and neutral expertise are the basis of those standards, and when discussion is put on that ground it is difficult to argue for anything contrary. Rejection of equal freedom and of expertise is oppressive and ignorant by definition, so how could it possibly be justified?

At bottom, the problem with the standards that now govern public life is that they deny natural human tendencies and so require constant nagging interference in all aspects of life. They lead to a denatured society that does not work and does not feel like home. A standard liberal response to such objections is that our reactions are wrong: we should accept what we are told by those who know better. Expertise must rule. Social attitudes, habits, and connections, it is said, are not natural but constructed. They are continually revised and reenacted, their function and significance change with circumstances, and their meaning is a matter of interpretation and choice. It follows that habits and attitudes that seem solidly established and even natural cannot claim respect apart from their conformity with justice—which, if prejudice and question-begging are to be avoided, can only be defined as equality. All habits and attitudes must be conformed to egalitarianism and expertise. To object would be bigoted or ignorant.

But why should we trust those said to know better in such matters? Visions of an emancipated future are not necessarily wiser than nostalgia for a virtuous past. If all past societies have been sinks of oppression, as we are now told, it is not clear why our rulers are likely to change the situation. They understand the basic problems of life no better than the Sumerians did. They are technically more advanced, but technology is simply the application of means to ends. Tyrants, who know exactly what they want, can make good use of technique, and if clever they will pass their actions off as liberation.

Advanced liberalism fosters an inert and incompetent populace, a pervasive state, and commercial institutions responsible mainly to themselves. Alas, the state generally botches large-scale undertakings, commerce is proverbially self-interested, and formal expertise is more successful with small issues that can be studied in detail than with the big issues that make life what it is. Experts can treat appendicitis, but they cannot give us a reason to live. They can provide the factual content of instruction, but they cannot tell us what things are worth knowing. Why, then, treat their authority as absolute?

We should not accept the official, and "expert," debunking of ordinary ways of thought. While popular habits and attitudes can be presented as a compound of prejudice and self-interest, so can official and expert views. Both expertise and the state are immensely powerful social institutions. They have their own interests, and there is no reason to trust them any more than drug companies or defense contractors in matters that affect their own status and position. Expertise is only a refinement of common sense, upon which it continues to depend for its sanity and usefulness. Thought depends on habits, attitudes, and understandings that we mostly pick up from other people and that cannot be verified except in parts. It cannot be purified of habit and preconception and still touch our world. Ordinary good sense must remain the final standard of judgment. Good sense, however, is the business not of experts and officials but of the public at large.

In fact, advanced liberal society is reproducing the error of socialism—the attempt to administer and radically alter things that are too complex to be known, grasped, and controlled—but on a far grander scale. The socialists tried to simplify and rationalize economics, while today's liberals are trying to do the same with human relations generally. The latter involve much more subtle, complicated, and fundamental aspects of human life. Why expect the results to be better? A look at what is on television or a conversation with an older schoolteacher is likely to suggest that the attempt to reconstruct life on abstract content-free principles has actually made life worse. The test must be experience. If the people in charge of affairs are so competent and intelligent, why the increasing cynicism about politics? Why the decline in so many aspects of social and cultural life?

We need not accept, as inevitable social change, what the state and its experts decide for us. When major institutions persistently act in ineffective or destructive ways while praising themselves for unprecedented justice and rationality, there is evidently something wrong with the outlook guiding them. For a better way of life to become possible we need to free ourselves from the views that are now conventional and find a different perspective. The problems of public life today go too deep for technical fixes. A fundamental critique of the principles accepted as authoritative is necessary so that our life together can fall more in line with what people find natural, comprehensible, and satisfying. The intention of this book is to promote such a critique and to explore alternatives.

CHAPTER TWO

Principles

Liberalism establishes a general schema for life in society that has thoroughly triumphed in the West and finds substantial acceptance elsewhere. Informal, tradition-based resistance to its claims has weakened and grown ever more inarticulate. Explicit movements of opposition—populism, radical Islam, East Asian authoritarianism—remain influential in some places, but they are localized and fall far short of the power, determination, and universal ambition of the radical antiliberal movements of the last century, such as Marxism and fascism.

So successful is liberalism, both politically and intellectually, that its triumph has led to a practical, and sometimes explicit, belief in the end of history.[1] In this sense, history is understood as the story of struggle against the oppression that preceded the coming of the advanced liberal state, the form of human association whose universal unconditional validity, manifested by enlightened judicial decisions and international human-rights conventions, makes history and particular culture irrelevant.

What Is Liberalism?

Such triumphalism would be impossible if liberalism were not a well-defined system that has become altogether dominant in Western political thought and public life. The overwhelming dominance of liberalism must reflect great strengths, including a persuasive set of fundamental principles deeply rooted in modern Western life. Before discussing those principles, however, it will be helpful to expand on what I mean by "liberalism."

From the perspective adopted in this book, liberalism is equivalent to the political, social, and moral understandings now most authoritative in the West. The term thus refers to the present Western governing consensus regarding the appropriate means and ends of government and social organization, to the abstract understandings behind that consensus, to the institutions and practices to which it gives rise, and to the liberal political and intellectual tradition that has led to all those things, at least when its history is recounted from an American perspective. That tradition begins with Thomas Hobbes and John Locke and extends through classical liberalism to John Rawls and beyond. It provides the common ground for American political discussion. At times the term "liberal" is also used, if there seems no danger of confusion, to refer more specifically to those who stand most clearly for liberalism so defined, and who are best able to claim to be enlightened and progressive and to dominate serious discussion of social and political issues.

The dominant features and tendencies of the system to which the liberal tradition has led can be illuminated by referring them to a very simple principle: equal freedom. As an ultimate standard, equal freedom rests on a denial of the political relevance of realities that transcend human experience and precede human choice. In the broad sense, all mainstream Western politicians are liberal today. Each claims to accept popular consent as the basis of government. Each promises above all to promote some combination of freedom, equality, and the satisfaction of preferences, in the form of prosperity, opportunity, security, consumer and worker protection, and so on. Other goals, such as "national greatness," "traditional values," or "God's will," are mentioned on occasion, but they are mainly symbolic, clearly subordinate, and opportunistically put forward. They also attract severe criticism in academic circles and the mainstream media unless they are clearly used as synonyms for liberalism and put forward for the purpose of co-opting alternative understandings of politics and bringing them into its service. As an example, "religion in politics" is thought good when the civil-rights movement does it but not when the prolife movement does it, precisely because the goals of the former movement are those of liberalism, while those of the latter are not.

Development of Liberalism

The current situation is the outcome of a movement of thought and social change that has been at work for centuries and is still sufficiently coherent and functional to be treated as an important factor forming the social world around us. That movement has combined an emerging commitment to equal freedom as the standard for public life with an evolving set of beliefs and arrangements that have grown out of the interaction of that commitment with inherited institutions and understandings. As time has passed, established beliefs and institutions have come to assert the basic commitment to equal freedom ever more directly and comprehensively— that is what it means to say that liberalism has been progressive—until the movement has gone to extremes that are hard to recognize as such because they are so much in line with what has already been achieved.

Growth

The gradually expanding role of freedom and equality in political and social life can be traced back to the High Middle Ages. The first developments were gradual and unconscious. Freedom has long been an ideal in
the West, where slavery largely disappeared before modern times and the
position of the middle classes has been improving since the end of the Mag-
yar and Viking raids in the eleventh century. The Protestant Reformation
and its emphasis on individual conscience and the priesthood of all believers brought the ideal of equal freedom closer to self-awareness. Hobbes
and Locke, with their analysis of society as a contract among individuals
for material benefit, introduced liberalism as a distinct outlook that made
the ordinary practical concerns of individual men the basis of social order.
The Enlightenment developed and spread the view that social standards
are human creations to be judged by reason and re-created at will. And at
length, the American and French Revolutions and the founding of liberal
political parties made general extension of freedom and equality an explicit
goal of practical politics, a status it has retained ever since, either in a radical
Continental form or an initially more moderate Anglo-Saxon form.

The century just past saw liberalism achieve its final triumph at
the level of public principle, a triumph that has led to radicalization and
the exclusion of inconsistent views from public life. The First World War
signaled the end of religion and tradition as stated principles of order in
Europe. The conception of legitimacy that finally vanished in those years
depended on customs and religious establishments that were no longer
accepted as the basis of politics. With the fall of the great monarchies of
Central and Eastern Europe, authority could no longer be viewed as di-
vinely ordered or simply as part of the way things were. Instead, it had to
base itself on the will of the governed. In the absence of God and natural
order, the will of man became the source of all authority.

What followed displayed the implications of man's enthronement. The Second World War meant the victory of egalitarian economic concerns over attempts to appeal to particularities that make men and societies what they are: race, nation, the state as an aesthetic or organic whole. That victory was inevitable. Divorced from rooted popular belief in a higher order in which man's need for explanation could find satisfaction, the particularities for which the Axis fought were too arbitrary to ground a stable and coherent social order. Particularism that stood for nothing substantial beyond itself lacked direction and resorted to violence as a substitute for transcendence. In the absence of a believable God the Axis concocted ersatz deities out of blood, thunder, and whatever national symbols were at hand. Not surprisingly, the attempt did not work. Equal satisfaction of wants and a corresponding conception of equal human dignity seemed compellingly rational by comparison, and Allied victory meant the end of the European Right as a serious force.

Since 1945, Western public life has been based on the practical supremacy of economics and the principle that social order exists to get men what they want rather than to express an essence or ideal. The sixties completed the establishment of that principle by purging from public life remnants of older ways of thinking—for example, the notion that the social order should retain a grounding in Christian tradition. Before the sixties an appeal to Christianity could be a unifying move. Churchill could describe the fight against Hitler and later against communism as a fight for the survival of Christian civilization. Afterwards such references were declared divisive, a sign that governing elites no longer recognized Christian tradition as even residually authoritative.

The fall of the Berlin Wall demonstrated the definitive victory of liberalism over other principles thought progressive by marking the end of order based on collective rather than individual purposes. In the West, similar tendencies led to the decline of the traditional working-class economic Left and its replacement by a new lifestyle and multicultural Left. The death of socialism was the triumph of the principle that society is a field of impersonal technical rationality oriented toward the satisfaction of arbitrary individual desire. That triumph was also inevitable. Once wants had become the standard of goodness, and whatever could not be reduced to sensation and desire had been put radically in doubt, men became dubious of "the will of the people" and other invisible attributes of collectivities. They wanted proof before giving up their particular desires, and found the shopping mall a more compelling vision than New Soviet Man.

The year 1989 also meant loss of faith in History, refuted by the triumph in history of a radically abstract and individualistic and therefore ahistorical principle. History, with a capital H, had abolished its own significance and could no longer serve as a substitute religion. As a result of these developments—the death of God, the reduction of the human essence to desire and technological reason, the dissolution of "the people," the end of history as a meaningful process—no substantive conception of the common good can be presented as authoritative in present-day public life. Values are thought to be simply a matter of individual wants, and maximum equal satisfaction is the only moral principle recognized as binding. What remains of history, from a liberal standpoint, is a sort of endgame in which the implications of maximum equal satisfaction as a supreme principle are perfected at home while some combination of social evolution, transnational organization, electronic communication, global capitalism, and Western military power brings down whatever barriers remain to the establishment of a comprehensive liberal system throughout the world.

Maturity

The goal of today's liberalism is a universal, technically rational system for the equal satisfaction of desire that is to constitute the sole publicly authoritative form of human association. Ethnic and gender distinctions are to be deprived of all effect, religion banished from public life, and a worldwide order established—based on world markets and transnational bureaucracies—that eliminates local distinctions and transcendent attachments in the name of human rights, international economic development, and collective security.

That goal can be understood in a variety of ways. Understood politically, it means the twin sovereignty of world markets and transnational bureaucracies as rational means for maximizing equal satisfaction of desire. Understood morally and even theologically, it implies a religion of individual man as the source of value, the doctrines of which are equality, autonomy, and hedonism. Such principles are accepted, if not always explicitly, by all significant public authorities throughout the West. Responsible leaders in church, state, and the academy now view cooperative effort toward a world ordered by them as their foremost responsibility. Dissent is all but criminal, since the alternative is thought to be poverty, tyranny, and bloody chaos. Romantic or populist gestures in opposition usually amount to little but political grandstanding and never achieve anything substantive.

The denial of public respectability to nonliberal principles, such as deference to traditional religious and moral beliefs, has led to peremptory demands for the full realization of liberal freedom and equality. Principled resistance has collapsed, and institutions have to be brought fully in line with maximum equal freedom to the extent possible. The demands go beyond economic welfare to substantive equality of position and status, or at least dissociation of inequalities from characteristics that are neither purely individual nor relevant to the functioning of liberal institutions. "Affirmative action," the requirement that underrepresented groups be equally included in major social activities and roles, is one such demand. "Political correctness," which requires that every group be given an equal share of respect, is simply the application of affirmative action to intangible aspects of social position. Although novel in some respects, it is a natural consequence of principles that have been long in the making and by now are well established. Complaints about it are utterly ineffective because they ignore the broader setting that makes it inevitable.

Transformations

While liberalism today can seem monolithic—if it did not, the concept of "political correctness" would make no sense—a striking feature of the liberal tradition has been its reversals on particular issues. The opposition between successive stages of liberalism has led some observers to deny that they can reasonably be treated as part of a single continuing tradition.[2] Points that once seemed basic have dropped from view: the respect for private property, the division and limitation of power, the recognition of an inviolate private sphere where the state has no business. How can an order be liberal, some ask, in which social planners reconstruct morality, or democratic, if government reconstitutes a people it finds lacking? Nonetheless, such transformations have been brought about by the same principles that have always made liberalism what it is. No change in fundamental principle has been needed, only a change in what institutions enjoyed general acceptance and what seemed possible.

The ultimate basis of liberalism is rejection of moral authorities that transcend human purposes.[3] To make contract the basis of social order, in accordance with the liberal myth of the social contract, is to make human goals the final standard of what we are to treat as good. A consequence of that standard is acceptance of the equal value of wills and their goals: if there is no authority higher than individual desire, then there is no standard by which to judge one desire better than another. Such thoughts have always been central to liberalism, at least implicitly, but their practical implications have depended on the setting and its possibilities. The evolution of the latter has been the evolution of liberalism.

Liberalism has always followed a path between conservative deference to whatever is established and the radical demand for aggressive social reconstruction. A view that makes individual preferences and equal freedom the standard must largely accept existing habits and expectations, at least until institutional change and reeducation have brought them more in accord with ultimate ideals. The combination of simple ultimate standards with willingness to defer closing the gap between ideal and reality has contributed enormously to the durability and success of liberalism, and to its ability to achieve profoundly radical results through step-by-step methods. It has enabled the classical liberalism of private property, parliaments, limited government, and equal laws first to overthrow the ancien régime and then to develop gradually, without change of ultimate principle, into today's socially radical big-government liberalism. As the source of liberal guilt, this combination has even supplied a motive for steady long-term support for liberal goals.

Early liberalism emphasized opposition to religious and hierarchical institutions that obstructed the equal right to do as one chose. It insisted on religious freedom and the abolition of formal privilege, so that property rights could replace status and established religion as a principle of social order. The result was the creation of a public realm in which, in principle, each could equally do what he liked. Rather than abolishing inequality and subordination, however, the effect was to limit these conditions to private life, the role of which expanded because of the new limitations on public action. The "private life" that was exempt from liberal standards was not private in function. It included economic and family life, as well as religion, scholarship, and the arts, and thus constituted by far the greater and more important part of social life.

The social order was therefore able to go on much as before, based on established sex roles, class distinctions, unequal property, and particularistic cultural and religious norms. Nonetheless, the liberal principle of equal freedom deprived such institutions of the secure legitimacy they possessed in earlier, more particularistic and hierarchical forms of society, in which they had been viewed as organic parts of an order established by God, nature, or history. They hung on mostly because they seemed necessary for social functioning, and once the possibility arose of replacing them they became hard for liberals to accept. The growth of the bureaucratic state seemed to reduce the role of particular cultural connections and to offer a way to reduce economic inequalities and sex distinctions. That possibility made it very difficult for liberals to continue to accept the sanctity of property, social arrangements that limited the equal freedom of women, or the privileging of the habits and preferences of whatever historical community happened to be dominant.

Establishment of formal equality was therefore followed in due course by government initiatives designed to advance equality substantively. These included the provision of social insurance, the promotion of economic opportunity, and the redistribution of wealth, leading eventually to the modern welfare state. Since then, the ambitions of the state have become ever more extensive, until today they have come to include suppression of whatever is thought to interfere with the equality and technological rationality of the social order, even such traditional constituents of personal identity as sex and historical community.

The attempt to reorder fundamental aspects of human life in the name of equal freedom has made government sovereign over social life. Arrangements that develop of themselves without official sanction—traditional family arrangements and ethnic ties, for example—are regularly suppressed in favor of those that can be designed, supervised, and reconfigured as needed to bring them in compliance with liberal principles. A tradition that once called for small government, property rights, individual responsibility, and bourgeois morality has come to demand guaranteed security, sexual freedom, and compulsory transformation of habits and attitudes in the interest of tolerance and inclusiveness.

The continuities of principle are nonetheless more basic than the changes. Those who claim that today's liberalism betrays liberal values by denying some favored freedom—free speech, free enterprise, free association, or whatever—overestimate how free, equal, and rational earlier forms of liberalism were. In all societies there are human distinctions that enable some to tell others what to do, and liberalism has always had to deal somehow with the contradiction between the demand for equal freedom and the human necessity for hierarchy and restraint. In classical liberalism the distinction between public and private enabled political life to be free and equal by restricting inequalities to what was considered private life. In contemporary liberalism, the concepts of human rights and expertise serve a similar function by restricting inequalities to the prepolitical process through which the content and application of human rights is determined, and to professional or economic settings thought to be determined by neutral technical considerations. Now as before, some people—whether husbands, clergymen, factory owners, social scientists, federal judges, or diversity consultants—tell others what to do and believe. In each case the compulsion is squared with equal freedom by treating it as a prepolitical matter of natural social institutions, human rights, or technical expertise, and by labeling people who question it as crazy, ignorant, or immoral.

Some continue to claim that welfare-state liberalism is an abandonment of the true liberalism of laissez faire, or that affirmative action and political correctness are an attack on the liberal principles of individual merit and free speech. Nonetheless, the great majority of those who call themselves liberals have come to accept politically correct managerial liberalism. It dominates the liberal tradition's institutional mainstream and seems consistent with the most basic long-term tendencies of the tradition and liberal society at large. That situation supports viewing the liberal tradition and its principles of freedom and equality as a coherent whole, and the thought of thinkers like John Rawls as the legitimate continuation of earlier thinkers such as Locke and Mill.

Power

An outlook that seems as firmly entrenched and apparently unavoidable as liberalism must have supports that go far beyond historical happenstance. One important support is the connection between liberalism and power. Every general political outlook is concerned with power, and liberalism could never have triumphed if it were not closely related to what confers it in the modern world. The relation between liberalism and power is at the heart of the position it now holds.

As a Standard

To a large extent, the strength of liberalism comes from applying to social and moral life the technological method of defining what is wanted and rationally organizing resources to achieve it. Modern bureaucracy and industrial organization apply that method directly to social functions and economic production, and modern markets, which enable desires to find their most efficient satisfaction through the medium of money and contract, also facilitate its activity. Present-day liberalism, more than any other approach to government, is fully integrated with such institutions. Their success enables liberal societies to out-compete others, and the association of liberalism with technique gives it the weight and prestige that comes with the success of modern natural science and industry.

The relation of liberalism to power is accentuated by its tendency to identify power and the good. Liberalism's selling point is "choice." As Judith Shklar puts the matter, "every adult should be able to make as many effective decisions without fear or favor about as many aspects of her or his life as is compatible with the like freedom of every other adult. That belief is the original and only defensible meaning of liberalism."[4] Liberalism is thus part of the modern attempt to put nature and the social order in the service of human will. As such it culminates the centuries-old attempt to replace custom and religion by human will and this-worldly reason as the basis for life and thought, other expressions of modernity such as Bolshevism and Nazism having destroyed themselves through irrationality, violence, and corruption.

The modern attempt to base social order on will is comprehensive. Science helps us control things physically, and what they are for us is molded by symbolism, social relationships, and biochemistry. People today believe they can manipulate such factors; they expect physical and social technology to permit reconstruction of all human reality and a large part of nature into a single rational system subject to man's will and devoted to its satisfaction. Such an orientation toward power makes advanced liberalism radically secularist and antiparticularist. Because the world is to be re-created with man's pleasure as the standard, human power, and thus the means of power—money, position, manipulative skill—are all that truly matter. History, tradition, biology, and religion become obstacles to be overcome or irrelevancies to be put to the side rather than part of an order of things to be valued and accepted. Power and pleasure become the ultimate goods, and other goods make sense only by reference to them. Body and soul are placed at the service of desire, contemplation debunked as an illusion, pushpin (now called "popular culture") declared as good as poetry, and religion turned into a "preference."

Educated and well-placed men today see rejection of a technological approach to human life as ignorant or disingenuous, and in any case dangerous. For them, assertion of limits on man's power in favor of principles transcending desire can only be obfuscation. Whatever people say,

their real purpose is to get their own way, so opposition to egalitarian hedonism can only be a rhetorical ploy motivated by the desire to supplant
what others want with what one wants oneself. Hence the emphasis on
equality as the supreme moral principle. Since power is the supreme good,
and nothing has value in itself that can limit the exercise of power, the
alternative to the principle of equality is thought to be unlimited use by
some of others for their own purposes. Traditional morality, which makes
some desires superior to others, is thus understood as a devious effort to
control others and becomes a stock example of immorality. It is understood as intrinsically oppressive, its ostensible concern with higher things
a hypocritical pretense.

So accepted is it that the point of human action is control and the
world merely raw material for our purposes that noninterference has come
to seem only another form of manipulation. All situations are interpreted
as human constructions that can be reconstructed intentionally, so that
failure to reconstruct is seen as choosing the existing situation over known
and equally available alternatives. Failure to reconstruct race relations is
"institutional racism," an instance of the more general vice of "social injustice"—failure to remake all social life in accord with liberal principle. Even
the traditionally minded fall into viewing the social world as a conscious
human construction, so that acceptance of tradition becomes a decision to
construct the world in a particular way. Since tradition is justified by the
impossibility of designing social order consciously,[5] those attached to it
become unable to explain their views even to themselves.

Technocracy

Because liberalism is a principle of government, its triumph arrives with
the triumph of the men and institutions favored by the arrangement of
power it proposes. It is thus the ideology of a ruling class. The victory of
liberalism is the victory of managers, experts, educators, media organi-

zations, and rationally organized bureaucratic and commercial interests. Such people and institutions benefit from large-scale rationalized organization of social life, which demands comprehensive systems of planning, training, indoctrination, and control, and of gathering, analyzing, and disseminating the information large formal institutions need to operate. Not all members of our ruling elites adhere to liberalism, and it also draws support from outsiders, but the reduction of politics to administration and technique puts power in the hands of those who find it most persuasive and do most to promote it. Liberalism advances their interests and they determine its content.

The technocratic society they prefer promotes liberal understandings. Market, bureaucratic, and industrial forms of organization abolish durable ties and treat everything as interchangeable. The electronic media destroy fixed character by continually fragmenting, reformatting, and repackaging experience. Modern communications, jet travel, city life, and the automobile make every person, place, and thing equally present to every other, so that each has the same environment and status. That situation destroys differences of implication and significance, so that nothing means anything definite and everything becomes either an object of simple desire or aversion, or else a resource to be used for some further purpose. Money, government decree, and technical rationality become the sole principles of order, and the whole of life—work, education, entertainment, everyday routine, the relations between the sexes and generations—is swallowed up by a universal rationalized system that treats the world as a resource to be exploited for the efficient equal satisfaction of preferences.[6] Under such conditions it becomes difficult for those discussing any issue to take nontechnocratic approaches seriously. Even common sense must put on technocratic garb to get a hearing: one cannot speak of the commonest and most evident features of daily life today without citing social science studies.

A technically rationalized process strives for clarity and perfection through standardization. Differences must be as few, well defined, and technically manageable as possible. When applied to society such demands yield liberal morality. They mean that the particularities of history, place, and human relation must be deprived of significance. Traditional ties, standards, and identities must be destroyed so that populations become aggregates of unconnected individuals who are easy to sort and manage and unlikely to resist rationalized training, marketing, and propaganda. Qualitative differences must be treated as differences in individual taste, so that attempts are made to treat prostitutes as sex workers who can be dealt with in the same efficient way as those employed in other industries.[7] "Discrimination," the recognition of serious nonbureaucratic and nonmarket distinctions, and "intolerance," the recognition that not all values can be turned into mutually independent and interchangeable commodities, become attacks on the basic principles of social order and thus on morality itself. Worst of all is "fundamentalism," recognition of an authoritative principle that cannot be reduced to the unified rationalized process that constitutes the technocratic order.

The great issues of the "culture war"—political correctness; multiculturalism; the struggle over sex and family life; the aggressiveness, intolerance, and growing dominance of the radical secularist Left—are all aspects of the campaign by technocratic institutions to make their power absolute by destroying, as manifestations of bigotry, other forms of social organization. Marriage, for instance, must be abolished as a specific institution with a natural and necessary social function and reduced to sentiment and nonbinding private commitment. To say marriage makes a difference is "discrimination," to say it has to do with some relations and not others is "intolerance," and to keep making those points when their opposition to technocratic understandings of rational social organization has been pointed out is "fundamentalism."[8]

Similar objections are lodged against all religious and cultural standards that do not simply repeat the demands of the technocratic liberal order. To give such standards any weight beyond recognition as private tastes is to engage in discrimination, intolerance, bigotry, and—to the extent a principle is asserted—fundamentalism or similar fanaticism. Such standards threaten the rationality of the system, because they interfere with conversion of the people into a mass of productive units and consumers with idiosyncratic tastes that can be efficiently managed and satisfied. They are therefore understood not as legitimate standards but as prejudice and bigotry: evil, irrational, and profoundly dangerous.

So great is the power of modern technocacy, and so close is the connection between liberalism and power, that liberalism comes to seem irresistible, almost a law of nature. All classes favor it. Political elites like what increases their power, the rich what secures and increases their wealth, experts what makes expertise the key to social functioning, idealists what conforms social functions to abstract rational principles, social climbers what makes them respectable, and almost everyone what makes for comfort. Besides, liberalism and technocracy present an illusion of limitless choice that allows us to deny life's limitations. The scientific conquest of nature, with which liberalism associates itself through its embrace of scientism, has been spectacularly successful, and people expect methods that solve some problems so well to solve all. Those methods have given us unprecedented physical power and economic abundance. Why should they not solve all other problems and give us whatever we want? If a political movement makes "give the people what they want" its creed, why not believe in it and view it as the most natural and inevitable thing in the world?

RATIONALITY

While liberalism is closely connected to practical functions and interests, it is not their mere appendage. There are interests that would benefit from every possible configuration of power and political outlook, and any particular interest could appeal to a variety of theories that would support it. At least in concept, the world could be governed by very different ideas while remaining technologically the same and retaining a generally similar type of social organization. Fascism and Bolshevism were also modern ideologies, East Asian authoritarianism seems to work well in some modern industrialized settings, and Islamic radicals are exploring ways to make strict Islam consistent with modern technology and bureaucratic organization. The needs and effects of power are not enough to explain the rise and development of liberalism.

Importance of Principles

Considerations rooted in general ways of thinking matter decisively. Life in a Western liberal society is not at all the same as in Japan or in a Muslim society, because people in those societies view life differently.[9] Rarely are we clearly aware of the fundamental principles of our own thought, which we state and apply variously, but without them our actions would lose coherence and institutions would lose the ability to function. Those principles establish the social environment of our actions by determining how situations are understood, what goals are thought to make sense, and how to go about resolving disputes.

Apart from such principles the social world becomes as incomprehensible as a book written in a language with no grammar and no settled meanings for words. The linguistic analogy is a close one, since fundamental social and linguistic principles both establish how we interpret and make sense of things and how we establish the common understandings necessary for cooperation. Ideas do have consequences. However materialistic one's view of man, it remains true that he participates in complex and extensive systems of common action coordinated by means of language. It is therefore not an idealistic misunderstanding of human nature to treat as decisive how words function within systems of language and belief, and thus what are ordinarily called ideas and principles.

To some extent, of course, it is simple efficacy that makes principles acceptable: we accept what seems to work. For example, we accept the outlook characteristic of modern technology very largely because it gets the results we want in so many situations. Nonetheless, the understandings accepted at a particular time are not a simple consequence of practical needs. Understandings determine efficacy as well as the reverse, since they determine what is thought to be needed and they make possible the cooperation that achieves results. The success of modern natural science does not of itself imply a technological approach to human relations. And other causes make "GDP" an efficacious standard for common action today where "divine right of kings" or "*mos maiorum*" might once have seemed more valid.

Basic concepts and principles are especially important in liberalism because it demands that power justify itself and because it strives toward explicit rational coherence. A deep and enduring conviction of the rightness of liberal views on the part of intelligent, well-placed, and public-spirited men has been necessary to the success of those views. Liberals experience liberalism as a rational and moral imperative, and they rule less through brute force, conspiracy, or even explicit common purpose than through coordinated action, without central direction, based on a common scheme of concepts and principles. While liberalism has elites and central institutions, it lacks a definite hierarchy and discipline, and therefore the ability to enforce views that fail to attract general elite acceptance.

Such a system could not function if it were not deeply rooted in fundamental understandings shared by influential people and if the populace did not acquiesce. For all its concern with power, liberalism defines itself by reasonableness and makes that its ideal. For the sake of reasonableness, it aims at principles acceptable to all. Anything less would force some to be subservient to others and thus be oppressive. The establishment of such principles is supposed to lead to a truly fair and consensual society. Liberalism is inspired by the dream of political principles that rule without oppressiveness because they have the universality, transparency, modesty, and power of logic. Equal freedom, like the principle of noncontradiction, is alleged to apply to everyone everywhere without interfering with anything anyone might legitimately think or do.

That dream of a truly free and rational political order is essential to liberalism. Power is to be maximized, but it is also made so equal and so devoted to human satisfactions that it seems to disappear. That is what liberals mean by "empowerment." The dream survives all criticisms, comes back from all defeats, and only grows stronger with time. Liberals may claim to be realistic, skeptical, multicultural, or postmodern, but all the rethinking and reformulation of their views, and all the actual inequalities, restrictions, and hierarchies liberal society finds necessary for its functioning, leave untouched the principle of equal freedom, which is beyond challenge. In the absence of substantive transcendent principle, which liberals do not accept, to reject equal freedom as the ultimate political standard would be to accept the power of some to force their preferences on others and so in principle to accept oppression. For a liberal to do so would be inconceivable.

Scientific Rationality

How to make power noncoercive and universally acceptable is of course a difficult question. The preferred strategy for liberals is to recognize man as the measure of things, so that what we want becomes the standard for social order. Such an approach, to the extent it could be carried out, would result in uncoerced support for public measures because it would bring them in line with what each of us wants already.

The attempt to make man the measure may seem self-contradictory, since it is hard for any sane adult to consider his own desires the measure of all things. It seems to most of us that life goes on as it does without much reference to what any of us thinks or wants. In addition, how things seem and what appears desirable differ from person to person, so no one of us can be the measure, and the majority can evidently be wrong as well. Nonetheless, man-the-measure has come to pervade the whole of life and thought, and even to be treated as basic to rationality. We know ourselves best, it is said, and the alternative to measuring things by ourselves would be measuring them by something transcending our experience, of which we can know little or nothing.

The principle of man-the-measure has been able to bear the weight placed on it in modern times because it has been reformulated in the terms of modern natural science. While the view that man is the measure goes back at least to Protagoras, in the form that dominates our world today it rose to power in the seventeenth century, an age marked by Descartes' decision to accept as true only what was clear and distinct to him and by Bacon's reconstruction of science on experimental principles for "the relief of man's estate."[10]

In this modern form, man-the-measure is made usable through insistence on rigorous formal reasoning and close attention to immediate experience backed by special training and expertise. Tradition and revelation are discounted, together with habitual common understandings, and what we can immediately and surely perceive, grasp, control, and make clear to others—things like sensation, measurement, logic, and technique—are accepted as the standard for what is real. That view has been accompanied by a broader movement from *contemplation* to *use* as the final goal of knowledge, and from *goodness* to *success* as the ultimate standard for action. The purpose and test of truth has become whether it helps us predict and control the world for our own purposes.

Such an approach to knowledge did not come from nowhere. It developed from a characteristic Western tendency to emphasize observation, logic, and critical thought. In social affairs that outlook favors contractual ordering, individual rights and initiatives, government by consent, and law. It has been traced variously to Greek philosophy, Roman law, classical civic life, Germanic love of freedom, and the Christian emphasis on the individual soul and the world as a rational creation. Whatever the particulars, it is evident that many of the tendencies leading to our current condition are long-standing Western distinctives[11] that have been immensely strengthened in modern times by the success of modern natural science, technology, industrialism, and rational bureaucratic and market forms of social organization.

In the natural sciences, making the trained observer the measure has been extraordinarily productive. The critical tendency and the focus on human thought and activity have meant an emphasis on observation, measurement, and model-building. Observation and measurement reduce things to simple units we can grasp completely, while model-building eliminates the need to talk about anything but measured quantities and our own theories. Such an approach minimizes commitments to things that might be doubted and gives modern natural science enormous power. It ties beliefs as much as possible to what we can clearly perceive, quantify, control, and make clear to others. When it builds on such things it does so as simply as possible, in accordance with Occam's Razor, and as much as possible in ways that can be clearly specified and tested. It is therefore as reliable as humanly possible. Perhaps more to the point, the usefulness of the method in attaining and holding power makes it impossible to belittle. Television and modern medicine, not to mention military jets and tanks, work everywhere, and men of all backgrounds can make effective use of them.

Liberalism is of course a moral and political doctrine, while modern natural science deals with other matters. But morals and politics do not exist in a vacuum. Modern science, which is oriented toward control of the natural world, and modern politics and morals, which are also oriented toward getting us what we want, go together. Science is the search for mechanisms of control, as the experimental method suggests, so the world it reveals is one with no supreme being or highest good, no objective standard of right and wrong, just ways and means of attaining our goals. It is a world suited to liberalism. If God made the world, and called it good because it was good, then "value" is not an add-on to a world that in itself is neutral but rather is part of the way things are. On the other hand, if there is nothing but observation and prediction, atoms and the void, then "values" can only be the desires you and I happen to have, and the point of social and moral life can only be their attainment.

Subjectivism

Even so, in social affairs man-the-trained-observer cannot, even for the modernist, be the final measure. Some other way must be found to make man-the-measure usable. The complexity and subtlety of human phenomena make measurement, modeling, and controlled verification mostly impossible. Furthermore, the attempt to reduce human realities to measurable appearances misses the things that are of greatest concern to us. In human affairs we are necessarily concerned with realities that cannot be controlled, experimented on, or reduced to our own measure; we are concerned with things as they *are*, not as they *are to us*. When I am dealing with industrial-grade borax I do not lose much by ignoring what it may be in itself, and talking instead about quantitative observations, mathematical models, and fitness for a purpose. The case is different when I am dealing with family, friends, and fellow citizens. I am called upon to deal with them as they are, and not with my quantifiable experience of them.

But what are "things as they are"? The phrase seems to refer to a self-subsistent order of things that is independent of our experience. The critically minded do not see how something independent of our experience could become known to us, since it seems we know things only as part of our experience, so they want to restrict the applicability of the phrase as much as possible. If reducing others to our own measure does not seem to work, the way to go beyond our experience, while recognizing as little outside it as possible, is to recognize the experience of others on a par with our own but to acknowledge nothing further, in particular no comprehensive moral reality that includes and orders experience in general.

If all we have to go on is how the world seems to individuals, with no given moral order transcending and comprehending them, we can choose between the view that each is his own measure and the view that some are the measure of others. If those are the choices, the first seems more rational and humane; it also leads to the view that each man's good is whatever he thinks good. The world, in effect, is here to satisfy the desires of all of us, so that giving each what he wants becomes the highest ethical and political aspiration. Human preferences—the desires and goals each of us happens to have—become the source of the values that merit social recognition. Since all preferences are equally preferences, they equally confer worth and should be equally favored. Cultures and lifestyles are collections of preferences, so they should be treated as equally good as well.

Such views are basic to advanced liberalism and give it much of its persuasive power. Subjectivism as to values seems to demystify ethical questions, establish freedom on a firm basis, let each of us get what he wants, hold out hope for the greatest possible wealth of human diversity, and make it possible for us to concentrate on the practical problems of living together rather than on speculation as to ultimate goods, speculation that often seems to go nowhere. They seem to leave the moral and spiritual world open for each to develop in his own way, at least if that way is radically individualistic. They point the way to the Supreme Court's comment, in a decision upholding the unlimited abortion right now viewed as fundamental to our legal and moral order, that "at the heart of liberty is the right to define one's own concept of existence, of meaning, of the universe, and of the mystery of human life."[12]

It is of course impossible to achieve equal treatment in all cases. Preferences are often inconsistent, so some must be sacrificed to others. If I like loud parties and you like sleep it may be impossible to satisfy us both. Nonetheless, the liberal conception of justice requires that the preferences to be sacrificed be chosen in a way that recognizes their equal worth. The simplest principle for doing so is utilitarianism, the greatest satisfaction for the greatest number. All desires are treated equally, and if enough people have a strong enough taste for electric guitars at 3 a.m., too bad for those who want to sleep. Democratic politics can be understood as an expression of that kind of utilitarianism, since it decides issues by the weight of numbers and to some extent by relative degree of commitment.

Strict utilitarianism is clear, direct, and useful in unsettling traditional moral conceptions. Nonetheless, liberals have come to reject it. The problem is that the equal worth of all desires does not in itself require that all men be treated equally: it might maximize general satisfaction, for example, to enslave an annoying minority and force its members to perform dangerous and unpleasant tasks the rest of us would otherwise have to do. Nonetheless, doing so would be highly illiberal. Those who identify what men want with what is good do so in part because they feel the commanding force of their own desires. Since strict utilitarianism deprives a man's own desires of any protected status, and in principle would authorize others to use him as a mere means to their ends, accepting it would require rejecting the sense that one's own desires have authority simply as desires.

In addition, the equal worth of preferences suggests equality among those whose preferences they are. Creating values is a godlike act, so in the liberal view the capacity to have preferences and thus create values confers a sort of divinity. We share equally in the capacity, so we share equally in the divinity.[13] That is one reason we are now called upon not only to tolerate but to celebrate diversity of lifestyle and culture. To do otherwise would be to ignore the divine effulgence now felt to envelop all desires simply because they are someone's desires.

The natural response to such concerns is a guarantee that the private desires of each person will be equally protected against others' claims. Equal satisfaction for each person, or at least equal treatment of each person with respect to his preferences,[14] therefore joins equal treatment of preferences, lifestyles, and cultures to form the liberal understanding of justice.

Nonetheless, it often happens that the preferences of one person must simply be sacrificed to those of others. If I am a divine-right monarchist, my wife an anarchosyndicalist, and my cousin a Maoist, it will be hard to satisfy the three of us equally. The liberal response is to make what seems the minimum deviation necessary from strict neutrality by turning neutrality itself into a substantive principle. Since not all goals can be accommodated, the nod is given to neutral ones, those that interfere as little as possible with the goals set by others. After all, if the conflict of goals is the problem, and each goal is intrinsically as good as every other, it appears reasonable to reward the goals that accept the situation and try to avoid conflicts, thus aligning themselves with social morality.

Such a principle seems as little substantive as possible, and accepting it seems in the spirit of Occam's Razor. Since equal freedom seems sufficient to give rise to an ethical system, to go beyond it in any substantive way would apparently violate rationality as now understood. Any value other than maximum equal freedom for all persons and preferences seems an arbitrary personal addition that cannot claim objective validity or serve as a public standard of what is right. Certainly people view the matter that way; "tolerance" in the current sense of respect and support for the goals of others, as long as those goals are themselves tolerant, is considered the highest form of morality. Every other substantive ethical standard is denounced as dogmatic and oppressive.

Moral Rationality and Goodness

To most educated people today, liberalism seems simply rational. Liberal understandings of freedom and equality flow reasonably and persuasively from man-the-measure and other understandings allied to modern natural science, the outlook now thought to define rationality. Just as our senses and ability to control nature are authoritative for modern natural science, what we want and how to get it are authoritative for modern morality. The considerations relevant to action that can be most readily recognized, measured, compared, and controlled are pleasures, pains, desires, and preferences—what works and what does not. Sticking to such things as much as possible seems a requirement of the scientific approach. Regardless of the problems to which they may lead, liberal arguments have become unanswerable. Each can do as he likes consistent with the equal freedom of others, and in case of conflict the more tolerant wins. Which part of that is to be rejected, and how?

Liberalism, like modern natural science, can claim to be good, and it attracts specifically moral support.[15] Both are based on principles that everyone, or almost everyone, recognizes as important—desire and aversion; the evidence of our senses; logic, technology, and cooperative effort to attain goals. People who disagree on any number of things can discuss such principles productively, agree on conclusions, and act on them together. By putting all goals on the same level of personal preference and technical possibility, such an approach seems to promote the possibility of compromise and cooperation, since one goal can always be traded against another to the extent that they cannot be made compatible. In this way, liberalism presents itself as likely to promote peaceful and productive social life.[16]

Indeed, liberalism and modern natural science can be viewed together as a form of secularized and rationalized Christianity. In a sense, both are unassuming and humble, because they tell us not to make claims that we cannot back up. By making everything equal they raise valleys and lower peaks. Furthermore, since they accept as true only what can be verified by anyone who has been properly trained and equipped (at least if we put aside certain basic presuppositions that must be accepted without question), they make thoughts and experiences that can be universally shared the standards of truth and goodness. They thus seem fundamentally social, and even suggest a kind of universal love—all are accepted, none is excluded, and each accepts the goals of all the others, subject only to the rejection of goals that refuse to take part in the system because of their intolerance.

IRRATIONALISM

But what about the irrationalist tendencies that have recently appeared within or perhaps in opposition to liberalism? Modernity, it is said, has been replaced by postmodernity, which has encouraged progressives to go beyond the Western concepts of reason and individuality on which liberalism is based but are now viewed as unfounded and oppressive. Freedom and equality, it is suggested, no longer require foundations or even intellectual coherence. Multiculturalism and the like will somehow destroy the oppressiveness of ideology and culture while promoting the flowering of individual and group identity. Habit, attachment to freedom, self-sustaining democratic traditions, non-Western and nonmasculine ways of thought, the way things work of themselves, or something unknown and unknowable will be enough to secure the functioning, continuation, and progressive development of the system.

Reason, however, is not so easy to escape. It is true that some tendencies within current liberalism, such as some forms of feminism and ecological consciousness, have anti-Western and anti-logocentric aspects. Others, such as a general sense that Enlightenment foundationalism has failed, put the whole of modern rationalism, including its liberal aspects, in doubt. However, the practical consequence of such tendencies is a more demanding rationalism that further radicalizes Western modernity. Multiculturalism, for example, is fundamentally a denial that one's acts can be judged by another's standards. The effect is that it becomes impossible to apply any standard to conduct except the liberal standard of equal respect for persons and preferences. If I belong to another group, you cannot judge me by your group's standards. Nor can I be judged by my group's standards, because if I reject them that simply shows that I am in a subgroup—gay Muslims, perhaps—that must be allowed its own freedom of decision. Judgments must nonetheless be made, so the consequence is that particular cultural standards become altogether unavailable and one falls back ever more single-mindedly on abstract logical criteria like equality.

The ostensibly anti-individualistic, antirationalistic, and anti-universalistic tendencies within contemporary liberalism carry the concept of everything its own measure to ever greater extremes. They extend "every man his own measure" to "every man, woman, homosexual, witch-doctor, and tree his, her, or its own measure." The result is to impose the most abstract individualism and rationalism imaginable on everyone everywhere. To "celebrate diversity" is to make ethnic, sexual, and similar categories irrelevant to social function, and as a practical matter it becomes the same as the compulsory imposition of rationalized uniformity. To do away with "master narratives" is to do away with myths, and is therefore an extreme restatement of scientistic literal-mindedness. Even to be anti-Western in the current manner is to demand that the West be purified from all particularity, and so to further the radical and universalizing side of the Western heritage.

Irrationalist liberalism cannot help but support universal rule by money and rationalizing bureaucracies, since no other arrangement can plausibly present itself as a neutral method of arbitrating incommensurable understandings and preferences. Postmodernity offers no alternative because it creates no institutions and cannot rule. Its adherents are mostly careerist academics, cultural revisionists who have given up caring who rules, political opportunists who apply its relativism only to their enemies and their own past missteps, and liberal apparatchiks profoundly satisfied with the current order who see no real need for political change. Its language is rhetorical and irrelevant to any real issue because it cannot give answers. When someone needs to deal with a real problem he reverts to modernist rationalism, which becomes even more than before the sole possible authority.

Postmodern liberalism does not destroy the legitimacy of all forms of discourse equally but involves a bait-and-switch. It denies that ordinary people, whose thoughts and words are now understood to lack settled cognitive content, can effectually criticize their rulers, who claim the special ability to represent all possible cultures and points of view. Since only experts can negotiate the ambiguities and contradictions of multiculturalism intelligently, only experts are allowed to speak, and what they say defines what must be accepted as public reality. Others must do as they are told and like it.[17] Postmodern liberalism puts the advanced liberal order beyond criticism, a necessary function in a hyperactive state operating in a media-drenched environment on principles that grow ever more difficult to understand or justify. It is not in-group snobbery but the maintenance of power that is the root of liberalism's intellectual elitism—although that very fact makes liberalism appealing to in-group snobs.

Beyond shutting people up and making principled opposition impossible, the irrationalist aspects of advanced liberalism provide a sort of stand-in for traditional aspects of Western life that have been destroyed by liberalism and modernity. The inhabitants of liberal society, like anyone else, feel the need for something that transcends desire and gives it a setting that puts it in perspective. Pure liberalism cannot easily do that for them. The easiest way to solve the problem is to find something vague—something like "humanity" or "the earth" or some obscure spiritual presence—that minimally transcends us and so supplies the need for something higher, but without making serious demands or indeed becoming more than a personal indulgence. Such substitutes lack stability, concreteness, and content, and thus authority, so they help stabilize technocratic society by providing a safe outlet for natural human impulses that might otherwise grow disruptive. Feminism, for instance, is concerned with the body and human connectedness, and ecology with man's setting in the universe, but neither in a way that can give rise to a nontechnocratic social institution. Instead, they undermine more substantive alternatives by obfuscating the issues and supplying palliatives. They are ornamental and not functional, but even ornament serves a function.

Irrationalism cannot be taken literally. Liberalism cannot dispense with justifications, because it cannot present itself as simply arbitrary, customary, or traditional. Government involves force and demands cooperation in projects that go against the personal interests of many of those involved. Because liberalism puts individual choice first, it insists that such demands receive specific justification. Irrationalist obfuscation can dampen criticisms to some extent but cannot do away with the demand for justification altogether. If no common culture can be assumed as authority, nothing is left but an appeal to perspicuously true universal principles. Without an appeal to such principles, liberalism would lose its claim to special legitimacy. It would also sacrifice the logic that defines it and so enables it to function and adjust coherently to varying circumstances without a unified hierarchical structure. It would stop being identifiably liberal and become an aggregate of ad hoc decisions by whoever holds power. It cannot present or understand itself in such a manner, so regardless of all criticisms and evasions it must continually come back to claims of universal reasonableness.

CHAPTER THREE

Institutions

THE CHARACTERISTIC INSTITUTIONS OF LIBERALISM ARE CONTRACT, REPRE-
sentative democracy, and rational bureaucratic administration within a
legal regime that makes equal freedom an overriding enforceable standard. Markets, the contractual arrangements of civil society, parliaments,
and state and transnational bureaucracies, all under the supervision of
courts charged with enforcing human rights, are thus basic to advanced
liberalism. Those institutions are intended to put man-the-measure and
equal freedom into effect. They give effect to will as such—as much and as
equally as possible—and for that reason have exclusive public authority.

DEVELOPMENT

Liberal institutions attempt to reconcile the ideal of equal freedom with
established habits, technology, and freedom as ordinarily understood,
each of which has a certain claim to respect from a liberal standpoint. As

we shall see, the manner and degree to which liberal institutions do so has changed as liberalism has developed. Over time, abstract demands and technological ways of thinking have played more and more the leading role, suppressing established arrangements and, in the end, freedom as ordinarily understood. As a result, institutions based on traditional components of personal and social identity, like sex, family, culture, religion, and historical community, have been deprived of legitimacy and sidelined or suppressed.

Abolition of Politics

The emphasis on abstract principles like freedom and equality means that form, concept, and process trump substance in liberalism. Public life must be governed as much as possible by a priori demands such as equality or facts backed by certifiable expertise and scientific procedure. Less formal principles, such as respect for tradition and even majority rule, are thought oppressive, no matter how numerous their supporters or sensible their particular demands, because they do not present a clear rational justification for decisions but simply let some wills override others. Liberal institutions thus tend to fall into a hierarchy, with those based on abstract principle and expertise ranking higher than those based on substantive choice. Human rights trump national politics, the Supreme Court outranks Congress, and Congress outranks local institutions that reflect more directly the will of particular communities.[1]

Potemkin Democracy

The insistence that concept trumps substantive choice has consequences that are greatly at odds with claims that liberalism is democratic. It means that liberalism has right and wrong answers. Since the people often choose the wrong answers, their actual views cannot be taken seriously and must often be ignored.

Equal freedom requires the satisfaction of as many desires as possible while giving them all equal weight. Not many people are able consistently to deal with public issues in such a way. Most of us cannot help but bring in other concerns. Popular involvement in public affairs interferes with the rational process of ascertaining the demands of equal freedom and maximizing its realization. That process can best be carried out if disputes are resolved by a disinterested third party who truly accepts and knows how to apply liberal concepts. With that in mind, government becomes ideally a matter of administration, technical skill, and interpretation of formal a priori principles such as equality and neutrality. Judges and bureaucrats decide important issues and develop their decisions into ever more detailed specifications for all aspects of social life. Majoritarian politics is limited to secondary matters such as the specifics of economic initiatives and public consumption choices, with public discussion and the decision-making process supervised by expert and media gatekeepers.

Liberal society nonetheless insists on its democratic character. It wants to serve human will, and it is awkward to claim that the people must be forced to be free. There are indeed important democratic elements that differentiate liberal from, say, Soviet society. Many specifics, such as the choice of the highest officials and the terms of the welfare system, are determined by electoral or representative politics, and the people can, if sufficiently outraged, exert a veto on particular government initiatives, a veto that lasts as long as the outrage lasts. Such elements are important and provide a reality check that helps keep the system comparatively rational. They give early warning when public reactions have been misjudged, and they help identify the most skillful political operators and the most acceptable ways of packaging liberal programs and putting them into effect. However, they rarely stop governing elites from doing what they want to do. In a society as complex and highly organized as ours the concerns of those professionally in charge of our national life prevail in the end over popular concerns that can be only sporadically expressed.

While liberalism claims to respect the will of the people, its standard is equal freedom rather than popular rule, so on issues that matter—intergroup relations; public moral standards; the nature of man, the world, and the common good—it tells the people what their will has to be. In a society in which the endlessly expanding demands of extremely abstract principles are determined and enforced by unelected officials insulated from popular influence by the support of the professional custodians of public discussion, it is not the people who rule. The categories in which discussion is carried on show the real situation. For the people to have a vantage point of their own, and for them to act in a somewhat rational, coherent, and decisive fashion, they must possess a complex of settled attitudes and understandings sufficient to guide decision. Such understandings and attitudes, which give the people their character as a people, are now referred to as "social prejudices and stereotypes." A society like our own, in which "prejudice" and "stereotype" are thought to imply "morally and legally impermissible," is a society that has decided that the people should not participate in governance in any serious way, but rather should be dissolved as a people and placed under the tutelage of expert, bureaucratic, and media explainers. "Multiculturalism" and "inclusiveness" are at bottom efforts to bring about such a result.

Nonetheless, the people cannot seem to be excluded from decisions affecting them without refuting the claim that in liberal society it is *their* will that counts. That is why basic issues are defined out of existence. They cease to be political issues on which public opinion has any bearing. Instead, they are treated as matters of human rights, social health, or rational management, and consequently dealt with through professionalization of social functions, a therapeutic approach to human relations, and continual expansion of human-rights guarantees. The appearance of discretionary political power is minimized by handing the most sensitive decisions over to the judiciary, which is shrouded in incomprehensible expertise yet represented as grounded in tradition and ultimately in the decision of the people to establish constitutions and laws. Popular participation is effectively reduced to the ability to favor one or another of the political parties accepted as legitimate because of their thorough acceptance of a strictly limited role for political decision-making.

Affirmative action and mass immigration illustrate how the system works. The people quite generally oppose such policies, but elites overwhelmingly favor them, and the elite view always wins in the end. In spite of occasional populist rebellions, established policy continues with only sporadic debate. On occasion the people are able to secure the adoption of measures they favor—as seen, for example, in voter initiatives against racial preferences or in favor of restrictions on benefits for illegal aliens—but the effect of such measures is almost always neutralized by judicial or administrative actions (or failures to act).[2]

The reasons for the difference of outlook on such issues are evident. Affirmative action makes it easier for those in charge to buy off possible trouble and maintain the appearance of equality, and it weakens local cohesiveness while extending the reach of the administrative state. Such features, which our rulers find attractive, trump the autonomy of local institutions and popular attachment either to fairness and merit or to established ways and connections. As to immigration, the people value the ties that make them a people and believe that the country should be run for their own benefit. Ruling elites, by contrast, are concerned with the power and efficiency of governing institutions, the status and security of those who run them, and maintenance of the liberal principles that support and justify their rule. It is in their interest to expand the human resources available to them, even at the expense of those who are already citizens, and to weaken the mutual ties that make it possible for the people to resist rational management and to act somewhat independently.[3] In addition, any moderately self-seeking ruling class prefers cooperating with members of the ruling class in other countries to representing the interests of their constituents. The practical result of such influences has been the suppression of immigration as an issue in the interest of an emerging borderless world order. Restrictionist arguments are scantily presented in the mainstream media, and concern with cultural coherence, national identity, or even the well-being of one's country's workers is routinely denigrated as ignorant and racist nativism.

The response of EU ruling circles to popular discontent over European integration provides a similar example. The EU joins officials, politicians, business leaders, and opinion-makers into a transnational ruling class answerable only to itself because there is no pan-European people coherent enough to hold it responsible. The appearance of popular control is useful to that ruling class, but to the extent possible the populace is not allowed to affect results. When the EU project encounters popular resistance, tactics are modified, public education or disinformation is redoubled, and the matter raised repeatedly until a more favorable answer can be secured. When the Danish refused to approve the Maastricht Treaty and the Irish refused to approve the Nice Treaty, further referenda were held and the votes were reversed, in the Danish case after modification of the terms of the treaty. When the French and the Dutch voted against the proposed European Constitution in referenda and further "no" votes were expected, the process was stopped, the provisions of the Constitution were repackaged with small changes as the "Reform Treaty," and the movement for adoption got back on track, this time with the firm intention of avoiding referenda. The voice of the people is no longer considered the voice of the sovereign, if indeed it ever was.[4]

Advanced liberalism thus ends in a guardian state that attempts to determine the results of social life from above and suppresses whatever cannot be made to measure up to its understanding of efficiency, equality, and rationality. The system allows some public participation, but it also includes extensive filtering mechanisms. And on anything that touches basic matters it severely limits participation as an interfering irrelevancy and possible danger. The resulting failure of democratic aspirations should not be surprising, since in mass society the common man cannot be the measure in any real sense. He can speak articulately only through those who claim to interpret his voice, and they will always have their own agenda. Since the people's will cannot be institutionalized, claims that government expresses it always hide the real situation.

Scientism and Tolerance

The justifications for limiting popular involvement in public life typically involve scientism and what is now called *tolerance*. Scientism is the view that modern natural science is the only way to obtain real knowledge. It has given rise to the view that formalized procedures carried out by those with special training and certification are the only source of knowledge worth bothering with. In that view, experts should decide as many issues as possible, and to dispute what they say is to take the side of ignorance and unintelligent brute force. Since the knowledge of the people is informal and often inarticulate, they should have no active role in public life other than to support the established order and, when relevant, to make their preferences known—at least when experts do not claim that they already understand the people better than the people themselves.

Crude political expressions of scientism, such as Marxism, once waged open war on the traditions and religion of the people. Contemporary liberalism, which supplements scientism with the claim of tolerance and popular consent, is more sophisticated. It accepts the right of tradition and religion to exist, but it trivializes them as mere personal preferences that cannot be allowed to affect anything that matters. Furthermore, the disciplines of mental health remain available to delegitimize popular preferences at odds with public policy. Those disciplines were used as political tools with Bolshevik crudity in the Soviet Union, but they have been deployed with greater finesse in the West. Classic examples include Theodor Adorno's critique of the "authoritarian personality," which allowed almost any sort of skepticism regarding liberal demands to be treated as a sign of psychological disorder,[5] and Richard Hofstadter's "The Paranoid Style in American Politics," which assimilated support for Barry Goldwater and dissent from the Cold War–liberal consensus to a pattern of political insanity that spanned centuries.[6] A more recent example is the term "homophobia," which turns adherence to traditional sexual morality into a mental disorder.[7]

Tolerance, in its current meaning, follows partly from the sense that individual feelings are sacrosanct and partly from scientism. It insists that things science does not deal with, such as substantive value, be treated as subjective feelings because they cannot be determined by neutral experts. It also insists that every opinion regarding substantive value must, to the extent possible, be equally respected and none permitted to dominate the others. To do otherwise would be to let some people dominate other people. That strategy aligns with the contemporary liberal claim to celebrate all preferences as such, from homosexuality to pan-Asian cuisine. The strategy is rhetorically effective: most people care only whether their own traditions and religion get valorized; few notice that the effect is to trivialize all traditions and religions, including theirs.

A consequence of such an understanding of tolerance is a tendency to insist that opinions regarding value, to the extent that they are not tolerant in the advanced liberal sense, be kept private. To allow opinions that insist that some preferences are better than others publicity and possible influence would unjustly burden other equally valid preferences. Advanced liberal society therefore discredits, neutralizes, or silences those who speak out about matters of good and evil, except committed liberals and those who undermine understandings of the good that compete with liberalism. Public presentation of nonliberal understandings is treated as oppressive and can be subjected to legal suppression as "hate" or "harassment," for just by existing it creates a social environment less favorable to some people and ways of life than to others. Examples include the imposition of fines and threats of jail time in Europe for mere criticism of Islam or homosexuality.[8]

Scientism and tolerance complement each other. Tolerance supports scientism by asserting the equal value of all the contradictory views ordinary people hold, and consequently the uselessness of those views and the need to rely on neutral expertise for any determinate answer. Scientism confirms the "tolerant" demand that traditional moral judgments be kept strictly private by debunking such views as ignorant, superstitious, and bigoted, and by asserting that everything that can legitimately claim to be knowledge supports the official outlook, bypassing or suppressing ordinary standards of scientific inquiry, if necessary, to do so.[9] The two principles thus define rationality and moral decency in a way that hands serious issues over to authorized experts and other functionaries who can be counted on to resolve them consistently with the overall liberal system.

Tolerance and Social Control

While, in theory, values can be freely chosen in liberal society, in practice some are disfavored. Sometimes the favoritism seems arbitrary, as in the case of the suppression of tobacco but not alcohol. In general, though, it comes about because some values are at odds with a regime that needs all values to be treated as interchangeable. It is thought a pathology to take love, loyalty, integrity, religion, or community affiliation seriously as standards that trump the right to choose. To do so casts doubt on the principles of tolerance and equal freedom, because it suggests that some person, group, status, relationship, or goal has a special position that trumps immediate personal preference.

In fact, liberal tolerance does not expand the range of goods or ways of life that are available. It suppresses some while favoring others in the interest of establishing an entirely rationalized system. It calls for a particular human type and way of life in which a combination of rational self-interest, emotional self-expression, and political correctness is the proper basis for social relations. Such qualities promote a tolerant outlook, and the demand for tolerance profoundly affects what ways of life are permissible. Choice, the basic principle of liberalism, can be free and equal for everyone only to the extent it relates to things that can be supplied interchangeably. Otherwise, the choices of some get in the way of those of others. Burger King's "have it your way," the right of each to choose absolutely independently among preset choices that the established system finds equally easy to provide, is the model of individual self-rule in advanced liberal society. Even the members of pierced and tattooed youth subcultures, who claim to reject the established order but in fact are thoroughly formed by it, show their allegiance to accepted understandings by identifying their pursuits simply as "alternative" and thus just another item on the menu.

The attempt to make human goods independent and interchangeable within a universal rational system of production, consumption, and governance makes career and consumption the central modes of participation in social life. Career allows people to offer themselves as interchangeable productive units within the system, while consumption lets them choose among the kinds of enjoyment the system finds convenient to provide. Those two modes of social participation become the decisive dimensions of freedom and identity. They give us our dignity: I shop, therefore I am. To lack customary consumer goods is to be denied human dignity, and to have a career is to make something of oneself and realize one's dream.

The advanced liberal state emphasizes freedoms relating to individual indulgence, granting them generously and indeed making them almost absolute. Such freedoms, along with those relating to career and consumption, correspond to the human goods liberalism recognizes, and they aid the operation of the system by keeping the people occupied and away from public affairs. The promotion of private forms of pleasure and expression not essentially connected to the concerns of others, and so readily commercialized and otherwise made manageable, becomes basic public policy.[10] Such an arrangement is not new: the Roman state kept the proletariat quiet with bread and circuses. Prosperity, electronics and social complexity have expanded the menu of diversions and soporifics but the principle is similar. If we have career opportunities, counseling, television, fast food, and pornography, the thought is, people will get what they want, their desire for adventure can be satisfied by visits to casinos, they will not get involved in pogroms or the Ku Klux Klan, and those who know better will be able to run the system efficiently and in peace.

Freedom thus becomes a matter of private license, while self-government disappears. Governing the people by encouraging them to be self-involved and self-indulgent even generates its own justification, since it makes them less able to rule themselves and so makes it more necessary for government to act as their custodian. The strategy draws support not only from experts, educators, and welfare-state administrators on the left, but also from businessmen on the right, who after all have no objections to careerism and consumerism. Since those groups dominate the main political parties, serious political opposition is minimal. Occasional populist revolts may be triggered by violations of what the populace *believes*—as we see, from time to time, among evangelical Christians—but these are soon extinguished by a system that gives them what they most immediately and reliably *desire:* consumer goods and lifestyle freedoms.

In contrast to serious matters like career, the prerational and unchosen connections and commitments that once defined who a man is—family, religion, historical community—become lifestyle options, consumer goods like any other.[11] To treat them otherwise would be to threaten the social order, and so to discredit oneself and become subject to various sanctions.[12] Discussions of women's roles make the view now established clear: to be a mother and housewife is to be oppressed, self-indulgent, useless, or socially nonexistent. In both Britain and the United States, it is actually illegal for a guidance counselor to suggest to a female student that she may prefer a career as a mother and homemaker to one in the formal public workforce.[13] Even religion, to be legitimate, must transform itself so that it simply restates established egalitarian, rationalist, consumerist, and careerist values. Its public face and authoritative principles must be decided by experts and emphasize tolerance, inclusion, and equality. Anything more concrete, particular, and at odds with a regime of centrally managed egalitarian hedonism must remain purely private. In particular, no religion can claim superiority over any other religion or over irreligion. Each must understand itself as an optional pursuit, and thus as not a religion at all.

To some extent, the resulting form of society conflicts with the liberal principle that substantive goods should be treated equally, since it favors worldly ambition and material goods over the joys of fraternity and the simple life. However, the contradiction troubles only a few antimaterialist hippies and other highly idealistic members of the liberal coalition. The brute fact of material self-interest is enough to keep most people from noticing the problem, and in any case prosperity and choice can always be presented as all-purpose goods usable for any goal, even the simple life. Just as Marie Antoinette played shepherdess at the Petit Trianon, yuppies can spend their extra dollars on ecotourism and free-range chickens.

Global Capitalism

The material basis of advanced liberal society is its ability to deliver the economic goods it treats as the substantive part of the *summum bonum*. High employment, prosperity, and a flood of consumer goods and electronic entertainment multiply private pleasures as well as the effort and attention spent securing and enjoying them, while reducing the need for local networks of mutual reliance and support and the likelihood of popular meddling with public affairs. A sated and entertained populace makes for a placid and indifferent citizenry.

In an ideally technocratic world, material goods might be provided by a rational unitary system, but the collapse of socialism has convinced even leftists of the continuing necessity of independent enterprises and markets, including capital and labor markets. Advanced liberalism thus allows a great deal of local and particular discretion with regard to moneymaking activities. The necessity of allowing considerable autonomy to private economic decisions limits somewhat the ability of the state to enforce the rationalization of social life in the interest of equal freedom, and it has led to an emphasis on the role of liberalism as a quest for social rationalization within the limits of a market economy.

But experience has shown that markets can easily coexist with state control of other aspects of social life, and shrewd liberals welcome the arrangement. It is no mistake that liberalism has always been associated with markets. Classic socialism aims at a uniformity that interferes with the growth and expression of diverse preferences, and therefore only makes sense for populations too poor to have formed them. It embraces a solidaristic ethos that can valorize reactionary working-class attitudes about gender relations, race, culture, and even religion. Socialism's focus on economics also denigrates the value of liberal assaults on traditional culture. For such reasons, among others, the Soviet Union had lost its position of ideological and cultural leadership on the left long before it fell.

Market economies, in contrast, provide a way to fund and extend the welfare state while multiplying preferences and satisfactions. They tend to dissolve customary connections and make all goods interchangeable through the medium of money, thus promoting rationalization on hedonistic and technological lines and simplifying the setting of state action. Large business enterprises, with their rational bureaucratic methods of hiring, training, management, supervision, and promotion, provide the state with a ready-made instrument for reeducation and other forms of social control. The only freedoms they require are the freedoms to cut production costs and to attempt to satisfy whatever desires people happen to have. Otherwise, they leave the state a free hand. Indeed, they often find that complex state regulation gives them a competitive advantage over smaller enterprises, whose more informal practices make compliance difficult.

World markets in particular are an immensely powerful engine of rationalization. They lay the groundwork for the comprehensive regulation of economic life, and eventually social life in general, by national and increasingly transnational bureaucracies. World markets help maximize economic efficiency, at least in theory, by making all resources—human, financial, organizational, and material—equally available to a worldwide system of production and distribution. They destroy less rationalized local patterns and authorities, which are generally integrated with particular cultures, and create a single global system of practical life that can be understood and managed as a whole.

World markets help promote what is in effect a worldwide union of the ruling classes. By liberating national ruling elites from the influence of their people they allow their activities and outlook to be integrated with those of elites worldwide. Marx thought that the global extension of markets would undermine nationality and establish common class interests leading to union among those playing a common role in the system of production. He was right, but (not surprisingly) it has turned out to be the rulers rather than the proletariat who are astute, effective, well-connected, and bold enough to see and act on the opportunities the situation offers. Since the simplest method of resistance to elite globalism available to the working class is often a return to the more nationalist policies of the past, the traumas of globalism tend to push the working class still farther away from the global solidarity enjoyed by the elite.

The welfare state is another basic means of rationalization that has become integral to modern liberal capitalism. It is most obviously intended to stabilize and moderate the results of profit-seeking and the free market in labor by transfers from rich to poor and by the supply of various protections and services to individuals. It has the further effect, however, of promoting the takeover of civil society by the state. While the intention is often stated as support for the individual, the family, and other nonstate actors within civil society, the welfare state provides this support by taxing, funding, and supervising such actors, by undoing the inequalities to which they lead on account of their autonomy and manner of functioning, and often by performing their functions directly.

The effect of such interventions is to make smaller, less powerful, and less formal institutions less independent, less effective, and less needed, and in the end to abolish them as material factors in social life. The liberal animus against Burkean "little platoons" is fundamental. Small informal institutions cannot be supervised and controlled in the interest of equality and social welfare, and they differ from each other in purpose, membership, resources, and effectiveness. The normal functioning of the welfare state, which involves the imposition of various measures and controls designed to ensure that social welfare is measured, secured, and equalized as comprehensively as possible, necessarily suppresses them.

The welfare system replaces individual, kinship, community, and religious ties and obligations. Family functions are replaced by subsidized day care, public schools, and old-age pensions.[14] The result is that people become altogether dependent on employers and the state, and other institutions disintegrate as institutions and become mere leisure-time pursuits.

Human Rights

"Human rights" are a final means of social rationalization, one that demonstrates how advanced liberalism turns all things to its purposes. Some conception of universal human rights is likely unavoidable today. Modern developments have shortened distances and enhanced human power, forcing peoples together and facilitating acts of extreme inhumanity on an enormous scale. Such a situation motivates moral agreement on urgent issues but is also likely to limit its scope. One natural response would be acceptance of a few principles that foreclose clear abuses and can be affirmed from as many moral, cultural, and religious perspectives as possible. The human-rights movement claims to stand for such a response, and many of the things it proclaims as matters of universal right—such as the proscription of genocide, torture, slavery, and extrajudicial killing—seem to fit the bill.

In the most direct and limited sense, then, universal human rights would consist of straightforward principles that protect people against gross abuses generally recognized as such. Everyday references to human-rights violations usually have to do with such abuses, and it is those things that the human-rights movement plays up in its public pronouncements. However, the human-rights standards now set forth in treaties, proclamations, and national legal provisions go far beyond any such universal agreement. In the face of an evident lack of consensus, their supporters have chosen to promote universal moral unity through an expansive interpretation of the few highly abstract principles upon which agreement seems possible. The drive for universality in the absence of agreement has led to an attempt to draw a complete system of public morality out of the abstract rights of human beings conceived as simply as possible.

The human-rights movement therefore bases its standards on the dignity of man as a being with desires and the capacity to form plans for the future. Freedom becomes the ability to pursue and realize individual desires, whatever they may be, and justice the equal claim of men and their preferences to fulfillment. Such standards amount to a restatement of contemporary liberalism as a comprehensive system of legal norms enforceable everywhere.[15]

While the abstract principles on which current conceptions of human rights are based likely play a role in most reasonable moral and political systems, the attempt to turn them into a complete system of social morality that trumps all other considerations is eccentric. As now understood, human rights are religiously and culturally intolerant in a peculiarly radical way. The requirement that we be treated simply as abstract agents pursuing essentially private goals leads to the peremptory demand that aspects of social identity—religion, historical community, and sex—that give us a definite social position and connect us to concerns that transcend us be deprived of significance. Traditional understandings of human relations and social morality must therefore be abolished. Governments, for example, are now required by international treaty to cut back radically on customary parental authority and to intervene to eliminate social and cultural patterns that recognize differing roles for the sexes.[16] Such requirements are evidently at odds with the family as an institution and indeed with basic aspects of social life everywhere.

From an organizational perspective such a result is, of course, not surprising. Human-rights standards are put together by experts and functionaries, and they make rule by such people all but absolute.[17] They are an extraordinarily imperialistic and centralizing force that extends the rationalizing activity of the regulatory welfare state to all human relations everywhere. From the beginning they were intended to become internationally compulsory. Since they are presented as fundamental principles, to whose benefits we are entitled simply as human beings, they are in concept peremptory and categorical, determinable by jurists and other experts, rightfully enforceable at the instance of any affected party, and not subject to political considerations. Their implicit aim is the comprehensive transformation of all social existence everywhere along advanced liberal lines. The simplicity of the principles on which they are based and their consequent unity and universality, together with the grossness of the human-rights violations that sometimes occur, gives them extraordinary rhetorical force, so that the fact that the Nazis murdered millions of Jews somehow gives compelling urgency to the push for "gay marriage." Rights proposed at international conferences, adopted by diplomats, and ratified by lawmakers impressed by "international standards" and inclined to join in union with their opposite numbers in other countries are to be made enforceable by judiciaries upon whom they confer broad powers of interpretation, by donor countries who threaten withdrawal of aid and other sanctions, and at times by direct use of force. While enforcement falls far short at present, the ambitions of the human-rights movement are enormous, and the expansive principles on which it is based and its alignment with the present needs of power seem likely to tell in the long run.

Nonliberal Institutions

An unavoidable issue raised by the liberal project of social rationalization is the treatment of traditional and informal arrangements that compete with the bureaucratic and market institutions liberalism favors. Traditional institutions that rely on ties and distinctions liberalism rejects, such as family, sex, religion, particular culture, and historical community, order human life in basic ways. They create the connections by which men normally live (and live normally), and they establish common habits, understandings, and loyalties that guide social functioning and facilitate networks of trust and cooperation. They are the basis of a natural form of society that pre-exists any attempt to impose a consciously invented pattern.

Discrimination

Nonetheless, such arrangements put some people at a disadvantage. No society or institution is egalitarian. Patterns of cooperation depend on connections and distinctions that are intrinsically unequal. People would not consider career so important if a CEO and a mail clerk were treated the same. In the case of liberal institutions such as the market, the state, and certified expertise, the inequalities, however radical, are integrated with rationally organized functions and can be justified as necessary for the liberal system to operate. In the case of other institutions that is not so, at least from the liberal point of view. Advanced liberalism therefore demands that the distinctions and expectations on which traditional institutions rely, which it considers irrational as well as unequal, be made irrelevant to everything of practical importance. That is what it means to say that it opposes stereotyping and discrimination.

As an application of liberal principle such a demand has great force. Once basic physical needs have been satisfied, our relations with others, including how they regard and treat us, are what most of us care most about. Liberalism insists that systematic inequalities regarding such things be justified in liberal terms, so that the only distinctions allowed to matter are clearly definable distinctions liberal institutions rely on, such as wealth, bureaucratic position, and educational certification. All others must be abolished, at least in their effects. That insistence is now considered a matter of basic social morality. Persons of every race, ethnicity, nationality, lifestyle, religious background, disability, sex, and sexual orientation must be able to participate equally in major social activities, with "ability to participate" measured by their achievement of roughly equal status, rewards, and respect. Conversely, every significant activity and institution must include such persons in rough proportion to their presence in the population. If it does not, at least when those excluded can point to a social disadvantage from which they suffer that suggests the exclusion may be discriminatory, the disproportion is considered a serious wrong that disparages the equal humanity of those disadvantaged, and it must be rectified by all necessary means.

It is hard to overstate how radical such demands are. Sex, religion, historical community, particular culture, and the like, which are the inequalities targeted by measures such as the Civil Rights Act of 1964, have always been fundamental to social organization. Such traditional connections determine almost inevitably how people understand themselves and relate to each other. While the state and other public institutions often have good reason to ignore particularities, less formal arrangements such as friendship, love, and family life notoriously discriminate on just such grounds. The enforcement history of the Civil Rights Act as well as simple reflection shows that any serious general attempt to do away with such connections as social organizing principles must quickly become aggressively radical.

To say that distinctions of sex and sexuality should have no significance, for example, is in effect to say that the family should have no settled nature, that it should not be a social institution surrounded by definite standards that support and guard it and enable it to function effectively and reliably, that it is just a name for any sort of domestic partnership. When so understood it no longer makes sense to tie the family to serious obligations. It must be replaced in important matters by formal education, childcare agencies, fast-food restaurants, the welfare system, and so on. To say ethnicity should have no significance is to make a similar point about historic community and particular culture: all the expectations, assumptions, habits, attitudes, memories, standards, and loyalties that connect those who share an inherited community and culture must be made irrelevant to all aspects of life that have public significance. Multiculturalism—the comprehensive effort to detach social life from particular culture and inherited community—is a necessary consequence of the antidiscrimination principle.

Since public life under liberalism must be based strictly on liberal principles, it can only be organized by money, bureaucratic position, and certified expertise. It is difficult to arrange things in such a way. Even if the difficulty of abolishing the effect of basic social connections and the damage likely to result from making them nonfunctional is ignored, discrimination is often quite rational in particular cases and for that reason continually reappears. Human beings differ, as do their affinities to one other and their ways of cooperating. Enough differences are related to characteristics such as sex and ethnicity for free dealings to lead to a degree of social differentiation even in the absence of intentional discrimination. Where such differentiation arises, the habits, social expectations, and ease of cooperation it engenders accentuate it, and when such things become self-aware they turn into full-fledged discrimination of a kind now considered intolerably invidious. Discrimination perpetually re-creates itself if there is no comprehensive supervening force constantly at work to ferret it out and suppress it.

The attempt to ensure that every type of person, belief, habit, and preference is included equally in all important settings requires comprehensive measures that continuously counteract the way people naturally view and deal with each other. All significant institutions must adopt inclusiveness and diversity as fundamental commitments justifying constant efforts at reeducation, and all human activities must be continuously supervised for compliance. As David K. Shipler notes in *A Country of Strangers* (1997), "This is the ideal: to search your attitudes, identify your stereotypes, and correct for them as you go about your daily duties."[18]

That may not be a severe requirement in the case of liberal activist groups, neutral rational bureaucracies, and purely profit-seeking enterprises. It is likely to reduce their efficiency somewhat, and may make them rather alienating as places to work, but their fundamental commitments can remain much as before. However, it places a serious strain on educational and cultural institutions that are concerned with substantive noneconomic goods. If such institutions are allowed to function on their original principles, they will almost surely engage in discrimination based on cultural attachments and ultimate commitments, and thus effectively on class, ethnicity, and religion. At a minimum, they will be more welcoming to those of some backgrounds than others, and they will violate the requirement that the terms and conditions of employment be made equal—and thus the workplace equally hospitable—for those of all backgrounds.

Educational and cultural institutions must therefore be transformed and their fundamental purposes radically altered so that they can be inclusive. Schools that once taught the liberal arts must abolish particular cultural connections and emphasize diversity above all else. Drama companies must emphasize "nontraditional casting," while art museums must get rid of connoisseurship, which depends on the acceptance of particular cultural standards, in favor of multiculturalism, left-wing social history, and confrontational pieces that subvert traditional standards. Here and abroad lawmakers increasingly require Catholic organizations to hire atheists, place adopted children with homosexual couples, and provide contraceptives to employees. In the name of freedom and diversity, all institutions must be forced to adopt similar goals, standards, and practices that may be wholly at odds with their reason for being.

No usable way of limiting such requirements has been proposed. In fact, the extent of these demands is often ignored or obfuscated, and the convention that what is called *diversity* be treated as a great and unalloyed good makes it difficult to discuss and criticize them. To the contrary, these requirements continually become broader, so that the list of protected characteristics gets longer and forbidden discrimination comes to include toleration of disproportionate outcomes. If you are not part of the solution you are part of the problem—that is the meaning of expressions like "institutional racism." Everyone is required to participate enthusiastically in a never-ending and all-embracing campaign for inclusiveness and against that acceptance of the reality of human differences which is now called *hatred*.

The totalitarian character of such a campaign is unavoidable, given its premises. By its nature it requires a comprehensive control over social life restrained by neither popular consent nor traditional limitations on the role of the state. It requires "affirmative action"—quotas and equivalent measures—since the only way to verify proper motives and eliminate structural inequalities is to look at results. Reeducation programs, sensitivity training, speech codes, and other forms of thought control become a permanent necessity, since the purpose of any serious antidiscrimination program is to prevent people from acting and making decisions in ways that seem natural to them unless their habits of thought are constantly put in question and reformed.

"Political correctness" has drawn attention as an eccentric excess, perhaps because it has to do with words and it is natural to talk about words. In fact, political correctness is simply that aspect of inclusiveness which deals with the purification of language, symbols, and images, and as such is necessary to the effort as a whole. The specifics are of course infinitely varied. Writers and public speakers must use "inclusive" language—for example, they must avoid using "man" and "he" to refer to human beings in general—and otherwise use the terms chosen for protected groups by their most vocal spokesmen.[19] Athletic teams must be renamed and illustrations in books and periodicals loaded with women and racial minorities in non-traditional and often improbable roles. Such matters become a matter of bureaucratic routine: committees meet, decide on guidelines, and incorporate them in style sheets and other authoritative standards. The rules often become petty and burdensome, as in the case of other rules relating to inclusiveness, since their purpose is to interfere quite comprehensively with the details of day-to-day life. Nonetheless, a desire to avoid constraint in matters that seem minor cannot, from the advanced liberal standpoint, justify the perpetuation of the oppression implicit in informal customary arrangements. If using "A.D." instead of "C.E." suggests the social authority of Christianity and so puts Buddhists at a disadvantage because of who they are or the preferences they live by, it is hard, from the standpoint of equal freedom, to view forbidding the term as oppressive.

Bigotry

The demand for inclusiveness becomes most intense when cast as opposition to the things now referred to as "bigotry": racism, sexism, homophobia, and the like. Such opposition is treated as self-evident and so rarely discussed analytically, but as a view accepted as fundamental to social morality and legitimate public policy it nonetheless has specific content. As such, it holds that there are definite things classifiable as "bigotry" that are backed by power and constituted by hatred and contempt for those who differ, and but for which relations among groups would be harmonious—if indeed differences were noted at all. Bigotry is thought to have no legitimate function whatever. It is pure pathology, like smallpox, and it transforms everything it touches. It turns insults into crimes and makes even atrocities more ghastly. The crimes of leftist regimes, which are not thought bigoted in their basic nature, are considered no more comparable to Nazi outrages than is a botched surgical operation to an ax murder.

Bigotry is seen everywhere, with or without specific evidence. As long as some groups are collectively unequal to others, the world is racist, sexist, homophobic, and otherwise bigoted, and the harder it is to find an explanation that can be presented without offending minority sensitivities and interests, the more fundamental and pervasive the bigotry is presumed to be. And since bigotry is presumed to be everywhere, accusations of it always stick, at least a little, and however reckless rarely hurt the accuser. Even false accusations are thought valuable, because they draw attention to issues that can never be overemphasized.[20] If nothing else, they demonstrate that someone feels marginalized and excluded—a situation that can never be ignored, accepted, or blamed on the victim.

The emphasis on bigotry as a supreme evil that must be fought in every way possible is a surprisingly recent growth that demonstrates a transformation of moral life. It first became important, and still is strongest, with respect to race. Emphatic opposition to racism, and the belief that it is pervasive and almost supernaturally monstrous, give the "race card" extraordinary potency. Any tinge of racism is now thought to discredit a man, practice, or institution. Nonetheless, the word racism apparently did not exist in English before the 1930s,[21] the 1968 convention was the first the Democratic Party held without whites-only delegations, and one of the first Roman Catholics to identify racial segregation as a sin died just a few years ago.[22] In earlier times, particular instances of racial oppression were recognized as wrong, but they were wrong in the way and for the reasons other oppression was wrong. Taking ethnic attachments into account in the ordinary affairs of life, when choosing associates for example, was not considered to be a radical moral evil simply as such.

American antiracism, which is now understood as basic to American identity, reflects profound changes in the nature of American nationality under the influence of liberalism and related trends. Americans began as overseas Englishmen, and thus as a traditional ethnic people defined by ancestry and inherited habits and loyalties. As John Jay, writing in *The Federalist*, observed, "Providence has been pleased to give this one connected country to one united people—a people descended from the same ancestors, speaking the same language, professing the same religion, attached to the same principles of government, very similar in their manners and customs."[23]

Independence distinguished Americans from their one-time compatriots, and their national identity became tied to the political theory that justified separation. The ideological component of American identity has since become ever more important, as immigration diluted common ancestry, secession and its bloody failure weakened and discredited local particularism, technology and economic development separated men from their roots, and American national institutions became more dominant and for their own purposes emphasized the universalistic aspects of American life.

The result today is that mainstream white Americans have come to understand ethnicity as something *others* have. They view themselves much more as free and independent individuals who are Americans because they accept ideals and institutions they understand as universally valid. More and more, for an American to return to his roots as an American is to become radically individualist, universalist, and anti-ethnic. Antiracism is a messianic version of the refusal to recognize distinctions based on particular culture and historic community, and as such it has become part of an Americanism that has replaced more particular identities as a focus for political and social attachment. Remnants of older and more particularistic understandings have become incomprehensible and give rise to guilt feelings that redouble antiracist zeal.

The evolving character of American nationality has foreshadowed broader changes in the world at large, as America has become less exceptional. The movement against bigotry has generalized and spread throughout the world as other countries have joined in the battle against discrimination, and as that battle has expanded from antiracism to opposition to sexism, homophobia, and other new offenses. The fundamental principle—the demand for the abolition of distinctions that relate to social arrangements other than markets and rationalized bureaucracies—remains the same, while its application has grown from the suppression of connections and distinctions related to historical community to the suppression of those related to yet more fundamental institutions such as the family.[24]

Today, resolute opposition to what counts as bigotry is no less a principle of the EU—and indeed all respectable institutions everywhere—than of America. That opposition is clearly not purely a matter of high ideals. Big business, finance, academia, and government, all intensely unequal and hierarchical, support the eradication of traditional distinctions and connections less because they love equality than because they want their own forms of inequality—financial, professional, or bureaucratic—to prevail. For a universal rational order based on global markets and transnational bureaucracies to dominate social life without resistance, populations must be transformed into aggregations of human resources and purchasing power lacking the cohesion, complexity, and noneconomic interests that might complicate the system and make it less manageable and efficient. As in other settings, moralism here distracts attention from obvious self-interest.

The strength of anti-bigotry is not, however, *simply* a matter of institutional self-interest. It is tied to broader changes that weaken family and community generally. Community normally involves historical, cultural, sexual, and similar nonrationalized ties that precede the specific choices

men make. Such ties are at odds with the modern tendency to question
things and demand plain answers, and to take them apart for reassembly,
packaging, and sale. As a result, standards of behavior not freely chosen
by individuals have come to be thought oppressive, and rejection of whatever transcends the concerns of particular men has become a moral norm.
Even a man's own culture, the understandings and habits he was born
to that make him what he is and connect him to those around him, now
seems an imposition.

Under such circumstances bureaucracies and markets can be defended as neutral rational ways of aggregating and coordinating individual preferences, but sexual distinctions and inherited and cultural ties are
incomprehensible. The relation of the sexes combines biology, psychology,
tradition, and social function in ways that are very difficult to unravel.
Historical and cultural ties are a mix of history, early upbringing, habits,
attitudes, connections, and loyalties that are more easily felt and acted on
than defined. They are social facts that do not reduce without remainder
to individual characteristics or conduct. That should not be surprising,
since social setting precedes individual qualities and choices. That is how
it becomes part of what makes us what we are and connects us durably to
others. However, the modern outlook is too narrowly analytical to deal
with such things. It finds sexual distinctions and inherited community
and culture lacking in any clear content and ultimately comprehensible
only as the fear of freedom, a will to dominate, or hatred for those who
differ. To make matters worse, moderns, who are fond of logical simplicity, interpret such things in the most extreme sense possible. Common
sense can only be the sense of a community constituted by tradition, so to
be fully modern is to be incapable of good sense and moderation. Doubts
about one thing become identified with insistence on its opposite, and
a rejection of simple comprehensive equality with the promotion of unlimited oppression. Hence the stereotypes of the "racist," "sexist," and

"homophobe": in the attribution of any significance at all to traditional nonrationalized connections and distinctions, moderns see limitless violent oppression.

Such changes in life and in social and political ideals correspond to a shift in basic philosophical understandings. Liberalism and modernity generally involve the denial of whatever transcends particular purposes. Such a denial implies that we create distinctions rather than find them, and that they matter only to the extent we make them matter. It brings about a setting in which classifying is simply an exercise of the will of the classifier, and attribution of stable character a manifestation of obsessiveness. In such a setting, extreme sensitivity regarding what is called bigotry is inevitable. If things do not have stable natures that precede our actions and purposes, classification is intrinsically oppressive; escaping it becomes essential to personal dignity. Since distinctions have no objective basis, the obvious motive for making them is the construction of one's own identity by arbitrary exclusion. To construct oneself as superior one need only treat others as inferior, and to make the distinction serious one enforces it violently. Classifying others thus becomes, from the modern anti-transcendental point of view, a kind of conceptual apartheid that leads directly to Nazism.

The contrast with previous understandings is striking. Universals were once understood to allow participation in the order of the world. To be a man, a peasant, or a king was to live in accordance with the innate order of things, to take part in the world made by God, nature, and history, and thus to have dignity. To be English or Thai carried with it a web of loyalties and standards that made possible a rewarding life in common. Even to be a beggar gave a man a recognized place. Such definite qualities gave reality and weight to things. They enabled men to escape the degradation of continual change and the nothingness of abstract characterless individuality. Stability meant life: change, decay, and death.[25]

All that has changed. If we deny universals, to be a king is to be imprisoned by the social expectations surrounding kingship. To have a particular IQ is to be defined as suitable for certain roles in the social machine, and so to be reduced to an implement to be used by others for their own purposes. Life and meaning lie in the escape from determinate being, in transition to something other than what one already is—the less definable the better. Like sex, drugs, ambition, and violence, change and diversity are this-worldly substitutes for transcendence. Anything, even change for the worse, is better than here-and-now reality and the requirements imposed by a specific community and way of life.

The movement against bigotry has come far and fast because of the crystallization of the conditions and understandings upon which it depends. Public recognition of the transcendent has collapsed. Even the churches, to the extent they remain socially respectable, have abandoned it in favor of this-worldly concerns, tolerance and inclusiveness first and foremost. The enormous growth of government social expenditures since the Second World War has brought radical centralization and bureaucratization to social life generally. Family forms and the relation between the sexes have become too indefinite for reliance, and children are now largely raised by a combination of electronic entertainment and government functionaries. Cheap transportation and electronic communications have powerfully enhanced globalization. Each of us today is constantly confronted electronically and in print with a heterogeneous assortment of persons and things presented by media functionaries or the Internet. We look at them not from the standpoint of our own concrete or inherited experience but from an artificial universal standpoint constructed by a perpetually shifting web of text, sound, and images. From that standpoint, the articulated distinctions that have constituted social order become baseless assertions. In particular, the social functions of traditional ties and distinctions vanish from sight. Instead, these ties appear to be a source of conflict, chaos, and oppression within a system functioning on wholly different principles.

Comparison with Other Regimes

Liberal institutions are often presented, especially by apologists, as basically procedural. They are a matter of majority rule, representative government, an independent judiciary, competition for office, a free press, a market economy, and so on. That view may have been reasonable when the task for those promoting equal freedom was to break down traditional habits and understandings intertwined with nonliberal procedures in public life, but it has long ceased to be valid.

In theory, liberals continue to put form and procedure first. In fact, the liberal concern with concept and form eventually becomes substantive rather than procedural, less a matter of fairness in elections than the enforcement of fairness as a general social condition. The contemporary liberal state is not simply a guardian of procedural fairness or a broker among competing interests. It is an enormous and all-pervasive system of power dedicated to the control and transformation of human life backed by a huge public sector; lower- and middle-class recipients of public assistance; accredited minority groups and their representatives; corporate recipients of various favors; and media, journalistic, and expert functionaries who draw their importance from the power of the regime they defend and promote.[26]

Liberal regimes claim to be far less involved than others in promoting particular social goods and a common outlook that supports them. In fact, the similarities are greater than they will admit. Like other approaches to government, liberalism rules in accordance with a particular understanding of man and the world, and it tries to bring social attitudes and beliefs in line with that understanding. That process is always a delicate business. All governments rely in the end on force, but they normally prefer unforced cooperation and rely on a variety of methods of establishing and protecting common understandings. Different governments emphasize different means: republics stress mutual persuasion among citizens, theocracies and ideological regimes persuasion by authority backed by sanctions, and traditionalist states common adherence to what has long been settled. All those are ways of reducing the number and intensity of disagreements by dealing with their substance, a process that is difficult but necessary if government is to promote values held in common.

What is unusual about liberal governments is that they claim to deal with inconsistent views on basic matters not by nudging or forcing them into line with the official view but by keeping them out of politics so each can remain as it was. Liberals say that such an approach leaves the mind and spirit free and allows political allegiance to be grounded not on the promotion of common goods but on letting each pursue his own vision of the good without interference. They claim that substantive moral neutrality of this kind is the only approach to government that can work in the present pluralistic age.

If such claims were true, liberalism would indeed be unique. But they are not true. While liberalism is certainly at home in today's world, its supremacy is due less to pluralism and the inability of particular substantive moral views to achieve dominance than to changes in the way dominance is established and maintained. It uses new methods of dominion that rely less on physical repression than on methods that centralize social life, destroy independent institutions and moral habits, keep fundamental principles out of the discussion, and maintain the illusion of open inquiry and popular rule.

The liberal state claims that it uses force only to guard individual rights that precede legitimate discussion in a regime based on freedom and equality. It is therefore impossible for a liberal regime to be oppressive as long as it is true to its principles: its actions, however forcible, minutely interfering, and opposed to the habits, desires, and expectations of those subjected to them, are by definition liberating. Such claims, backed by the machinery of public information and institutional expertise, give liberalism a "stealth" quality that enables it to rule without effective opposition by making issues seem to disappear: there is nothing to discuss. Liberalism boasts that it is "transparent"—open in its workings and free of procedural distortions introduced by irrationality and special interests. In fact, its fundamental quality is not transparency but invisibility, the ability to keep the substantive nature of the ends on behalf of which it exercises power out of sight, thus preventing challenges to its dominance from even being raised.

Liberalism has always been characterized by a reluctance to admit that government makes important decisions that might well have been made otherwise. Under classical liberalism, the need for the appearance of neutrality meant that everything had to be a matter of property rights. To answer a question, one asked what the holders of the relevant property interests wanted. Today, the supposed neutrality of property rights and legal procedures is supplemented or supplanted by the supposedly less rigid and arbitrary neutrality of experts, consultants, technicians, therapists, ethicists, social scientists, constitutional lawyers, transnational bureaucrats, and human-rights advocates, all here to help us and none (supposedly) exercising significant discretionary power. Government activities, even when backed by an enormous system of coercion, are presented as assistance, therapy, or the defense of individual rights, while resistance is viewed as harassment, violence, or psychological pathology.

The advantage its stealth quality gives liberalism in public discussion has so far been insuperable, and the need to maintain that advantage affects every aspect of its rule. Basic features of the liberal regime work together to define, inculcate, and enforce the common understandings on which it depends while avoiding any suggestion that those understandings might be debatable. This tendency gives liberal rule many of its specific features—for example, its reliance on judges and other functionaries authorized to rule certain arguments and measures out of order on the basis of expert knowledge and legal principles that few understand but everyone must accept. To reject them, it is thought, would be to reject both rationality and basic social commitments already agreed upon.

Europeans used to complain that American conformity and its enforcement by popular sentiment made men timid, and venturesome thought all but impossible. Today the same conformity has established itself on both sides of the Atlantic, but it is enforced less through popular sentiment, which now plays a subordinate role, than through political correctness, the increasingly bureaucratic organization of life, and the reign of expertise—which, as a system of mutual certification, involves its own pressures toward conformity. Even though the mechanisms are different, the function is still the same: to prevent difficult topics from arising in societies that want to maintain public order without the visible use of force, arbitrary decisions, or disputable ideological commitments.

Throughout the West, compulsory conformity is presented as diversity, indoctrination as neutral expertise, and rules that set strict limits on what can be said as the suppression of "hatred" and "bigotry," and hence as liberation. Such a system of control is made possible by a centralization of intellectual life that makes molders of opinion—experts, educators, media people, entertainers—integral to government. The saying that such people constitute a "Fourth Estate" should be taken literally. This power over opinion puts them among our rulers, and it brings with it disciplines and incentives that promote cohesion and help make their rule effective.

The result is that the republic of letters has become less republican and more bureaucratic and hierarchical. Thought and knowledge are no longer left to chance or individual initiative, although these remain important as a reality check. What counts as serious intellectual life is carried on by a state-supported bureaucracy comprising academics, foundations, makers of grants, professional associations, think tanks, arts officials, and so on. Mainstream news reporting and analysis are in the hands of professionals employed by a few large organizations that are acutely conscious of their power and responsibility as integral parts of the process of government. Experts determine what counts as reason and truth, and mass-communications media enable a small number of well-placed professionals to flood the world with the opinions, interpretations, information, and sound bites they think appropriate. Even the things children once learned at their mothers' knees have been socialized. The young are now reared largely by each other, with the aid of concerns, themes, and ideals supplied by mass-market entertainers and an increasingly unified state education system that processes them for a larger and larger part of their lives.

The effect has been radically to reduce intellectual independence and make genuinely dissident views seem provincial, ignorant, or insane. The only dissidence accepted as legitimate is that of the Left, whose demands for social justice amount only to demands for further extension of state power and activity. The few places actual dissent exists freely, such as talk radio and the Internet, are amateurish, socially marginal, lack discipline and coherence, and are seen as centers of disruption, misinformation, and hate that threaten everything decent. While talk radio and modestly dissenting blogs have had some influence on public discussion of particular situations, and the new media may ultimately have a much greater effect, so far their role has been less to change the basis and focus of public discussion than slightly to improve its rationality on particular issues. It is now somewhat more difficult simply to ignore the obvious. In that regard their function has been much the same as that of those academics, experts, and journalists who offer some dissent from the views institutionally dominant while respecting the limits necessary to continue as recognized legitimate participants in the discussion.

In spite of the talk of pluralism, diversity, and government as a mere provider of services, the outstanding feature of the current regime is its power, especially its power over social standards and the minds of men. The fact is that modern conditions make it less important than in the past for government to avoid assertion of radically unpopular positions regarding the principles governing our lives together. "Political correctness" with regard to issues such as religion and homosexuality shows that it is now possible to establish as authoritative social and moral views that are profoundly at odds with long-established understandings, as long as those who dominate public discussion are committed to them.

A state that is committed to the open-ended reform of all social institutions and spends a third to half or more of the national income is a very different and far more pervasive presence than anything known in the past. The air we breath is media-drenched and statist. The normal functioning of the contemporary liberal state deprives independent local institutions such as the family of function and recognition, while the requirements of "tolerance" and "inclusiveness," enforced on all significant institutions by law, professional standards, and the requirements of public relations in a media-driven age, destroy any remaining social basis for resistance. Any significant organization that does not celebrate the advanced liberal version of diversity and make its promotion a basic institutional objective finds itself a target and very likely in court.

There seems to be no place to hide, no setting—without going to extremes like the Amish and Hasidim—where basically different forms of life can establish themselves, maintain their independence, and show that an alternative is possible. The Catholic Church was long the main opponent of liberalism in the West, and as an international religious institution with a celibate and therefore socially detached clergy it still retains some immunity from state coercion. Yet the widespread emphasis within it on ecumenism, openness to the world, and "pastoral" approaches—not to mention tolerance, social welfare, and human rights—indicate a pervasive sense that what is real and important today is determined by reference not to anything metaphysical or transcendent but to the universal unitary this-worldly scheme of things constituted by liberal principle and secular technological society.[27] Technocratic liberalism, which was supposed to leave ultimate issues alone, has ended by becoming the ultimate principle constituting human reality.

CHAPTER FOUR

Through the Looking Glass

An examination of liberal principles and institutions, and a consideration of liberal society generally, suggest that their logic leads to results very much at odds with their apparent promise. In trying to secure and expand freedom, equality, and tolerance, liberal society becomes unfree, unequal, and intolerant. Such pervasive anomalies in matters so basic to our present way of life demand further exploration.

REVERSAL OF MEANINGS

The reversals are implicit in basic liberal concepts, which cannot rationally become the basis of government. If man is the measure it cannot be right to tell him what to do. We cannot be forced to be free or ordered to be equal. Neither theoretical refinements nor practical compromises can resolve such basic contradictions or keep them from leading to unprincipled and irrational conduct that eventually proves self-destructive.

Positive Neutrality

Many contradictions within liberalism spring from its claim to eliminate conflicts through a system of public neutrality. The presence in society of opposing understandings as to how to live is said to demonstrate that liberalism must triumph for the sake of social peace. That claim is now considered an irrefutable argument on its behalf.

The argument is puzzling. Moral diversity is common to all societies of any size and complexity, and almost any view—not just liberalism—would establish social peace if everyone accepted it. Liberal initiatives can generate conflict, and peace has often been maintained without them. It is unclear, then, what is special about liberalism and why today's situation requires it. Liberalism is thought to be universally acceptable to reasonable men. It is also radically at odds with traditional cultural and religious understandings of human relations. Are all such understandings unreasonable? Does everyone now reject them?

Liberals describe liberalism as if it viewed things from a superior position that lets it supervise other views while leaving them just as they are. Only a liberal could accept such a description. Liberalism is a comprehensive scheme of government, and as such it has pervasive implications for human affairs. It puts forth an ideal of life, at least implicitly, just as other social and political views do, and it has limited tolerance for opposition. Of necessity it decides issues that bear on how we should live and what things are worth. No government can be neutral between the services abortionists provide and the lives Operation Rescue defends, and the choice between the two is a choice between understandings of life. Contemporary liberal government spends a large part of national income on activities as value-laden as education and family support. Simply as government it must claim the right to confer honor, disgrace, and punishment, and it must demand a loyalty that extends to matters of life and death. To deal with such responsibilities in an intelligent, coherent, and effective way is to adopt a comprehensive moral stance.

Liberal society forces liberalism and its consequences on all of us just as other forms of society force other views on their members. In place of communal and family arrangements that mostly run themselves, it gives us social programs, market relationships, antidiscrimination laws, and the managerial state. Such institutions have pervasive implications for all our lives. Liberalism demands reform in matters as close to home as the relations of the sexes and the rearing of children. Its program of fine-grained social transformation requires even thought control. Equal-opportunity laws are not likely to achieve their goals unless people are induced to reject natural inclinations that continually reappear if left to themselves. A continuous program of propaganda, reeducation, and stigmatization of dissenters is therefore a necessary part of any contemporary liberal regime.

Whether such measures are good or bad, they are radical, and putting them into effect gives enormous power to institutions dedicated to the supervision and fundamental transformation of habits and attitudes, institutions that are of necessity exempt from popular control. Claims that liberalism leaves us free to choose whatever goods we prefer are unpersuasive when it relies so much on propaganda and bureaucratic control and in any event forces us to live in a society that radically limits the goods available by insisting that goods become nonsocial. A society in which the freedom to choose normal stable family life and a favorable social environment for raising children is as hard beset as our own is much less free than it imagines. There is no reason for someone who is not a liberal, and who believes it important to be able to choose such basic human goods, to accept such a society.

Liberal neutrality began as a collection of limitations on government power intended to deal with particular abuses, but it is now imposed on social practices generally. When it becomes a positive principle in that manner it stops being neutral. It is now a principle of potentially universal applicability that promotes an unprecedented extension of government power. Instead of narrowly restricting what government can do it now narrowly restricts what "society"—each of us—can do. It means that every institution that hopes to remain respectable must suppress substantive standards that transcend individual desire, even when doing so gravely weakens the institution, is radically at odds with its mission, and outrages its most loyal supporters. Nothing of importance is allowed to remain as it was. Educators convert education into the pursuit of goals such as tolerance and inclusion, career success, psychological adjustment, or whatever subjective interests the student may have. Even the Catholic Church has reconfigured the mass so that its most common form has become to all appearances an expression of the solidarity and sentiments of those gathered together. From the standpoint of the experts and professional managers who now dominate all significant public institutions, the resulting loss of integrity and effectiveness is as nothing compared to the absolute need to bring every institution in line with liberal neutrality.

It is not objectionable in itself that liberal government adopts a comprehensive moral stance with profound implications for human life, since other governments do so as well. What is objectionable is that liberals claim their views are neutral while all others are aggressive and intolerant. Governments cannot be neutral on basic principles. They can be moderate, but moderation is a much more limited affair. A moderate government would show respect for divergent views because it recognizes the difficulty of attaining moral agreement and the importance of arrangements that ease cooperation when agreement is shaky. To that extent, it would likely have some liberal features. Such features would be a matter of practical wisdom consistent with almost any understanding of the ultimate purpose of politics. A theocracy might choose some degree of accommodation over an attempt to extirpate opposing views by force, and to that extent it would be moderate. A liberal regime might also be moderate. If so, it would be lukewarm in its promotion of social justice, since the liberal conception of social justice requires thwarting so many human tendencies. If people were attached to nonliberal principles it would let them have their effect, rather than trying to suppress them in the interest of inclusion and the liberal conception of justice. Liberalism today is not moderate in that sense.

In practice, a claim of neutrality with respect to a scheme as comprehensive as modern government is hard to distinguish from a claim of absolute righteousness. It is a statement that those who disagree with the established order are oppressors who deserve only suppression or reeducation. Liberalism calls its demands "rights," makes them absolute and categorical, and treats principles of limitation—such as respect for natural tendencies and settled understandings—at best as temporary practical obstacles. Without stable limiting principles its demands become all-embracing. Since the alternative is thought to be oppression, they become enforceable by any means necessary. To consider such a system neutral is absurd.

Forced Consent

The principle of basing government on consent creates more contradictions. Liberalism has trouble making sense of authority. It treats human will as the standard, even though authority is needed when wills conflict and cannot serve as the standard. It tries to get around the problem by deriving authority from contract, but the question remains why contract obliges. Some transcendent principle is needed, but liberalism is reluctant to recognize such a principle. It is therefore unable to explain coherently why anyone should obey the laws it imposes.[1]

Whatever the theoretical problems, consent remains the ostensible principle of liberal government. As such, it is a principle with two faces.

When liberalism is out of power, the demand for consent is a demand against government, a demand that it justify itself by reference to popular support. When liberals govern, it becomes a demand against the people, a demand that they wholeheartedly support the government's orientation and policies. The transformation is unavoidable. A government that makes choice the highest principle cannot tolerate people choosing the wrong things. If individual preferences are the basis of morality and legitimate social relations, then the mere fact of dissent destroys authority, for it puts it at odds with what someone wants. No government can allow the casual destruction of its authority. To base government on consent therefore means that government must insist on consent and get it however it can. Consent becomes ritualistic. If the people reject liberal government, they must at all costs be induced to change their mind, because otherwise government by consent becomes impossible and the alternative, from a liberal standpoint, is oppression and chaos.

Liberal authorities insist that basic liberal understandings be put beyond question. They view nonliberal and therefore nonconsenting views such as those held by right-to-lifers and the traditionally religious as a public danger that naturally leads to violence. The September 11, 2001, terrorist attacks enhanced the belief that religion is essentially irrational and violent, and it led to denunciations of imperfectly liberal Christians as equivalent to Muslim terrorists. Among prominent and respected liberals such attitudes long predated those events. For instance, Anthony Lewis of the *New York Times* said in 1993 that "the murder of a doctor in Pensacola, Fla., tells us the essential truth about most anti-abortion activists. They are religious fanatics, who want to impose their version of God's word on the rest of us. For them the end justifies any means, including violence." He declared all anti-abortionists, simply as such, outside the political community: "In this country we have a constitutional bargain about religion. Individuals are guaranteed the right to choose their faith, but they may not compel others to accept their views. . . . The bargain is essential to our form of democracy, which requires compromise and does not work when there are ideological certainties. The anti-abortion activists are outside the bargain. They have all the certainty—the cold-blooded certainty—of an Ayatollah Khomeini."[2]

Liberalism ends by demanding adherence to its principles as well as obedience to its laws. The result is that official culture becomes thoroughly propagandistic and invades the whole of social life. Anti-harassment rules control the thoughts expressed in the presence of others. The schools become engines of indoctrination before all else,[3] and journalists, educators, experts, and other professionals recognize and enforce a social responsibility always to promote the official understandings. Those understandings—diversity, tolerance, inclusiveness, and the like—have become the inevitable content of all public celebrations and holidays, of all education that is not strictly technical, of all respectable religion, and of all art that claims to be serious, notably officially subsidized art that proclaims its own adventurousness. Contrary views, including all nonliberal religious or philosophical views on the nature of man and moral life, are caricatured, trivialized, kept strictly private, subjected to compulsory revision, or suppressed altogether. They become fair game for almost any kind of abuse.

Instead of religious tests, Sunday closing laws, and laws against blasphemy, there are diversity programs, speech codes, and the Martin Luther King holiday. Words take on new meanings: "hatred" comes to include opposition to liberal initiatives, while "inclusiveness" requires nonliberals to abandon their principles and even identity. "Tolerance" treats objections to liberalism as attacks on neutrality that are oppressive simply by being made. "Diversity" means thought control, "openness" means shutting the door to recognition of differences, and "getting government out of our bedrooms" means sexual-harassment law, training children to use condoms, and insisting that homosexuality be treated as equivalent to heterosexuality. Fear and hatred of "fundamentalism and intolerance"—of the belief that there are goods that do not reduce to human desire and distinctions that cannot be rationalized on economic and bureaucratic principles—becomes basic to public moral sentiment.[4]

Many people believe the new order is better than the old, but it is no more consensual in any ordinary sense. If it were, the bureaucracy, regulations, and reeducation programs it features so prominently would make no sense. The nature of advanced liberalism can be inferred from those who support it. Throughout the West the most well-placed and respectable men and institutions are regularly liberal, while those who reject liberalism are tagged as ignorant, provincial, and lower-class. It is simply not believable that in a society based on the consent of the people, special attachment to the official system of belief would be considered a mark of elite status and rejection as crudely populist.

Censorship as Freedom

In some ways it is surprising that liberalism should end as a system devoted to the control of belief and expression. Freedom regarding such things has been at the heart of liberalism. Belief and expression have to do with meanings—the significance things are understood to have—and liberalism wants to leave meaning up to the individual. Anything else would subject him to a spiritual authority outside himself and so fly in the face of the most basic liberal aspiration.

A liberal society tries to make freedom of expression open-ended and expansive. In some respects it is. You can say, write, and publish almost anything you want on topics that have traditionally been held sacred. You can attribute almost any significance to anything, call art whatever you present as such. You can dunk a crucifix in your own urine and have a photograph of the result treated respectfully by critics and displayed in museums. Nor is freedom of expression limited to speech, the written word, and the arts. It extends to "lifestyle," the expressive aspects of how we live. In the case of sex, for example, freedom has come to trump moral principles that have always seemed fundamental to the most basic human relations and so to social order itself. Whatever the effects of sexual freedom, to oppose it would be to prescribe the meaning of something that touches us deeply, which would now be considered an outrageous act of oppression.

Nonetheless, control of thought and expression follows from the basic dynamic of liberalism. Freedom and equality, like anything else, impose requirements. They require equal respect for what each holds dear, and thus for the meanings each sees in things. Promoting equal respect is an open-ended task that has special implications for freedom of opinion and expression, since expression is an act with consequences. To express a view publicly is in some degree to impose it on others and to suppress possible contrary views. If I am allowed to say "Merry Christmas," that places you in a setting in which Christian holidays have a special status. Why should you have to put up with that?

Advanced liberalism must therefore subject expression to limitations so that one man's meanings do not suppress another's. That is especially true of expression related to public affairs and social relations, which by nature tends to affect the world at large, and so other people in the aggregate more than oneself in particular. Advocacy of nonliberal views, or even presentation of facts at odds with liberal dogma, is treated as a sort of harassment. It is considered a gross violation of equal respect, for example, to suggest that there are legitimate objections to homosexual conduct or that there may be an explanation other than discrimination for group differences in income and position.[5] The effect is that freedom of speech becomes first and foremost freedom to support liberalism and attack nonliberal beliefs and attitudes.[6] You can burn a flag but not a cross,[7] debunk Martin Luther but not Martin Luther King, lampoon Christianity but not Islam.[8] In the end, equal respect limits political expression no less than respect for royal or ecclesiastical dignity once did, and free expression becomes more a private right to pornography than a public right to discuss politics and social affairs.[9]

The fate of liberalism is displayed in the fate of words like "diversity" and "tolerance." Contemporary liberalism honors diversity and tolerance above everything else, but its diversity excludes and suppresses people with a traditional understanding of normality, and its tolerance requires speech codes, quotas, and compulsory training in correct opinions and attitudes. *Tolerance* has traditionally been understood procedurally, as letting people do what they want. Contemporary liberals understand it substantively, to require equal respect as a fact of social life. Procedural tolerance calls for laissez faire, while substantive tolerance requires pervasive administrative control of human relationships. Liberalism has chosen the latter, so that tolerance now means that only committed liberals are allowed to live as they choose.

Secular Theocracy

In the end, liberalism requires that nonliberal views be driven out of the most private affairs and even the human soul. Our views on fundamental issues cannot help but affect our relations to others, and the drive for perfection implicit in the one-sided abstractions upon which liberalism is based means those effects cannot be ignored forever. When we discuss and deal with the most important realities—life and death, family connections, whether children should be born and how they should be raised—the liberal state demands that we treat our most basic commitments and understandings as a dispensable matter of personal opinion. Advocacy of orthodox Christianity, for example, contributes to a public environment in which the way of life of atheists and homosexuals is routinely called erroneous and objectively disordered. Such a result cannot possibly be legitimate in a political order that takes liberal social justice seriously.[10] A view that can be allowed no airing at all must in effect be eradicated. For if it is wrong to act on beliefs or even to express them publicly, they lose their connection to the world at large, and therefore any possible claim to truth. Liberal inclusiveness demands in the end that nonliberals, including all serious adherents of any traditional religion, effectively apostatize and convert to liberalism.

Liberalism as a Religion

Liberalism, which began as an attempt to moderate the influence of religion in politics, thus ends by establishing itself as a religion. That should be no surprise. Our religion is our understanding of what at bottom is real and right, and we cannot help but believe that some of the things of which we speak are simply real and some of the things we do simply right. Something that functions as religion is a necessary part of any overall system of thought and action. In particular, legitimate government must be backed by something of the kind. Unless it is based on a common understanding of principles superior to the human will that are rooted in the nature of things, government is simply one man telling another what to do. Such an understanding, however, is essentially religious.

The fundamental political question is the nature and purpose of authority, and thus the nature of man, the world, moral obligation, and the human good—in other words, which religion is correct. Liberalism cannot get by without answering that question. Paradoxically, it extracts an answer from its claim of moral ignorance. We do not know what the good is, it tells us, so respect for equal human dignity compels us to treat all desires the same. The satisfaction of all desires, with each desire treated equally, becomes the unquestionable good. Man becomes the measure, and individual will the source of value. The limitations on knowledge with which the liberal outlook began lead to a definite result and become constitutive principles of moral knowledge rather than limitations on it. In short, they become the basis of a religion, a fact concealed by the moral doubt that liberalism claims as its first principle.

This new religion, a system of moral absolutes based on a denial that moral truth is knowable, consists in nothing less than the deification of man. To refuse to talk about the transcendent, and to view it as wholly out of our reach, seems very cautious and humble. In practice, however, it puts our own thoughts and desires at the center of things, and so puts man in the place of God. If you say we cannot know anything about God, only our own experience, you will soon say that there is no God, at least for practical purposes, and that we are the ones who give order and meaning to the world. In short, you will say that we are God.

Skepticism unavoidably turns into dogmatism. We cannot help but act, and if skepticism makes all action nonrational we will nonetheless act on some principle or other. If, because we are skeptics, we cannot take arguments in favor of other principles seriously, we will treat our arbitrarily chosen principles as absolute and denounce those who question them as a threat to peace and public order. Less skeptical systems that accept an element of faith can also introduce an element of rationality into basic issues since their understanding of reason is broader than that of liberalism and enables them to reason about faith. Liberalism also proposes a faith—man-the-measure as the highest truth and preference satisfaction as the *summum bonum*—but cannot discuss what it is doing or why. Any reasons it could give would fall far short of the clear demonstration it demands. Rather than engage other beliefs it must obfuscate its position, claim that it wins by default, and declare other faiths out of bounds. To put liberalism beyond question in such a manner, though, is to establish an absolute fideism as the basis of social order.

Liberalism becomes theocratic by its own definition: it bases public order on a particular dogmatic understanding of ultimate things that refuses to submit to public reason. Furthermore, it is likely to be more intolerant than a traditional theocracy. The goals of civil-rights lawyers are more readily achieved by force than those of more traditional theologians, and the *summum bonum* of the lawyers will not be realized at all unless it is achieved here and now in daily life, so there is good reason to expect them to be far less tolerant of human flaws and social imperfections than theologians generally are. Nor, since they lack a transcendent standard by which, even in concept, their cause could be measured and found wanting, are they likely to be more doubtful of its justice.

The practical strength of the liberal approach is that it conceals what it does, claiming to be a simple matter of "openness and tolerance," and so it is able to demand an extremely high standard of proof for opposing principles while avoiding the need for explanation and defense in its own case. Eliminating the possibility of criticism makes thought impossible, however, and thoughtlessness in basic matters is costly. The religion liberalism establishes has substantive weaknesses to match its polemical strengths. In the end, that religion fails to deliver because it makes no sense. It makes man the measure, but men are weak, mutable, prone to error, and at odds with each other. Basic incoherence leads to incoherence in detail: liberal neutrality is one-sided, liberal tolerance is dictatorial, liberal hedonism denies us what we want, and liberal freedom centralizes power, undermines standards that make free social life possible, and destroys our connections to others, making us dependent on universal systems utterly beyond our control. In the name of giving us what we want liberalism denies us everything worth having. It does not solve but creates anew and even exacerbates the problem of intolerant public claims of ultimate truth leading to ideological tyranny.

Persecuting Zeal

As an established religion grounding a political order, liberalism tries to eliminate competing systems of religion and morality to the extent they cannot be reconfigured as representations of purely human aspirations and so converted into poeticized versions of liberalism itself.[11] The effort is inevitable. Liberalism relies on claims of pellucid this-worldly rationality. Treating liberalism and equal freedom as simply rational, however, means that those who recognize other standards must be treated as irrational and not properly part of legitimate political discussion.

The triumph of liberalism puts the traditionally religious in an all-pervasive setting the basic principles of which deny their faith and require its eradication. Transcendent religion and traditional morality become sins against reason, truth, and charity. They sin against reason and truth by arbitrary assertion, since they make claims that are not demonstrable, and against charity by elevating the preferences of some—to the extent that they take effect, those of the powerful—over those of others. Simply by existing, transcendent religion and traditional morality are oppressive, since they affect the social environment by making it less tolerant and inclusive. They must be suppressed.

Suppression most often takes the form of insistence, backed by nagging and social pressure, that traditional faiths accept transformation into something radically different and, at bottom, trivial. They must be "tolerant," and "come to terms with modernity," which means that they must subordinate themselves to an official outlook that aspires to reorder the whole of human life. And they must accept their status as purely private pursuits with no implications for social relations or understandings of reality. Things can go farther than nagging and ridicule, of course. In Europe and Canada, assertion of traditional morality or the superiority of one religion over another can now be treated as criminal. The "liberalism of fear" (liberalism based on fear of illiberal persecution) could, it seems, well be replaced today by a conservatism of fear. After all, who knows how far liberals will go?

Advanced liberalism believes itself tolerant, but its tolerance is intolerant in somewhat the way the Taliban are intolerant. As prominent spokesmen define the issues, it often seems that we are in the midst of a world struggle between two quasi-totalitarian religious movements: radical Islam and advanced liberalism.[12] Where the Taliban believe themselves called to do away with all social authorities but the Koran and shari'a, today's liberals believe themselves called to eliminate all authorities other than expertise, rational bureaucracy, and markets. Both views demand a radical purification of social life on simple principles, and the similarity in purpose leads to similarities of method and style. Islam distinguishes the Dar-ul-Islam, the realm of peace in which Islam rules, from the Dar-ul-Harb, the realm of unbelief and war, and it looks forward to the unification of the world in a single community of believers under a single divine law. Similarly, contemporary liberalism insists on the rightful universality of its own realm of peace and justice where liberal principle and human-rights conventions prevail, outside of which there is no legitimate authority but only institutional violence. Like radical Islam, liberalism strives to make its realm of peace and justice universal by imposing it on everyone everywhere by all available means. Both movements accept the legitimacy of war, whether jihad or humanitarian intervention, to extend their sway and establish a new order by force. Liberalism is gentler, as a general rule, but the pervasiveness and efficiency of its regulatory net make up for its comparative softness.

The Universal Individual

The intrinsic contradictions of liberalism extend to its claim to promote the interests of the individual. Liberal individualism, like liberal freedom, ends by destroying what it intended to protect and foster.

Destruction of Identity

To all appearances, liberalism empowers the individual by letting him choose what he wants and get what he chooses. However, choice is useless unless distinctions make a difference, and "diversity" and "tolerance" mean that distinctions must be treated as interchangeable matters of purely private taste. As a result, advanced liberalism becomes freedom to make choices that are not permitted to matter. The glitter of unlimited choice dissipates when we find that nothing significant has changed because equality has deprived all changes of meaning. Cheap and easy travel seems wonderful until television, world markets, mass tourism, and immigration make all places alike. The same principle applies when other objects of desire lose their distinctiveness. The consequences of such experiences, repeated in all the affairs of life, are boredom, depression, and addiction to intoxicants that distract us from a featureless here and now.

Not only the objects of our choice but we ourselves lose our identities in liberal society. Our identity exists as part of a general system of identities. We understand ourselves and others by reference to particular things, persons, and relationships. Liberalism attempts to destroy the effect of basic social aspects of identity—sex, religion, historical community, particular culture and connections. Such things no longer have a legitimate social role: who a man is can have no relevance to how life is for him or to social relations that matter. If identity can have no effect, though, it is not identity. If everything becomes interchangeable, and all persons and their preferences must be treated the same, then identity loses significance and definition.

Liberal society claims to let us be what we choose, but it simultaneously forbids us to be anything distinct with a recognizable position and value, because that would deny the equal position and value of other possibilities. There can be no heroes, because heroes call cowardice and mediocrity into question. Nor can there be honest men, because honesty denigrates the stratagems of the oppressed. Distinctions in moral worth, after all, correspond to social hierarchies. "Respectable" once had to do with the middle class, "honest" with feminine chastity, and "frank" with a military ruling class. How can distinctions connected to such things be allowed in a liberal society?

Standards must go. Advanced liberal society insists on equal status for pop culture and the classics, abolishes school dress codes, instructs children in alternative sexualities, and puts Christmas and Kwanzaa on the same footing, all while making arrangements to keep such things from affecting anything that matters. Equal respect becomes an equality of compulsory irrelevance indistinguishable from equal contempt. Liberals end by favoring a social order that eliminates or at least puts to the side the human qualities men care most about, because if nothing they care about affects how society functions there will be fewer conflicts and hurt feelings.

For all its desire to give us what we want, advanced liberalism in fact imposes on us the greatest possible deprivation—the loss of what we are. If we can be whatever we want we can be nothing in particular. What, after all, am I? A man, someone with definite connections, history, and moral character, a member of this family and that people, an adherent of some system of ultimate understandings that defines the world and my place in it. A liberal regime recognizes me as a good citizen only to the extent that I agree that none of those things matter. I am allowed to give them whatever private significance I want, but the permission is all but meaningless since equal freedom requires the effect of such private preferences to be reduced to the vanishing point. Liberalism frees children from parents, women from men, the poor from the charitable, inferiors from superiors, all so that each can choose his own life. By making our connections to others insubstantial, however, it deprives actions of effect, and we end with perfect freedom to flail about in a vacuum—or, perhaps more accurately, since the system does require us to respect the conditions of its functioning, the perfect freedom a gear in a machine might have to choose the color it is painted.

Today's "identity politics" show nothing to the contrary, since their point is to turn social identity against itself. They are intended to make all identities equal and interchangeable, thus destroying them as identities. Latinos are rewarded for adopting a bureaucratically invented Latino identity. The point, though, is not to help them maintain a distinct position and way of life based on a functional Latino culture, but to give them claims against the state and against their fellow citizens, and to dethrone the culture of native white Americans so that they too are unable to rely on it and must also become clients of the state.

Liberal Identity

Nonetheless, there is of necessity a conception of identity that grows up and takes hold in liberal society, if only because we can think about ourselves and our actions only by reference to what we are. The effect is that liberalism replaces strong and stable identities with weak and problematic ones. As always, we define our identity by reference to common goods our community recognizes. If I say I am American, the claim is insignificant unless Americans are united by something they recognize collectively as good. In liberal society, however, the only thing recognized in common as a substantive good is the goal implicit in all individual desire: the ability to get what one wants. That ability is most readily recognized in the form of money, power, and success, so liberalism turns society into an assembly of individuals related by those things.

A liberal world is one in which the authoritative social reality, the thing by reference to which we are what we are, is a hierarchy of money, power, and influence that excludes all substantive values and so is strictly quantitative. We are allowed public recognition simply as employees and consumers, as nodes in a universal network of production and consumption, individuated and ranked by organizational charts, bank balances, and consumption choices. Under such conditions we lose substantive connection to others. Social and personal identity become hierarchical or quantitative, and self-realization becomes the pursuit of financial and hierarchical superiority or conspicuous consumption.

To the extent systemic imperfections allow traditional identities to have an effect, our identity as employees and consumers is supplemented by the sole identities liberal society recognizes as a legitimate alternative: oppressor, victim, or the good liberal who supports the system in its efforts to perfect itself and us in accordance with its own principles. The hedonism and careerism of advanced liberal society is thus supplemented by resentment, guilt, and a perverse co-opted idealism. The overall effect is that liberal society is pervaded by an obsession with money, power, position, and enjoyment corresponding to its technocratic hedonism[13]—which it must disguise and deny because of its egalitarian moralism. That obsession is all the more fascinating because of its irrationality, emptiness, and radical opposition to proclaimed morality. It is experienced as demonic and obscene, as a constant temptation to oppression and source of victimization. It returns us inwardly to a primitive state in which there is no distinction between power and the good, the accursed and the sacred, in which the fundamental spiritual problem is separating ourselves from the evil to which we are bound and by which we are fascinated, and the necessary response is denying it in ourselves and transferring it to another so that it can be driven out in the person of the scapegoat—the man who rejects freedom and equality, the "greedy," the "hater," the "bigot," the "extremist," the "fundamentalist."

That scapegoating creates an almost metaphysical inequality between those who think and feel correctly and are counted as part of the moral community, and those who do not and are not so counted. The resulting hatred and contempt for those counted as bigots serves a necessary function. It gives solidarity to a social order that lacks sustaining goods in common and so needs an enemy to define itself. And it provides an irrefutable justification for the rule of the class that defines correct thought. Since incorrect thoughts are quite common among the people at large, the actual people need be counted as part of the political people, and their desires and views treated as legitimate, only to the extent they support the regime and its principles. The position of the ruling class thus becomes impregnable.

FUNDAMENTAL CONTRADICTIONS

As we have seen, liberals have a vision of what human relations should be, the conviction that their vision is unquestionably correct, and the will to insist it be followed in all significant human affairs. As an abstract logical concept of unlimited applicability, equal freedom must be defined and imposed by authority in ever broader ways without regard to human nature or popular understandings. It must, in short, be tyrannical. The principle of equal freedom creates a dictatorship of intrusive functionaries to which everyone is forced to submit whether he likes it or not.

The conceptual problems that lead to such a result can be variously stated. Most basically, perhaps, the problem is that the attempt to make freedom the ultimate principle of social life makes no sense. Freedom is always freedom to do something, so it must be subordinate to some other good that motivates it and makes it worth having. When taken as a final standard, the opposing possibilities it seems to offer cancel each other out so that it loses all meaning. Abstract equal freedom makes anything anyone does that affects others presumptively an unwanted imposition and so an act of aggression. A minute and comprehensive system of control therefore becomes necessary to prevent oppression and to make us free. The only actions that remain permissible are those which leave others unaffected and those which directly support the system. The result is suppression of the things most worth having. Freedom becomes freedom to be self-involved, self-indulgent, and politically correct. Anything else is oppression. Love and loyalty become a threat to the system, because they interfere with rational administration and create the possibility of bias and enmity. They must be suppressed. Hence, for example, the liberal attitude toward relations between the sexes: they must be based on continuing untrammeled choice and have no effect on who we understand ourselves to be. They must, in short, be trivial.

Such an understanding of good social order and government makes no sense, and in a system that emphasizes logic as much as liberalism the contradictions only multiply. Liberalism presents us with sordid idealism, bigoted tolerance, mindless expertise, moralistic permissiveness, dogmatic agnosticism, mainstream extremism, rigidly uniform diversity, radically elitist equality, totally administered freedom, and compulsory established rebellion. It promises moderation but gives us overreaching. It prizes freedom of thought but insists on correct attitudes and suppresses contrary opinion as ignorant, irrational, oppressive, and dangerous. In the name of autonomy, it makes the state control everything. Rather than popular rule, it promotes distrust of the people and reliance on elites answerable to no one. Instead of benefits for women, minorities, and children, it delivers family collapse, children with no fathers, feminized poverty, and one in eight young black men in prison.[14]

If people thought and expressed themselves freely and clearly such a system would become unstable, so liberalism comes to base itself on obfuscation, indoctrination, ritualistic treatment of democratic forms, and the medicalization of dissent. The modern liberal state is only limited in the sense that it is not authorized to deviate from liberalism. Respect for the views and habits of the people is no longer a serious principle. What presents itself as enlightened and limited government becomes in practice obscurantist tyranny.

CHAPTER FIVE

Are Objections to Liberalism Overstated?

MANY PEOPLE RESIST THE NOTION THAT THERE IS SOMETHING CALLED "liberalism" whose inner logic leads to particular results that contradict original intentions. After all, liberal views are not fixed. They have changed over time and will change again. Very few actual liberals and no actual liberal society fit my description without contrary features. Everyone holds some liberal views, few hold all of them, and most normal people who hold them cut back on them in various ways. Grand concepts like "equal freedom" play a role among actual liberals and in present-day society, but so do many other things.

As an actually existing system—or rather series, family, or assemblage of beliefs, attitudes, and practices—liberalism can always be seen as more limited, varying, complex, hard to summarize, and dependent on local particularities than I have presented. It can be anarchic as well as tyrannical, legalistic as well as antinomian, puritanical as well as relativistic, averse to power as well as fascinated by it. It can be restated in ways that seem to avoid this objection or that. There can even be a modest practical liberalism that serves to moderate the nonliberal principles that continue to order life in all societies. Besides, many of the results attributed to liberalism can be attributed to other causes, including nonideological developments such as prosperity and mobility. So why not forget strawmen and stereotypes and just look at particulars?

IDEAS HAVE CONSEQUENCES

Such objections fall short, because general tendencies of thought and social organization exist, matter, and must be discussed. Differences among particular liberals do not show that there is no such thing as liberalism. Moral and political life is not an arbitrary heap of independent factors that can be changed at will in any direction. It involves arrangements of fundamental principles of social cooperation that form enduring functional systems with tendencies that need have very little to do with what their adherents intend or expect.

Like other grand social and intellectual movements, liberalism is not wholly manifested by any of its phases, and what this or that liberal says about it is no more final than what a particular scientist says about science or a particular industrialist about industrialism. To call liberalism progressive is to say that it is less a matter of particular thinkers, politicians, institutions, and schools of thought than of fundamental tendencies and implicit principles that link such particulars into a long-term movement with its own logic, line of development, and implied goal.

How people think affects what they do, and ways of thinking are no less systematic than languages. Each has its own "grammar": its own system of fundamental abstract principles that determine what makes sense and how particulars are to be classified. Such principles have consequences independent of the concerns and goals of those who live by them. If Descartes finds that he can accept only those truths which seem perfectly clear to him, or Bacon decides that knowledge is a matter of experimental study of nature for the purpose of learning how to make it do what we want, and those views catch on and come to determine what is thought rational, they will have enormous effects on all aspects of life, effects that need have nothing to do with their originators' intentions. The same applies to Hobbes's decision to treat society as a contract among self-interested individuals.

Those who study liberalism must therefore develop an understanding of what it is and where it is likely to go that is independent of what its proponents and theoreticians say and goes beyond cataloging commonalities and variations. They must, in short, identify its basic principles and ways of acting and trace their implications. Conceptual considerations are often shrugged off in politics on the grounds that events can be explained in a variety of ways, and material interests and particular circumstances matter more than abstract principles. This objection is weak, particularly in the case of a movement that emphasizes reason as much as liberalism, and it becomes weaker as liberalism advances. Modern conditions tend to simplify and rationalize human society, doing away with opaque particularities of sex, class, nation, and particular history and culture, and turning society more and more into an aggregate of interchangeable units ordered by abstract legal, financial, and bureaucratic principles. Liberal principles encourage that process and treat it as part of how the world should be. They insist on explicitness, reason, and universality, turn all issues into a matter of enforceable rights, and concede no ground to other tendencies. Formal institutions and rules become the effective and only legitimate principles of order. If liberal concepts did not carry enormous weight as such, it would be hard to understand why it seems so obviously *right*, to so many experienced, responsible, educated, and influential men, to make a demanding code of liberal principles mandatory for all societies everywhere as a matter of international law, under the rubric of human rights, even though nothing like the society those principles demand has ever existed.

In such a setting, logical coherence is at a premium and conceptual issues are likely to become quite practical. If such a description of modern society makes sense, and contemporary liberalism has a certain integrity as a system for understanding and organizing human life, its nature and properties have to be discussed and taken seriously. The logic of accepted concepts does not determine everything, but over time it is immensely influential. It matters that understandings of what is good are now seen as purely subjective valuations, which because they are subjective are equal in status. It matters that rationality is now understood as a combination of formal logic, scientific theorizing, and means-ends reasoning—so that substantive goods seem to be merely personal preferences, and arguments based on seeing them as such always seem better founded than opposing arguments.

All major tendencies of thought in the West have converged on contemporary advanced liberalism—progressivism and patriotism in America, Marxism and contempt for America in Europe, mainstream Christianity and Judaism among the religious, irreligion among skeptics.[1] Such a development needs to be explained. It seems less illuminating to view it as a collection of accidents that all happen to lead to a single consistent result than as a working out throughout Western society of the implications of some basic principle. If all roads lead to Rome, it is not because of the peculiarities of particular building projects but something more general.

One possible explanation for such a situation is the growing influence within all traditions of thought of a combination of technology and the ideal of equal freedom, both arising from the modern world's turn away from transcendent realities and toward this-worldly constructivism. Such an explanation makes sense of liberalism by seeing it as based on extraordinarily simple principles firmly grounded in fundamental understandings generally accepted in the West and widely influential elsewhere. To the extent that approach makes sense in describing past and present, it is reasonable to expect it to make sense in describing future developments as well, and for the trends it reveals to continue to play out within Western public life. It is useful for understanding our situation to discuss where those trends point us, even though neither they nor anything else can explain all particularities. A single discussion cannot deal with everything. My descriptions of the society we live in are unavoidably simplified and incomplete, and my explanations cannot capture all relevant factors. Even simplified and incomplete explanations are valuable, however, if only because in politics and social life nothing else is ever available.

Fine-tuning

Although liberalism is highly conceptual, problems with it cannot be solved merely by adjusting liberal concepts so that they avoid raising the problems. As a fundamental movement of life and thought that is functionally tied to other vast movements, such as the rise of modern science and the modern state, liberalism has its own way of acting that cannot be changed by exhortation or redescription. Its concepts are not philosophers' inventions but basic rules of classification and decision that function as fundamental principles of social cooperation. Philosophers' theories may describe and clarify them, but they do not change them any more than the theories of grammarians change the grammar of a language or the theories of economists change what money is or how businessmen act.

For example, someone bothered by the plebeian aspects of liberalism such as its tendency to treat pushpin as equal to poetry might try to present it as a matter of autonomy or even heroic self-creation. Its guiding spirit, he might claim, is respect for human dignity and the ability of each to live authentically in accordance with his personal vision of the good. Liberalism makes every man his own Nietzsche—only with health insurance, a retirement plan, and protection against discrimination. Such higher interpretations may help reconcile ardent souls to a system unavoidably opposed to higher inspirations by obfuscating its true nature, but they do little else. A liberal society cannot institute a practical distinction between preferences and "visions of the good," or between satisfaction of desire and living authentically, without an understanding of human nature and the good far more specific than anything it could adopt while remaining liberal. Liberalism may occasionally appeal rhetorically to moral heroism, but it is incorrigibly low-minded. Romantic aspirations toward spiritual authenticity may acquire political support in some respects and affect a few symbolic issues like support for the arts or minor features of public education, but such things are ornamental rather than functional. In the long run, the point of liberalism is to give us what we want and not to improve us except by making us more perfectly liberal—that is, more exclusively concerned with the equal satisfaction of desire simply as such.

Is Liberalism Limited?

A reader might object that the demands of liberalism are much less comprehensive than I say. Liberal standards, he might assert, are authoritative only for limited public purposes, while in private life, and with regard to ultimate explanations, each of us is free to choose and act on the standards he likes best. Presumably, something of the sort is involved in the proposal of John Rawls that liberalism be viewed as a "political conception" and not a "comprehensive doctrine."[2] This argument is not persuasive. It is true that the demands of liberal neutrality do not apply to the absolutely private, and that liberalism allows one to hold and act on a variety of ultimate theories so long as they give the right answers as a practical matter. The former point is central to the claim that liberalism is not an oppressive system of power but a system of mutual accommodation that leaves the self uniquely free and untouched, while the latter is consistent with liberal (and modern scientific) concern with observable consequences rather than anything that transcends them.

It is unclear, though, why liberal protection of the strictly private and purely theoretic matters so much, when modern government is so pervasive, human life and meaning are so strongly interpersonal and theory-laden, and government cannot touch the mental or strictly private in any case. An ethical doctrine is not a personal taste or abstract speculation. It is a teaching as to what it makes sense to do and avoid. By their nature, such teachings claim to be part of practical reason and so to be public and authoritative. A purely private or theoretic understanding of right and wrong with no public implications would be as trivial as a purely private or theoretic understanding of good engineering practice. Man is social, after all, and he has few important goods that do not essentially involve other people and the common moral understandings that join him to them.

The right to hold and act on any doctrine one chooses as long as it is consistent in practice with the official political conception cannot have much scope in a society in which government feels called upon to reconstruct social life and culture. Liberal doctrine is the basis of everything recognized as authoritative today. It views the transformation of social attitudes and customs as a basic public obligation, and everyone in advanced liberal society is pressed to act as if he accepted it unreservedly with all its implications.[3] When accepted as a political conception, and so made authoritative for the whole of public life, it spills over and conditions private life, severely limiting what, as a practical matter, we are allowed to believe about human relations and the good. The extent to which public standards emphasize subjectivity as to values, for example, affects the principles to which we can appeal in our dealings with others and determines much of the order of private life and the goods that can be realized within it.

The mixing of public and private is especially unavoidable in an age in which so many of the functions of life—including those as basic as the rearing of children—are carried on through market and bureaucratic institutions directly subject to public standards. While one's "comprehensive doctrine" may provide private guidance with respect to questions public dogma leaves open, the advance of liberalism steadily reduces the significance of such questions. Given the pervasiveness of liberal institutions, the freedom to explain or add to liberal doctrine in personal or theoretical ways is not so different from the freedom enjoyed by a Catholic monk sworn to obedience and subject to discipline to choose a personal theology or hold various optional pious opinions. Such freedom is no doubt valuable, but it does not justify treating liberalism as a specially tolerant doctrine.

Maximal Freedom?

One might nonetheless argue that liberal morality genuinely promotes freedom, within the limits of practicality, because it gives as wide a scope of expression to as many schemes of value as possible. One might claim, for example, that liberalism does so by protecting "privacy interests"— conduct that is close to the heart of what makes us what we are. Doing so, however, requires a theory of what makes us what we are. Such theories are no less contentious than theories of the good, and are in fact largely identical to them. Which makes us what we are: acting on sexual impulse, or living in accordance with common moral understandings that integrate impulse with stable personal relationships and other concerns? One answer would make restrictions on sexual conduct an attack on what we are;

the other would fault a lack of institutional support for sexual restraint. There seems no neutral way to choose between the two, and with the world so interconnected and government so active, a public choice cannot be avoided.

Others might claim that liberalism promotes freedom because it allows an action unless it interferes with others in a concrete and particularized way. For example, the right of lifestyle choice is said to override the right to an environment in which traditional standards prevail, because the latter is more likely to involve a scheme of concrete interference. The claim becomes less plausible as liberalism advances and spreads its reformist net ever more widely. In Iran, a man can be prosecuted for sodomy; in the EU he can be prosecuted for saying sodomy is wrong. Why is one a more concrete interference than the other? In any case, no actual government accepts the principle of minimizing concrete interference. All governments recognize that law may forbid intangible injuries and defend a beneficial system of conduct or suppress a harmful one, even when individual infractions do not cause identifiable concrete harm. One man's smuggling, tax evasion, or use of leaded gasoline may benefit him a great deal without having a discernible effect on anyone else. The principles governments actually live by would rationally allow legal support for traditional morality simply as morality just as they allow support for aesthetics as aesthetics. Offense to traditional moral and religious sensibilities is an injury that makes us morally callous and so weakens a social order based on self-government. Why, in principle, can it never be forbidden?

Such questions go to the heart of liberal public morality and its claim of unique transparent rationality. Liberalism deals with them by repeating itself, calling names, or changing the subject. The result is the same as establishing any dogmatic system: liberals say that they oppose divisiveness and extremism rather than schism and heresy, but the meaning is the same.

Radicalization

Liberalism is cautious in some respects. A view that is opposed to compulsion must oppose many kinds of extremism; a view that makes the liberation of individual preferences the standard must accept settled habits, to a degree; and a view that hopes to have an enduring effect must prefer established authority. For a long time, the tendency of liberalism to cooperate with existing arrangements and emphasize specific reforms substituted for principled moderation. It slowed the development of the implications of liberal principles and gave liberal society relative stability.

However, that tendency could not prevent slow radicalization, because the limits it recognized were not principled but pragmatic and therefore transitory. A preference for moderate reform is not a sufficient restraint when fundamental principles are simple and infinitely demanding and every failure to follow principle is a violation of rights. Even though its preferred manner may be moderate, liberalism recognizes no long-term limit on the pursuit of its kind of perfection. Nothing but practical difficulties, which ingenuity and effort can presumptively overcome, can stand in the way of doing what seems clearly right. Human cloning and genetic manipulation, which promise to make man truly his own self-creator, symbolize the infinite ambition of the movement of which liberalism is the political face.

Liberalism can act as a check on governments constituted on non-liberal principles, but not on itself. It rejects any authority that transcends it, views whatever does not conform to it as illegitimate, and acknowledges no restraining principle on the endless extension of equal freedom other than practicality. Principled accommodation of other views involves relating them to larger shared truths that none fully comprehends. Liberalism cannot do so because it makes morality a self-contained and fully knowable system defined by logic, technology, and human will. There is no larger truth that none fully possesses but in which all participate. Rather, there is only an open-ended and never-ending process of social transformation on behalf of abstract goals. As ever more comprehensive interpretations of the requirements of freedom and equality crystallize, their demands become absolute and trump even common sense—"deeply rooted social expectations," as the phrase now has it. Common sense, after all, is a matter of settled popular preconceptions—"prejudices and stereo-types"—that liberalism treats as oppressive because there is no clear rational procedure behind them.

Like other ideologies that attempt to reconstruct society on simple principles, liberalism eventually tries to extirpate whatever it does not prescribe. Indeed, its comparative prudence and moderation in tactical matters has meant that in the long run it could go to greater extremes than seemingly more radical approaches to government. The Bolsheviks wanted to do away with the family but had to backtrack. The more gradual liberal approach is attaining results that seem far more solid.

The difficulties of dealing with human concerns by means of the slender resources liberal principles provide have not made liberals more cautious by forcing them to consider that other principles must also have some legitimacy. Instead, the difficulty of full compliance with liberalism has radicalized liberals and led them to view their own societies, which always fall short of liberal demands, as unjust, oppressive, and unworthy of preservation except as sources of raw material for the construction of something more free and equal. Lacking substantive principles, liberalism can accept only abstractions like equality and public order as limitations on freedom. Such abstractions are too intangible for common sense to find a foothold and strike a balance. To avoid incoherence, one of them becomes the sole operative standard and the others are reinterpreted so that they no longer offer resistance. A single standard with comprehensive implications for all human affairs thus ends up at the center of political life.

The result is monomania: first of freedom or equality and in the end of bureaucratic control, which attempts to enforce equality by tyranny and live-and-let-live by reconstructing human nature.[4]

In recent years, the slide of the West into monochromatic liberal tyranny has accelerated. The evidence is everywhere: an increasingly assertive and intolerant atheism, the criminalization in Europe of mere criticism of homosexuality and Islam, the conversion of much of what is called conservatism into an aggressive one-world ideology. Among educated and well-connected people, no legitimate place is now recognized for principled resistance to the attempt to end sexual distinctions, abolish historic cultures and peoples, mainstream homosexuality, and drive all authority that cannot be reduced to desire and technical expertise out of what passes for public life. Diversity, openness, and tolerance, understood in a radical sense, are claimed to be the very essence of America, the West, and ordinary decency, and those who resist them in any way that amounts to more than mumbling and foot-dragging are considered fundamentalists or proto-Nazis and not legitimate participants in public life. No matter what happens, the answer is always to abolish traditional standards and understandings. The response to AIDS is celebration of homosexuality. The response to radical Islam is praise for Islam and demands that traditional Christianity be turned into a restatement of liberalism, excluded from public life, or otherwise debunked and suppressed. When Muslim immigrants in Europe riot, the problem is said to be insufficient inclusiveness and the answer therapeutic intervention to dissolve whatever (apart from political correctness) makes Europeans European.

Restraining Principles

Liberalism has developed beyond the point at which attachment to principles such as free speech can be counted on to maintain free public life and head off extremism and tyranny.[5] Speech might be protected for several reasons—as one of the activities people like to engage in, as a way of arriving at truth, or as a safeguard against government abuse. None is sufficient from the current liberal perspective. To base protection of speech on fondness for speaking calls for an explanation of why that preference is more important than others. To base protection on the seeking of truth would undercut a fundamental principle of the liberal regime, that the good is a matter of what is desired rather than what is true. The strongest argument for protection of speech within liberalism is procedural, that it is a safeguard against government abuse. Many who consider themselves liberals insist that a free and tolerably just society requires concrete political rights, such as free speech, that are not subordinate to other goals, even the freedom, equality, and well-being of others.

However, it is not clear what is unique about speech as a check on government. At times a similar role has been proposed for other restrictions on government power, such as hereditary rank, landed property, states' rights, jury nullification, absolute popular sovereignty, free association, and the right of the people to keep and bear arms. Such arguments have lost respectability as liberals have acquired uncontested power and undertaken increasingly radical social reforms that require comprehensive administrative control over society extending even to the reform of thought. The absolute concrete rights that were once useful in battling traditional hierarchies have become, from a liberal standpoint, irrational and retrograde. They make it possible to resist liberal hierarchies, and so protect irrationality and oppression.

Free speech, like other barriers to government abuse, is an irresponsible power placed in private hands. If it is ineffectual, protecting it can have little benefit. If it is effective it can injure, and it seems to need regulation no less than other private powers. It is often used for illiberal purposes, and it is most powerful in the hands of those powerful enough to make their speech heard. Speech regarding political and moral issues has traditionally been thought to present the strongest case for protection, but its results can easily be oppressive, as when it results in illiberal public measures or creates by its presence an environment unfriendly to some ways of life. It follows that its suppression should often be viewed as a liberating act. And in any event, it is not clear why freedom of discussion among the people is so important when knowledge and policy have become a matter for accredited experts. The point of campaign-finance reform is to purify public discussion. Why not purify it further?

Not all influential liberals have yet accepted such arguments. American courts have rejected liberal attempts at the regulation of speech,[6] just as they frustrated earlier liberal reforms in the name of constitutionally limited government, contractual freedom, and various other private rights.[7] Nonetheless, in the development of liberalism every attempt at line-drawing in favor of limited government—property rights, family privacy, constitutionalism, freedom of association—has eventually been discredited as a hypocritical and intolerable shield for oppression. A government that feels called upon to reform social attitudes will find it difficult to stop short of controlling speech. The logic of the development of liberalism, which proved too strong for established legal doctrine in earlier cases, will in all likelihood do so in this case as well.

However numerous the points of resistance, they are only islands in an ocean of change. While courts do not literally follow election returns, their understanding of rights is based on the moral and social outlook dominant in American ruling circles and not on the text of the Constitution or an autonomous legal tradition.[8] Our mainstream intellectual, cultural, and religious institutions display the politically correct outlook of our elites. Even liberals who support free speech agree with their more advanced brethren that politically incorrect speech is morally illegitimate. Free speech accordingly rests on little more than a distrust of government that is already compromised by suspicion of private power and by the enormous authority granted government in general. In the moral world of contemporary liberalism, how long can free-speech liberals (and the Supreme Court) stand firm, especially in the face of the increasing internationalization of legal thought regarding human rights?[9]

Dubious Gains

Continued faith in liberalism is supported by the common view that whatever its flaws, American society today is much more fair and decent than in the past. The correctness of that view is quite doubtful. Past discriminations led to many evils, but the triumph of advanced liberalism in the sixties has meant worse. Recent social changes have taken mothers away from their children; forced children to grow up without fathers; led women to destroy their children before or during birth; taught boys there is nothing specifically good about manhood or respectable about women; told girls that they are victims, predators, and commodities; destroyed common culture and common sense; multiplied crimes and prisons; increased economic disparities and the working week; imposed pervasive bureaucracies of racial preference and thought control; and led to rabid and mindless political partisanship, a radical decline in intellectual and cultural standards, and the degrading entertainment now seen on television and in theaters. There is nothing fair or decent about forcing people to live, and young people to grow up, in such a setting.

Recent moral progress is an illusion. What has happened, in effect, is that fairness and decency have been turned into nationalized industries. Instead of people having to treat each other decently, each does what he wishes and society at large is expected to supply the decency. From the standpoint of the managerial state, which even mainstream conservatives have come to adopt, the consequence is that fairness and decency have finally come into their own. The actual consequences have been those common to all nationalized industries: inputs have shot up, while outputs have dropped in quantity and still more in quality. Petty tyrants get cushy jobs as economic planners or diversity consultants while the people suffer from crime and abusive conduct. Things no one cares about like celebrations of diversity are overproduced while things desperately needed like integrity and trust are impossible to find. Why should nationalization work better in the case of something as hard to force and easy to fake as fairness and decency than it does in the production of shoes?

A survey of what are considered recent triumphs of social justice suggests that the two situations are indeed similar. Many people are persuaded that the welfare state is a plain requirement of morality because it guarantees protections to the poor and vulnerable, but examination reveals otherwise. Human life is subject to a variety of hazards, external and self-caused. The welfare state creates formal public institutions designed to protect us reliably and comprehensively from those hazards. It therefore substitutes expertise, bureaucracy, and state coercion for the complex combination of personal obligations, social connections, and ideals of life by which men have always lived. That combination, however, is what makes us civil and social. To supplant it and deprive it of its function is to undercut the worth and dignity of human beings by nullifying the importance of their actions and the habits and relationships that enable them to act well in affairs that matter.

The welfare state makes us clients rather than actors. It makes us useless to each other. It separates conduct from consequences and undermines personal responsibility. It weakens connections between the sexes and generations by insisting that dependence on particular persons is wrong. It deprives personal loyalty and integrity of their place and function by making us rely on the system as a whole rather than on ourselves and each other. The result is that people feel alienated and lack civility, couples do not stay together or have children, the ones they do have are badly brought up, and men and women do not know how to treat each other. In the long run—with the growth of crime, corruption, abusiveness, and other social disorders—costs soar, efficiency drops, dependency outruns productivity, and the system loses the ability to achieve its basic end of securing a reliable minimum of security and physical well-being.

Feminism is likewise thought a basic requirement of human decency and even rationality. In fact, it is the tyranny of brutally simple concept over complex human reality. Relations between the sexes are normally a balance among many things, and the balance constantly shifts. The question is not whether the position of the sexes should have stayed exactly as it was in 1950, 1850, or 1350, or whether flexibility and accommodation to modern circumstances should be allowed. Antidiscrimination laws and affirmative action are not needed for the changes and accommodations people find necessary in their daily lives. The real question is whether common habits and attitudes should be allowed to evolve consistent with natural tendencies as well as current needs—in which case much of the past is likely to be carried forward in some way or other—or whether the extirpation of sex as a principle of social organization has to be forced on everyone everywhere by all necessary means. Nonideological accounts of actual life written for purposes unrelated to sexual politics make it clear that the past was not a pit of misogynistic horrors from which equal-opportunity commissions had to rescue us. Whatever changes people generally wanted could have been made by local mutual accommodation. The obvious issue as to the benefits of feminism is whether relations within the family and between men and women are happier and more functional now than they were forty years ago. It seems clear that they are not, that the decline has something to do with feminism, and that the result is that women (along with men and children) are worse off than before.[10] After all, why should the intentional destruction of the habits and understandings that ordered and secured the personal and family relationships that women have always found their stronghold, and their replacement by the formal adversarial relationships men dominate, make women or anybody else happy?

With regard to the civil-rights revolution, which is used as the absolute trump card for the advanced liberal state, many of the same points apply. The basic issue is not liberal progress against frozen traditional injustice, but liberal ideology against the traditionalist assumption that change is normally an adjustment within a complex reality in which many things do not change and others are already functioning in ways that ought to be respected and encouraged. If conditions are bad in some way, as they always are, which approach fits human nature and therefore works better? Which will reduce clear evils without destroying nearby goods? Which is less likely to introduce new abuses to replace those it suppresses?

Barring conditions of poverty, social isolation, and forcible control difficult to maintain in present-day America, human beings largely make their own world, individually and collectively, through their own lives and the lives of the communities in which they participate. Before the changes of the sixties the economic, social, and cultural position of black Americans had been improving for many years. After those changes, the long-term black economic advance relative to whites continued a short time but then stopped,[11] and in other respects the problems of black society grew far worse.[12] Today we have Colin Powell and Condoleeza Rice, one the light-skinned son of West Indian immigrants and the other a daughter of the old black bourgeoisie, but also millions of ordinary American black men dead or in jail, black women without husbands, black children without settled family life, and hip-hop as black culture. The successful beneficiaries of affirmative action are plagued by suspicions, insecurities, and real or imagined slights, and on the whole are far from happy about their situation.[13] Whatever the specific explanation, it should be obvious that there is something very wrong with the standard story of a pre-civil-rights movement society marked by monolithic racism, oppression, and hopelessness undergoing a radical healing through judicial and legislative activism, with remaining problems demanding the same medicine. Might it not have been better to follow a more piecemeal approach, involving initiatives for removal of particular abuses, barriers, and legal distinctions, but no attempt to force comprehensive equality that in the process would dismantle black communities?[14]

The changes brought about by the radicalization of liberalism in the sixties and thereafter have hurt the weak and marginalized more than anybody. The liberation of women and of sex has deprived women of masculine support, feminized poverty, and turned girls into sexual commodities. The fact that their lack of any definite position, combined with feminine responsiveness to social context, induces them to cooperate in their own commoditization makes the process more rather than less degrading.[15] Gay lib has liberated conduct that destroys lives by glamorizing acting on weaknesses and facilitating preying on the confused. Black progress slowed or reversed in most ways for most blacks after the sixties, the period that was supposedly a new dawn in fairness and decency on racial issues. None of that is progress, any more than it is progress to make people generally worse—less social, loyal, and disciplined, and more grasping, cynical, and self-involved[16]—and to deprive them of concrete models and standards for a good life. All those conditions have been consequences of a post-sixties order emphasizing social justice and consequently downplaying the need for people to keep their own lives in order and to treat each other well in daily life.[17]

The Triumph of Tolerance

The growth of "tolerance"—indifference or aversion to traditional distinctions not required by liberal institutions—is considered a profound and unequivocal social and moral gain that overshadows any flaws in post-sixties society. It is unclear why that should be so. Distinctions of wealth, ideology, formal position, and expertise have not disappeared but have grown in importance,[18] so "tolerance" has not led to greater human brotherhood. Furthermore, the attack on traditional distinctions has meant destruction of the arrangements that connect people to each other and bring their similarities and differences into relation with the whole range of human concerns and so civilize them. Men and women still form couples, parents look after their children, common interests lead to common enterprises in which different people play different roles, and the rich, well-placed, and powerful have dealings with those who are less so. By abolishing recognized distinctions of sex, class, and particular culture, however, advanced liberalism has abolished ways of dealing with such connections and distinctions—ways of humanizing them. It has done away with ladies and gentlemen, but not with the relations that made such ideals of gentility necessary.

Technocracy—the attempt to order human life solely by reference to concepts modeled on those of formal logic, bureaucracy, market economics, and the modern natural sciences—runs against the grain of human nature, and calling the suppression of other ordering principles "tolerance," "inclusiveness," and "rationality" does not make it otherwise. The progress of inclusiveness is the progress of alienation. To say that what I am should have no effect on my position in the world is to say that I should have no essential connection to the social order of which I am part but should be estranged from it. Why is that good for anyone? In the interest of the market and bureaucratic institutions now dominant and a conception of morality that makes them absolute, liberalism has abolished the significance of traditional institutions like family, religion, and local and particular community that give concrete moral substance to a man's life and meaning to whatever autonomy he has. It has bulldozed and paved over the social and cultural setting in which ordinary people make their homes and find dignity and meaning, reducing them to powerlessness and degradation, while raising the aggressive, capable, and powerful to secure and comprehensive dominance.[19] Pop culture—glitter for the few and trash for the many—is its worthy symbol. Why claim that such changes have made human life better?

Before the radicalization of liberalism in the sixties, and the globalization that is part of liberalism, people lived in a public environment that for most was far less alienating than the one they are now forced to inhabit. Their mutual relations were easier and less fraught. They were more able, on the whole, to talk in their own ways about what they found important and to comment freely on public affairs. They could find work and housing and support their families without giving up everything for their careers. A woman had fewer choices of employment, which for most women are simply choices among deeply subordinate and often insecure positions in large and uninspiring organizations. In exchange, though, she had much more freedom to avoid economic dependence on an employer, and much more freedom to become the wife and mother of a stable and functional family and raise her children in a safe environment in which she felt at home. Blacks were much more free than today to have a normal family life, to be cared for by their parents when young, to marry and stay married when mature, to raise their children with confidence that they would have a productive life, to stay drug-free and out of jail, and not to be murdered by their neighbors and associates. Such freedoms should be taken no less seriously than the egalitarian advances and expressive and lifestyle freedoms now emphasized.

Nor has advanced liberalism been needed for whatever good can be obtained from the conception of human rights. Very little theory is needed to enable those who hold a variety of views to cooperate in dealing with things they agree are gross abuses. And, to the extent that the radically liberal theory that now inspires the human-rights movement makes a difference, it actually defeats its own ends. Gross human-rights violations are more likely to result from attempts to transform human nature in some unprecedented way—from a Great Proletarian Cultural Revolution or an attempt to construct New Soviet man—than from a willingness to live with the world as we find it. To insist on radical equality with regard to traditional distinctions such as religion, sex, class, and ethnicity deprives man of the particular qualities that give him a specific viewpoint, a concrete place in the world, and a set of alliances and interests that go beyond purely individual concerns. It isolates him and makes him powerless, with his liberty and dignity wholly dependent on bureaucratic and financial institutions. By eliminating the stable network of personal connections needed for enduring loyalties and even culture to exist, it promotes a conception of humanity that is too abstract to be usable except for manipulative purposes. It abolishes the most important social barriers to tyranny.

THE REALITY OF LIBERALISM

It is important to be clear about liberalism and its implications. Minimizing its logic permits its defenders to explain away its most egregious offenses as individual anomalies. Many of those who recognize the tendency of liberalism toward extremes hope that in the end tolerance, compromise, and common sense will prevail, and that advanced politically correct liberalism will become more humane and willing to let those who differ with it live in accordance with their own conceptions. Their hope is forlorn. The issues are too important, too morally laden, too much a matter of basic principle, and at the same time too intertwined with crude considerations of money and power for angularities to soften. Compromise must be based on a sense of unity that goes deeper than the points at issue, but the teaching of liberalism is that there is no principle of unity deeper than the right to equal freedom, respect, and consideration. Temporary truce is the most that can be hoped for as long as advanced liberalism co-exists with other views.

It sounds extreme to call liberalism "tyrannical" or even "totalitarian," or to say that liberal society, apparently so open and pluralistic, is in fact a closed ideological system that exists through its extraordinary ability to disguise its nature. The goal of liberalism, after all, is to enable us to control our own lives as much and as equally as possible. Abortion access flows from the right to choose. The welfare state makes available the resources needed for the exercise of ordinary choices in daily life. Affirmative action tries to give women and blacks the same practical choices that white men have. "Gay marriage" gives equal rights to nonstandard intimate relationships. There are objections to such things, but at first glance they hardly seem despotic. How can it be illuminating to lump together a variety of governmental and private actions with widely accepted ideals and their various expressions, call it "liberalism," and complain that when all those things are put together they constitute a comprehensive scheme of control that amounts to tyranny? Social attitudes and institutions, taken collectively, always severely constrain what one can say and do. Why label the current setup as tyrannical?

There are no secret police and few government spies in America. The judiciary is independent and private property generally safe. Trials are public and procedural safeguards observed. Elections with universal suffrage ensure that if voters at large feel seriously oppressed they can do something about it. Anyone can run for public office on any platform, and anyone can write or say what he wants without fear of prison or confiscation. Tenure protects scholars with unpopular and even conservative views. If the Amish want to live as such, they are allowed to do so, and the government is even willing to change the law to accommodate their rejection of social security and high school. Informal restraints on thought, expression, and action appear matched by similar restraints in other societies. And above all, life is comfortable, which was hardly the case in Nazi Germany or Stalinist Russia. The differences between the American regime today and the regimes usually called tyrannical or totalitarian are obvious and fundamental. Critics used to complain that liberalism was relativistic and permissive. How can they now call it dictatorial?

The differences between contemporary liberal societies and recent extreme tyrannies, important though they are, should not mask similarities that are also fundamental and justify some similarity of descriptive language. Totalitarianism is a consequence of the modern abolition of the transcendent and the deification of human will. Why not expect the same cause to create similar tendencies within all modern political systems? It should be obvious that there is no such thing as openness or pluralism in the comprehensive sense contemporary liberalism proposes. Every society functions on definite principles viewed as basic to public order and the common good, and every society ensures in one way or another that those principles are inculcated and obeyed.[20] The widespread conviction that liberal societies are different proves only that things are not as they seem and that something is being overlooked or concealed. An analysis of liberal society must therefore be based on something other than that society's self-presentation or the ideals of its proponents.

"Tyrannical" and "totalitarian" do not mean "brutal." Lack of freedom can take a softer form. A tyranny is an irresponsible government not limited by law or binding custom. A totalitarian regime is a tyranny based on an all-encompassing theory that does away with all institutions other than those controlled by a ruling elite able to make the governing theory mean what its interests require. On those definitions medieval monarchies were in general neither totalitarian nor tyrannical. They were limited by law and custom, other institutions retained independent authority, and the Christian outlook that justified and limited the social order was in the hands not of the king but of the church, a body distinct in fundamental ways from secular rulers, often at odds with them, and bound by authoritative texts and traditions and ultimately the will of God.

In contrast, the contemporary West inclines toward tyranny and even a sort of totalitarianism, at least if one recognizes (1) the nature of liberalism as a self-contained and all-embracing scheme for life in society, (2) the ability of ruling elites to reinterpret that scheme and change its practical meaning, (3) the barriers to political action at odds with that scheme, and (4) the degree to which the centralization of social life and pervasive regulation make all significant social institutions agents of the state. Western countries are governed by liberal elites and institutions that reject custom as a standard and whose power to define liberal ideology and force it on society is not limited by any substantive external point of reference. They claim to be bound by ideals of freedom and equality— by the popular voice—and by law. Freedom and equality, however, are content-free and can be made to mean anything when taken as ultimate standards. The popular voice can be managed, and in any case is subordinate to basic legal principles. Furthermore, the judges who define the law are themselves part of the elite and draw their power from the liberal ideology to which they are committed.

The minuteness and comprehensiveness of the social controls available today make up for the comparative mildness of the sanctions they impose. The softness of a tyranny, its reliance on bribes, obfuscation, petty regulations, and voluntary cooperation among ruling institutions and elites rather than force, does not altogether do away with its character as tyrannical or even as totalitarian. One should look, rather, at consequences. Because man is social, tyranny can inhere in the relationship between an irresponsible ruling class and its society as well as between a government and the individual. A man who arbitrarily imprisons me or confiscates my property is a tyrant. Institutions and general ways of thinking that destroy the social institutions and relationships that make me what I am; that attack the family and abolish gender distinctions, communal ties, and traditional moral standards; that drive religion out of public life and tell private associations what members to choose and why—these are also tyrannical. Imprisonment and exile are punishments because they deprive a man of his social setting. The intentional destruction of that setting is plainly worse. Genocide was originally defined to include the intentional destruction of the essential foundations of the life of national groups.[21] Liberalism does that to all national groups by abolishing the constituents of nationality. How can that be acceptable? When everyone must praise such actions as incontestable demands of justice, when it is all but impossible to make protests heard and critics are treated as enemies of humanity, when the existence of any higher standard is denied, then the tyranny, however maintained, takes on a totalitarian quality.

The advanced liberal state is able to do such things almost invisibly because of the very scope of its power. It is to a traditional tyranny what conquest is to common theft. It does not bother with instances but seizes whole institutions and the very principles of their being. Old-fashioned tyrannies invaded households, confiscated estates, proscribed eminent men, and exiled dissidents. Advanced liberalism does better—it redefines property and the family; eliminates eminence through quotas, sensitivity training, and the devaluation of values; and destroys every homeland by eradicating borders and particularities. By abolishing all sense of an authority that transcends human institutions, it makes its outlook and institutions a self-contained absolute. Opposition becomes almost metaphysically impossible. Because it dominates the bureaucracies of knowledge and communication and expands their dominion by destroying other authorities, it acquires the ability to redefine facts, moral standards, and even language. It thereby makes effective objection all but impossible. What *should not* be a fact *cannot* be a fact, or so it is believed. The erstwhile fact drops out of public truth as authoritatively defined and cannot be discussed.[22] If you accept advanced liberalism you can treat your views as truth, speak out publicly in their favor, act on them in affairs that affect other people, and attempt to enforce them wherever you want. If you reject advanced liberalism you cannot. To assert seriously the superior authority of transcendent truth or to reject "inclusiveness"—to say, for example, that homosexuality or the cultural effects of immigration are a problem—is to be excluded from respectable public life, viewed as potentially violent, treated as a threat to social order, and subjected to social, vocational, and occasionally (especially outside the United States) criminal sanctions.

In theory, the popular election of top officeholders should mean that government must defer to the will of the people, so that any tyranny would have to retain majority backing and thus be subject to limits. However, popular influence in government should not be exaggerated. The practical ability of elites to force fundamental changes over strong and rooted opposition from the people as a whole is illustrated by mass immigration, compulsory "diversity," and the exclusion of religion from public life. In any event, the formulation and effect of popular views is deeply affected by the framing and presentation of issues and information. It is also affected by public education, widespread dependence on government benefits, the human tendency to imitate the famous and powerful, the growing disorderliness of popular culture and informal human ties, and the tendency of world markets, huge bureaucracies, and electronic media to distance us from the realities that condition our lives and put us in a world of images that can be spun to make anything seem true. Such conditions make popular views more an occasional reality check than a continuing guide for those who govern us.

The reader may still think my complaints overblown. Nonetheless, there are plain grounds for concern about the future. Free government requires a settled widespread distribution of power, respect by government for popular loyalties and understandings, and cohesion among the people at large so that they can hold their rulers to account. Today's liberalism undermines all those things. Unlike traditional forms of society, which also restrict action and expression, liberalism is at odds with settled habits and natural tendencies. It establishes a far more centralized and active scheme of supervision and control, one that disarms criticism as uninformed and beside the point.

More generally, liberalism is one of several modern political movements that deny human nature. It makes the nature of man a matter of human choice and technology, as communism made it a matter of economic evolution and fascism of human will and national struggle. In each case the motive has been to eliminate human nature as an obstacle to the re-creation of the world. Unfortunately, the destruction in concept of stable and rooted human nature has led more than once to the concrete destruction of very large numbers of actual human beings. The sequence seems natural. If *man* does not exist, why should it matter whether *men* exist? Liberals do not take the threat of such inferences seriously, but it is not clear why. If "human" is content-free, a mere social classification the point of which is determined politically, and if it is irrational to recognize a radical difference in rights between a man and a dog—both of which seem to be the emerging liberal views—the stage seems set for horrors. Why should such considerations not concern us?

CHAPTER SIX

Irrationality and Self-Destruction

LIBERALISM IS AN ESSENTIALLY CRITICAL OUTLOOK THAT TRIES TO ORDER social life without having the substantive content needed to rule. It must therefore avoid obvious issues. It must claim, at least implicitly, that it is the simple embodiment of reason, that it can rule without requiring sacrifice, that enforcement of its demands is not really coercion, that punishment and war are anomalies which can be obfuscated in principle and done away with in practice, and that objections to liberalism should be ignored or suppressed. It lacks the ability to deal with new situations and its own internal problems. In the end, its inability to deal with reality leads to self-destruction.

INSUFFICIENCY OF LIBERALISM

Liberalism claims to resolve conflicts by applying formal principles like autonomy, private property, or "to each his own" that take no position on the content of the good life. That cannot be done. Formal principles cannot resolve substantive questions without smuggling in help from elsewhere. What, after all, is "one's own"? Whether it is control of one's body or an imperial throne, a thing can count as such only if there are common understandings that make it so. Rights are not simple presocial conceptions independent of particular understandings of human life. They become definite and usable only in a larger social and moral setting. They cannot by themselves serve as master principles for resolving basic issues.

Liberalism tries to establish the larger setting necessary to orient decisions by making neutrality a substantive requirement: goals are legitimate only when they give other goals equal respect. Overriding the goals of others is right, it is said, only when the effect is to promote a system of "tolerance"—that is, a setting in which all goals are nonaggressive and mutually independent. This maneuver fails. Substantive neutrality cannot define a moral order because whether a goal is tolerant depends on what goals have already been determined to be acceptable. Insisting that others recognize a relationship between two men as a marriage may be tolerant in a liberal society but it is absurdly aggressive in a Catholic or Muslim one.

The basic inability of liberalism to resolve issues in accordance with its stated principles causes it to raise questions it cannot deal with and must ignore or silence. Examples are everywhere: if every society must be intolerant in defending its leading principles, how can tolerance be a leading principle? If government is to give us what we want, do we want hedonism? If I have a right to pursue my desires, and I desire to live in a society guided by traditional understandings, do I have the right to pursue that goal politically? If not, why is an environment free of racism and sexism a worthier goal or even one more conducive to everyday freedom and equality than one free of atheism and immorality as traditionally understood? Such questions cannot be avoided, and in the long run they make the liberal claim to special fairness and rationality absurd.

Scientism

The inability of liberalism to resolve conflicts or even deal with them rationally is incurable because it stems from the inadequate conception of reason on which it is based. Human life refers to things beyond itself. The consequence is that liberalism loses its connection to reality and human nature and so its ability to function.

Modern natural science and its social-science imitators are now considered the only authoritative way to ascertain genuine facts and principles. All else is opinion that each may take or leave as he chooses. Moderns therefore demand that authority align itself as much as possible with science and its methods. Liberalism attempts to do so, and it limits the considerations it will recognize as much as possible to those which are universally demonstrable in the manner of the modern natural sciences, supplemented when need be by the most minimal and content-free principles possible.

Modern natural science can limit itself in such a way, and thereby achieve great reliability in its results, because it normally deals with matters that are much simpler than human social relations, and because it accepts that it is a limited enterprise, an effort that might or might not be successful to discover principles that enable us to predict and control nature. It is under no obligation to explain everything.[1] In contrast, government and social morality cannot remain silent when, as is almost always the case in human affairs, rigorous principles yield no sufficient conclusion. They must deal with man and society as a whole and provide usable answers for whatever comes up, however complex and subtle: questions of life and death, personal responsibility and punishment, the education of children, and the relation between the sexes.

The scientific outlook cannot be much help here. The features that make that outlook effective on its proper ground make it unusable as an approach to social life and morality. It succeeds in the physical realm by isolating systems, reducing problems to numerical terms, and solving them one at a time, avoiding considerations of context and quality as much as possible. Liberalism attempts to do the same in the moral and social realm. It promises happiness by satisfying particular desires, ignoring their value and the overall setting in which they operate. Indeed, it destroys that setting—traditional social patterns and understandings of the natural and transcendent—the better to isolate desires and allow them to be dealt with effectively and equally.

The result is the destruction of what men value most highly. Liberalism is centered on man but denies what he is and attacks what he cares about. It serves humanity by rooting out the natural inclinations, concrete loyalties, and aspirations toward the transcendent that make us human, the better to tend to the particularities of individual desire. As the liberal state develops it sharpens its opposition to arrangements that reflect ordinary habits, perceptions, and needs—arrangements that therefore have become traditional—because it cannot recognize their logic but must insist on its own. The current campaigns to eradicate "racism," "sexism," "homophobia," and the like are so thoroughgoing as to become in substance attempts to destroy normal moral ties—those consisting in obligations to particular men based on specific affiliations such as family, history, and religion—and replace them with the abstract bureaucratic and market arrangements that are alone thought rational.

But man is not a machine. His good cannot be realized through an industrial process or determined by adding up the particular desires of individuals. Nor, in the long run, will he support a system that insists on doing so. Bureaucracy, contractual relations, and abstract altruism have their uses, but they cannot take the lead in organizing social life because they simply do not have the same force as concrete obligations to family, friends, and faith. The attempt to rationalize life on market and bureaucratic principles destroys goods that cannot be managed, commodified, and made equal. It weakens our sense of mutual obligation and higher purpose, leading to cynicism, corruption, crime, general ill-feeling, and endlessly rising costs for social services. The liberal state cannot do anything about such issues or even recognize them without recognizing considerations and goods with which it cannot deal effectively. Such a recognition would destroy its claim to unique rationality and therefore its right to rule. The problems therefore remain unremedied and grow worse, eventually compromising or destroying social cohesion and the ability of institutions to function.

The Good

Another way to state how liberalism is rendered irrational and in the end self-destructive is that it has a grossly insufficient understanding of the good. There is nothing mysterious about our need for an adequate conception of the good. A "good" is a reasonable goal, one worth choosing after consideration of what it is and the relevant circumstances, while "the good" is whatever general quality it is that makes goals reasonable to pursue. Cooperative social life depends on agreement as to goals and thus goods. Everyone agrees that some goals are better—more worth choosing—than others, but there are different views as to what those are. A scheme of action that affects life as comprehensively as modern government can hardly avoid favoring some such views over others, and when it does it will inevitably judge that the goals preferred are worth preferring because they are better in some way. To claim that government should act without taking a position on such issues is either to embrace political irrationalism—the view that we should live together socially in certain ways with no idea why—or to impose the authority of certain goods while denying doing so.

Discussion is needed to bring about agreement as to goods and to relate that agreement to concrete measures that preserve and foster the goods in question. For example, it is impossible to discuss laws relating to family life sensibly without taking the goods characteristic of marriage into account. Liberalism cannot support such discussions, because they require standards that transcend desire and create a common moral world within which thought and discussion can evaluate conflicting desires and bring them into order. Liberalism cannot recognize such standards, at least not openly, because such recognition would be at odds with the limitation of reason to formal logic, modern natural science, and means-ends rationality. It therefore tries to resolve conflicts among goods, when they cannot be traded and bought off, mainly by finding grounds for ruling one side out of order and silencing it. Discussion of basic goods, and therefore free and rational political life, becomes impossible. To say that values are equally worthy, as long as they are tolerant in the sense currently demanded, is to deny the possibility of rationally discussing which to choose, and thus the possibility of rational action in politics and eventually even in personal life.

Hedonism

In fact, liberalism does have a theory of the good, albeit one that is minimal, inarticulate, and unargued. To attempt to treat all goals equally is to judge that each is as good and worth pursuing as every other. On such a view the good becomes satisfaction of individual preference simply as such. Equal satisfaction becomes the highest standard. As such it is equivalent to equal freedom, at least if we accept that equality of result is equivalent to equality of opportunity.

Liberalism is thus hedonistic: preference is the thing that determines rational action, so the good, by definition, is what pleases us. Such a position does not make sense, because it makes every consciously chosen action equally reasonable. Because it is consciously chosen, the action brings about a preference and therefore a good. If the choice is equally a choice, the good is equally a good. Since it is choice itself that makes something good, we do not choose things for their goodness but merely because we choose them. Our choices become arbitrary, and our actions essentially nonrational. The rational component of morality is reduced to the therapeutic task of clarifying choices and the technical task of securing their satisfaction equally and efficiently.

Such a result is deeply inconsistent with the way we actually deliberate about action. It is the outlook of a psychopath, someone with no moral connection to other people or to any system of goods outside his own desires. Treating our goals as the final standard just because they happen to be our goals turns the entire procedure of choosing goals and pursuing them into a pointless waste of effort. Why chase after something whose value is simply that we have decided to chase it? Would it not be more reasonable to become a Buddhist whose one desire is liberation from the dependency, burden, and degradation of having goals at all?

If goodness were a matter only of desire, the most effective way to realize it might be to manipulate desires chemically so that they center on things that can be reliably delivered to everybody. A combination of drugs and electrodes in the brain might be the direct path to the *summum bonum*. No humane and reasonable person accepts such a view, however consistent it may be with some aspects of the new biotechnology. The hedonism on which it is based is useless to us because we are not at bottom hedonists. By giving us "whatever we want" hedonism fails precisely to give us what we want. Our good, and for that matter our deepest desires, depend on what we are, and we are rational and social. Man does not desire to get what he wants just because he wants it. He wants what he wants, but he also wants to recognize it as good, as something that should be desired because it contributes to a scheme of life the worth of which does not depend on his desires alone.

All men by nature desire to know. "Knowledge" includes moral knowledge. As rational beings, we are not satisfied unless our lives are based on an enduringly valid understanding of which goals are right. Nor, as social beings, can we be satisfied unless that understanding is shared. Goods wither when they are understood as merely individual goals with no right to social support. Even the disinterested love of truth and beauty needs common support so that it can be seen to relate to something objective. Liberalism disrupts that support by denying public recognition to any good but satisfaction of desire. It thus denies the reality of all that concerns us most deeply. It claims to let each of us create his own standard of the good but might as well claim to let us flap our arms and fly. When it tells us to choose our own moral world, it turns its back on the public moral world needed for choice to have meaning. We value liberty because it enables us to choose and realize goods, but if no goods are objective, freedom loses seriousness and becomes indistinguishable from willfulness. How can choice be so important if what is chosen matters not at all? Or if it is choice itself that matters, why is willfulness not the greatest virtue?

The problem is more than theoretical. People care about things other than hobbies, consumer goods, purely private indulgences, and the triumph of liberal principle. They care about complex and often hierarchical social goods that require a common recognition of enduring obligations that trump particular desires. Marriage, for example, is more than what two people choose to do privately. It involves objective duties and social definitions on which the parties are entitled to rely. To define it as the chance parallelism of two wills, each with its own purposes, is to destroy it. If John wants to marry Suzy, he cannot achieve his goal unless marriage *exists*—that is, unless it is socially recognized as an institution involving objective duties defined and guarded by specific attitudes and customs. Otherwise, it is a personal hobby or fantasy and not a marriage at all. Liberalism suppresses such attitudes and customs and the institutions and goods to which they relate. It gives special justification only to equality and self-centered satisfactions that do not require others to give of themselves. Things as basic as love and loyalty lose their sanction and become morally questionable because they impose enduring demands and obligations. Marriage, among other things, becomes impossible even though the name may remain. To the extent society becomes liberal it becomes inhuman, and as the process approaches completion the society becomes unable to function or survive.

Hedonism does not even work in practical procedural terms—that is, as a clear method of deciding what people want so that they can be kept contented and quiet. The attempt to maximize satisfaction runs into insoluble problems. Satisfaction cannot be computed and depends on variables that cannot be controlled. There is no way to add up satisfactions that differ as radically as reading Plato, playing Chinese checkers, viewing pornography, and climbing mountains. Nor does satisfaction follow any simple logic. Struggle can be enjoyable and unalloyed pleasure a bore. When John and Suzy differ it is usually impossible to tell whether satisfaction would increase if John gave in to Suzy or the reverse. Quite possibly each would be happier giving in to the other. O. Henry's story "The Gift of the Magi," in which a young wife and her husband find bliss when she sells her hair to buy him a watch chain and he sells his watch to buy her a set of combs, is a familiar example of the situation. Matters become still more complicated when one attempts to deal with the complex satisfactions of millions of very different people, with the effects of what people do and think on the situations in which desires arise and find fulfillment, and with the further effects on social life and happiness of government attempts to take over responsibility for such things and engineer them to make them manageable. How can the difficulties possibly be resolved except arbitrarily, by falsifying the nature of happiness and how it arises or by imposing the interests and preferences of those in power?

Even if such problems could be solved as a practical matter and government could achieve an adequate understanding of what constitutes human satisfaction, hedonism could not be relied on to support the liberal regime. The world does not obey our will, so prosperity and social protections eventually give out. We may run out of oil, the climate may change and require hard decisions, war and terrorism may make life difficult and insecure, social indiscipline may make cooperation difficult and cause the government to rely on the stick rather than the carrot as a way of achieving its goals. Some of those things will eventually happen. When they do, upon what will liberalism, the philosophy of subjective individual fulfillment, fall back for support?

THE TWILIGHT OF LIBERALISM

Until recently, the indefinite advance of liberalism seemed inevitable. Liberalism alone seemed able to maintain the voluntary cooperation needed for efficiency and social peace. Once an issue had been raised, any nonliberal resolution seemed irrational. All liberals had to do was to dramatize what they considered oppression and victory was assured. The dominance of liberalism and the apparent impossibility of changing or reversing it have led some to say—and many implicitly to assume—that we have reached the end of history, that since liberalism is altogether dominant and cannot essentially change it has won forever.

That conclusion mistakes the imaginative limits of liberals for the limits of reality. The owl of Minerva flies at dusk. The possibility of comprehensively formulating advanced liberalism, first realized by John Rawls,[2] and the difficulty of imagining anything beyond it, are signs that its possibilities are played out. The principles of liberal modernity are too simple and authoritative and their implications too clear to allow for changes even when those principles become obviously self-destructive. Liberal conceptions of justice and rationality strive for ever greater clarity, consistency, and independence of cultural prejudices. Once a restriction or inequality has come to seem illegitimate and the attempt to abolish it has begun, a proposal to accept it once again seems an utterly intolerable embrace of oppression. That dynamic has given liberalism extraordinary enduring momentum, but it also makes it impossible to reform. Advanced liberalism lacks the complexities, ambiguities, unspoken higher standards, and other internal resources that would permit renovation. One can fiddle with its institutions in comparatively minor ways, but the implications of the basic principles that define them and give them coherence and legitimacy eventually become quite clear, and when they do they overcome all objection and stubbornly resist change.

Self-demolition

Adam Smith noted that there is a great deal of ruin in a nation. The same principle has notoriously applied to liberalism. Predictions of its impending collapse and overthrow have repeatedly been falsified. One could shrug off today's predictions by pointing to liberalism's durability and continuing spectacular successes. It has more than once bounced back from apparent weakness and decadence, and today it seems more prosperous, stable, and dominant than ever. Its pragmatic success is such that in the foreseeable future, dissolution from within seems the only thing that can seriously threaten it.

If radical problems are implicit in liberalism, one might ask, why has it been as successful as it has for so long? It seems unrealistic to think that something so dominant will go away and be replaced by something more like what preceded it. What are the candidates for succession? Where will they come from? Besides, liberal arguments seem unanswerable. The current order makes satisfaction of preferences the key, and gives people their particular desires better than any alternative. People may hate it on the whole, but they love the particulars and refuse to give them up. Liberalism resolves disputes by letting each do as he pleases consistent with the equal freedom of others. Which part of that arrangement is to be rejected, and how? A fundamental deviation from liberal principle would require a source of knowledge regarding the good that most educated commentators believe unavailable. What would that source be and how could it be validated?

Nonetheless, the strength of liberalism as a principle has eroded with its triumph as a ruling rather than critical outlook. In the long run, inner weakness matters. Today liberalism must give answers rather than criticize those others give, and on examination its answers are not persuasive. "Let them do what they want" cannot be a principle of government, and the promise of social peace through endless accommodation, which has been the liberal trump card, becomes less persuasive when further accommodation must come at the expense of the liberal system itself.

The difficulty of presenting or even imagining an alternative will not keep liberalism going forever. If anything, it will make its collapse all the more sudden and complete. Pride goeth before destruction, because it cannot see what lies before it. A constructed this-worldly order of the sort liberalism progressively institutes cannot provide a pattern of human life that works, because human knowledge and skill is limited. The liberal regime can exist only because it is incomplete. Residual preliberal habits and attitudes, as well as material prosperity and technological prowess, mask its moral and cultural consequences and maintain social functioning. Those habits and attitudes are not an automatic outcome of freedom, self-interest, and universalizable reasoning but rather depend on inherited nonliberal patterns of life and thought. The victories of liberalism destroy those patterns, and in the end will destroy liberalism itself.

Liberal society rests on trust, which is itself based on common beliefs, habits, and attachments. It needs domestic and social relationships that promote moderation, self-control and mutual respect, and legitimate particularity that allows a variety of independent perspectives to supplement and correct each other. It needs tradition: liberal tradition to define its commitments and nonliberal tradition to foster the nonliberal qualities needed both for social survival and to ensure that progress toward liberal commitments is slow and cautious. It needs loyalties that attach the people to the public order and elites to the public good. Such loyalties normally rely on ties of locality, community, class, culture, nationality, and religion.

Liberalism loosens and disorders the connections and particularities on which it depends. It cannot keep from doing so, because it is progressive and idealistic. The aspiration toward a totally rational, self-contained, and equal system of human life has always been basic to liberalism. That aspiration demands progress toward an idealized future that cannot be clearly imagined and is based on abstract standards of freedom and equality that cannot be satisfied. Liberalism insists on an all-embracing justification for the political order of a kind that is impossible because the social world cannot be fully grasped in thought. Impossible goals set never-ending tasks. As liberalism develops, consciousness is raised, the remaining illiberal aspects of the social order become plain, and liberals, in order to remain liberal, must attempt to eradicate them. Attempts to get rid of particular inequalities bring to the fore others, so that liberalism continually radicalizes itself. The elimination of hereditary privilege and the weakening of family connections is purchased by acceptance of inequalities based on market success and formal qualifications that seem more acceptable because of their relatively impersonal rationality. Then they, too, come to seem like arbitrary impositions. Wider schemes of reform are needed to mitigate their effects, as well as the effects of natural distinctions such as sex and historical distinctions such as ethnicity.

As a result, liberal societies reject ever more sweepingly the particular connections on which they depend. All particularities come to seem irrational. They seem to stand in the way of physical and social power and the liberation of the individual. Also, Western dominance requires justification on principles that have no special connection to the West. Our particularities must be judged by the standards of our science and technology, which are viewed as rightfully universal. The outcome of such demands is the abolition of traditional and informal patterns and their replacement by a pervasive system of control—necessarily irresponsible—that passes itself off as a neutral and transparently rational system of freedom and equality. That development destroys liberalism, because it destroys local diversity and autonomy and the prerational ethnic and religious ties that make free political life possible. Without local diversity and autonomy there can be no stable and effective devolution of power and no limitation on the subject matter or goals of politics. Without prerational ties there can be no reliable basis for public spirit and no limit to how far disputes can go once started. The destruction of such things means the disappearance of a public order based on discussion and cooperation, and with it the ideals of rationality and objective truth that have made liberalism itself possible.

Neoconservatives and others have noted the problem and proposed that advanced liberalism reverse itself and allow a certain degree of autonomous authority to cultural tradition and religious faith, enough to hold families together and to maintain a degree of loyalty, discipline, and public spirit. On its face the idea has some merit. Liberalism has shown a great deal of flexibility in some respects, allowing and even subsidizing political opposition while finding ways to manage it. When needed for efficiency and rationality, it has allowed necessary changes, such as economic deregulation.

However, traditional authorities are more difficult than markets to domesticate and to subject to a system of supervision. They are at odds with such basic liberal tendencies as individualism, rationalism, and hedonism. They are informal, opaque to supervision and resistant to bureaucratic fine-tuning. A decision to bring them back would go fundamentally against liberal principles. Those who run the advanced liberal state share a genuine belief in liberalism that profoundly affects their actions. Causes like abortion, gay rights, and mass immigration serve the interests of governing elites, but they are also felt as genuine moral imperatives. Liberalism could not exist as it does if liberals were not truly convinced of the correctness of their moral views. Advanced liberal society therefore tends to view cultural traditionalism and substantive religious faith the way the Soviet state viewed economic liberalism—as an enemy with which no compromise is possible. Whatever enthusiasm liberals have had for the welfare state, they never suppressed advocacy of economic liberalism as "greed" in the way they now suppress advocacy of ethnic cohesiveness, traditional views regarding sex, or nonliberal religion as "hate."

Nor can the people moderate the liberal regime and save it from itself by insisting on a commonsense accommodation of ideology to the ordinary conditions of life. The reign of expertise and formal modes of organization have become too pervasive for them to clarify their views and articulate them effectively when those views oppose the official ones. In a media-drenched age, official understandings seep into popular thought and determine the language the people feel they must use to make themselves understood. The result is that criticism by nonexperts becomes confused and blunted unless some special doctrine and discipline enables them to hold firm in opposition, in which case they are excluded from public life as fundamentalists or extremists. The only acceptable thought is academic thought, which has the same defects as academic art. Its overemphasis on formal criteria suited to institutional needs disables it from dealing adequately with basic realities.

End Game

As time goes by, the growing irrationality and oppressiveness of the liberal regime will weaken its attractions and ability to function. In the absence of a common culture, it will fall back on force and group assertiveness as principles of organization, with liberalism functioning at most as a rhetorical justification for actions that are generally quite unprincipled. Under such circumstances, the once-liberal state is likely to depend less on efficiency or rational or popular appeal than on abolition of the social base for public life and other forms of social organization, so that no alternative seems possible. It is to that end that liberalism is now tending. Prosperity, the world market, and electronic communications loosen personal and cultural ties. The blurring of sexual distinctions and restrictions dissolves the family. The welfare state deprives of their functions the informal personal connections on which nonstate structures are based, and high levels of taxation and regulation weaken them further. Multiculturalism abolishes the functions of particular culture and historical community and turns them into pure principles of opposition that must be mediated by the state to avoid communal violence. The centralization and professionalization of intellectual and cultural life make it impossible to raise questions about fundamentals and have them taken seriously. Life and thought become trivial.

Leo Strauss and others have claimed that since the Wars of Religion,[3] statesmen have been able to build solidly because they have aimed low, at stability and prosperity rather than at any transcendent good. The problem with such a strategy is that if the good has no place in public life the low eventually becomes very low indeed. Politics wholly divorced from the transcendent aims at the abolition of the things that make us human, because those things complicate administration and markets and get in the way of the satisfaction of desire. It is no longer war but the degradation of the people that is the health of the state. To satisfy the demands of tolerance, the people are required to make individual pleasure their final standard and to abandon the human connections and concrete standards that make them what they are.

We cannot live that way forever. While the weakening of informal moral connections makes resistance to the liberal regime more difficult, and to that extent entrenches it, it also destroys the loyalty and discipline needed for public order, rational discussion, sacrifice of private interest to the public good, and even ordinary social functioning. The liberal regime cannot justify non-consensual authority and feels bound to undermine it as oppressive, whatever the consequences. Technology cannot provide a replacement. Scientific management cannot eliminate the necessity of sacrifice by the people—which can range from the demands of ordinary honesty to willingness to risk everything in war—or by officials constantly tempted to abuse their positions.

In any event, government has to govern, which requires prudence. Advanced liberalism kills prudence by killing thought. It suppresses the free discussion of public affairs intelligent decision requires, and by making human desire the measure it ensures that unpleasant facts get ignored. It depends on competent elites, but it is reluctant to recognize human differences and institutes affirmative-action programs that make it impossible to deal with questions of relative competence.

Most fundamentally, perhaps, an outlook based on independent individuals pursuing their own interests cannot deal with issues that go beyond their lives as self-interested individuals—reproduction and child-rearing, loyalty and sacrifice, life and death. Such issues are basic to social survival, but liberalism can only treat them as matters of individual preference. The consequences include suicidally low birthrates, children growing up without parental care, immigration and social policies that presume that culture does not matter and that cultural particularity must be extirpated, and a military bureaucracy that cannot deal with casualties except by turning every conflict into a universal crusade for an abstract cause that can never be achieved.

Eventually the burdens of moral and intellectual decline outweigh their benefits to the regime. The resulting disorders permeate social life, and as the generations succeed each other orderly government and social life become progressively harder to maintain. In the absence of loyalty and faith, official corruption, popular disregard for the law, and general cynicism take over. Government is driven to maintain itself by dogmatism and unprincipled use of force. It stops being liberal.

The vices of liberalism are intrinsic, progressive, destructive, and irreversible. The liberal regime cannot change fundamentally or stop progressing on its chosen lines. Lack of moderating principles means that it cannot help but overreach, eventually catastrophically. What might seem the remote theoretical consequences of liberal principles become quite practical issues indeed. Three centuries after John Locke, these issues confront us everywhere. When it proves impossible to base human relations on further extensions of equal freedom, the regime will face insuperable problems. The more bureaucratic the system and the more incontestable its principles the less the ability to muddle through based on common sense, luck, illogic, and the possibility of a turn for the better. A state that has become thoroughly irrational, corrupt, and unable to call on the loyalty of its people can hang on if other social institutions continue to function. The advanced managerial state, however, makes all institutions thoroughly dependent on itself. As a result, administrative decadence can lead to a sort of social malfunctioning far more pervasive than any found in earlier forms of society. In the Soviet Union, the impossibility of comprehensive central administration of social life, combined with an insistence on abolishing competing institutions, led to gross social and economic failure and eventually to collapse of the regime, followed by mafia rule and demographic decline. Something similar may happen to us in the West.

Part II
Up from Tyranny

CHAPTER SEVEN

Blind Alleys

THE ADVANCED LIBERAL ORDER PRESENTS MODERN POLITICAL LIFE IN ITS most developed and characteristic form. It is fully integrated with current understandings of reason and reality and appears to leave no line of development open except the further extension of its own principles. Its claim to be the sole rational way of ordering politics and morality is generally accepted among the educated and influential. Those who recognize standards superior to human purposes, or even natural limitations on equality, are seen as dangerous bigots who want to oppress others in the name of some arbitrary principle. However, nothing human lasts forever; man is not the measure; our wishes and perceptions do not determine reality. The liberal order has lost touch with the world it governs and is destroying itself. In looking to the future we must put our hope in something different.

Stay the Course?

But how can we go forward to something better when it seems impossible to imagine even the possibility of change? The domination of public discussion by liberalism, the overwhelming success of the scientific style of reasoning with which it is associated, and its rigorously critical attitude toward other modes of thought make it seem impossible for other ways of thinking to function as public standards. How can something transcendent serve as a standard, when those thought to know better insistently debunk it as an irrational and oppressive fantasy? How can natural limitations be recognized, when technology overcomes nature and it can always be disputed what is natural? Rather than propose something basically different, it seems easier and more sensible to modify liberalism a little or to move toward something that is closely related to it.

Leftist Responses

Most of those who seek a solution to the problems of advanced liberalism maintain a general allegiance to Enlightenment understandings of reason and reality. They may blur those understandings somewhat, but they do not propose a definite alternative. More often than not they try to distance themselves from what is already established by adopting a leftist as distinct from a liberal perspective. While generally sympathetic to recent tendencies, they complain that they do not go far enough. Academic leftists, who wish to build on liberalism by further radicalizing it, are a prominent example.

However, such critics have difficulty making it clear how they propose to improve upon what already exists. The distinction between liberalism and leftism has generally been fuzzy. The two mostly agree on what is ultimately desirable but they have differed on style, tactics, and their sense of what is possible. Where liberals are reformist the Left is radical and uncompromising. Both are constructivist, hedonistic, and anti-transcendental. The triumph of liberalism and the maturation of liberal society have meant that liberalism has absorbed some leftist positions. Experience has shown that others—such as the outright public ownership of industry—are unworkable. The consequence for liberals and leftists has been a blurring of mutual distinctiveness, a loss of direction as the possibilities of further basic change have become obscure, and a tendency toward paralysis and irrationality. Neither has anything solid to propose, even though the world they see around them is very far from the utopia of which they once dreamed.

Leftists, who tend to live by their cause and treat it very much as a religion, want to do something radical right away. The question is what that is to be, what would constitute progress in an age in which their principles have been generally accepted and all basic alternatives to the current very partial and unsatisfactory realization of those principles seem to have been explored and found unworkable. They have answered such questions in various ways, none persuasive. In general, their response has been to step up their denunciations of existing arrangements, at least in the West, and to emphasize cultural issues, mostly those involving the destruction of remaining traditional distinctions. Here the academic Left serves again as a notorious example.

Irrationalism

Going beyond a mature political doctrine like present-day liberalism, with its clear principles that leave little room for variation once their implications have been worked out, requires either adopting a new conception of reason or justice, or giving up on reason or justice altogether. The easiest choice for those for whom the leftist and liberal understanding of justice is fundamental is to give up reason, so there has been a decided move on the left toward political irrationalism. People do not see how to change modern standards of reason and reality, but since those standards no longer seem to show leftists a way forward, they have come to place their hope in unreason.

Unreason can take many forms, among them the crude form of ignoring obvious facts and accepting fantasy as reality. There is plenty of that on the left today. The idealization of Third World peoples, movements, and regimes is one example. Another is the insistence that traditional institutions and distinctions are at the root of all social evils, so that the abolition of boundaries and change simply as such are regarded as obviously good things that will bring about a fundamentally better world.

A slightly less crude form of irrationalism, one that for many people makes up at least temporarily for the lack of any idea where to go or what to do, is faith in creativity—the arrival of unforeseeable answers from who knows where. An appeal to creativity can have a variety of meanings. It might be just an appeal to a less formulaic way of thinking. It could be an assertion that not everything can be planned in advance, and that experiment, improvisation, or blind luck might lead to something surprisingly useful. Or it might be the observation that a pessimistic analysis can turn out to be incomplete or wrong, and something unexpected might yet turn up.

Nonetheless, there is often no more than any of this to contemporary talk of creativity. An awareness of a void at the center of things that must be filled—even though there seems no way to do so—can lead to a faith in creativity that trumps reason and morality. Creativity can seem a sort of magic capable of overcoming even basic logical contradictions: its cult has led to mindless action, at times even terrorism, that attempts to transform an oppressive situation and open up possibilities by acts of pure will that disrupt the order of things. Such attempts can do a great deal of damage, but they go nowhere, and after the initial excitement they are likely to trail off into repetition, formula, careerism, pretense, or mindless vandalism and personal abuse.[1]

Abandonment of Justice

One can also try to deal with the crisis of liberalism, while maintaining a general attachment to the current understanding of reason, by abandoning the aspiration for justice in favor of pure willfulness. In a time in which getting one's way is the *summum bonum*, that possibility can be put into effect immediately and with very little thought or effort, even by those who call themselves liberals or leftists. The theoretical abandonment of justice has taken the form of claims that argument and truth reduce to rhetoric and power, while its practical abandonment has led variously to the idealization of will and struggle; to a politics of image, spin, and self-aggrandizement; and to rejecting politics altogether in favor of self-indulgence. At lower social levels, abandonment of justice has resulted in what is called the underclass, while at upper levels it has taken the form of careerism and yuppie moral nihilism—personal hedonism, conspicuous if supposedly tasteful consumption, and the amoral pursuit of success, sometimes mixed with sentimental altruistic gestures.

Such responses offer no principled resistance to liberal excesses. A society that accepts them is likely to do badly, but they do have the effect of making the application of the advanced liberal conception of justice more erratic and less effectual, and to that extent they may make the world more livable. When established political conceptions become totalitarian, self-seeking and corruption become forces for moderation. They can even function as virtues. The illegal economy kept the Soviet Union going, and congressional paralysis due to political self-seeking has likely spared us much bad legislation.

A less radical move, at least from a conceptual standpoint, would be to retain the liberal idea of justice as equal freedom while restricting it in some simple way—for example, by weakening its universality. One might argue, for example, that justice is primarily a concern within one's group, defined by some connection like blood, history, or social class, and that outside the group the standard is simply self-interest. A view of morality based on social or biological evolution or the way morality has actually functioned within particular societies might support such a conception. Examples of this approach include national socialism and the Marxist conception of class morality.

A problem with such an approach is the arbitrariness of the group within which justice primarily holds. Most groups are not absolutely clear-cut. We belong to a variety of overlapping groups with regard to which a particularistic but still rational perspective would impose varying obligations, none of which trumps all the others from a moral standpoint. It is impossible to sort out such a situation without an understanding of justice that transcends every particular connection, contrary to the original goal of clear-cut radical particularism.

Because neither liberals nor the Left seem to have much to offer, and because the various forms of irrationalism, amoralism, and arbitrary particularism evidently go nowhere, intellectual and political entrepreneurs have tried to concoct a variety of "third ways" between right and left. The offerings have involved more gesture and rhetoric than substance. One example is communitarianism, which proposes a centrally managed nondiscriminatory particularism that is hard even to imagine: if people run their own affairs based on local ties and institutions, how will the system assure equal treatment for the marginalized? How will racism, sexism, and various local chauvinisms be excluded? How will rights and welfare be equalized among communities? Other proposals are similarly rhetorical and nonsubstantive. They either fail to present anything coherent and concrete, or else they repackage, with slight changes, the mix of market and bureaucratic ordering characteristic of all advanced liberal societies.

A basic problem for all "third ways" is that liberalism and the Left are defined by the programmatic replacement of tradition and faith by social technology and equal freedom. To reject any substantial part of the progressive program is to join the Right, since a rejection of modernist reason, freedom, and equality almost always implies (except in the cases of irrationalism and arbitrary particularism) an acceptance of tradition, hierarchy, inherited faith, and the particularities and substantive goods that are intertwined with them.

SIMPLE CONSERVATISM

If a move to the left does not work, if there is no "third way," and if serious conceptions of reason and justice are necessary in public life, then a turn to the right seems necessary. In principle, such a turn would involve modification of the liberal understandings of reason and justice, not so much by limiting their universality as by broadening them to include things known through tradition and faith and needed to deal with particularity and the transcendent.

Conservatism recognizes principles that apply universally. However, it cuts back on the direct applicability of such principles to make room for connections and distinctions—like those related to religion, family life, and historical community—that cannot be brought into a unitary managed system. We learn about such connections and distinctions, and the moral world they help constitute, more through experience than through the kind of reasoning associated with the modern natural sciences. For example, a father has special obligations to his children, as does a citizen to his country. Similarly, men and women may have somewhat differing duties, just as soldiers and civilians do. Such particularized duties apply to others similarly situated, but they cannot be generalized to all persons. Since they are not fully determined by abstract reasoning, social understandings of what they are vary somewhat, and we must rely on particular traditions to determine what they are. For that reason conservatives accept tradition, faith, and particular loyalties as part of what we need to be reasonable and just.

It is not easy to question basic understandings of reason and justice, especially when they are backed by as much social authority as liberal modernity and when change would involve recognition of principles and circumstances that cannot be completely grasped and demonstrated. Those who are put off by liberal neutrality and hedonism but find it difficult to break with them fundamentally have found it easiest to avoid analytical difficulties and become simple non-theoretical conservatives. The form of conservatism they prefer attempts to limit the development of liberalism and blunt the ruthlessness of its logic not by modifying its principles but by a refusal to take them altogether seriously, justified perhaps by mild skepticism or a somewhat nonconceptual way of thinking. The intended effect is to create room for a continuing moderate attachment to goods inspired by memory, common sense, and residual transcendent attachments, and to avoid the extremism to which liberalism tends.

The result is a minimal form of conservatism that does not want to be explicit about what it thinks and so tends to be more procedural than substantive. A substantive conservative is attached to his tradition because he sees truths embodied in it that he needs but cannot demonstrate. In contrast, a procedural conservative is conservative because he prefers what he is used to. He shrugs off the logic of liberalism because he does not trust it, and he likes change to be slow, deliberate, and clearly needed. If change is slow and somewhat disfavored it is likely to be more intelligent and less disruptive, he might argue, and so is likely to permit a degree of stability that enables people to organize their lives productively.

Simple procedural conservatism is a view for moderate worldly men attached to what is established but willing to accommodate new developments that seem sensible or inevitable. It aspires to a sort of mixed society, in which there is a place for the most helpful aspects of liberal as well as nonliberal tradition. On ultimate standards, however, it is agnostic, with no final reference point other than what people do. As a result, it tends to drift, and when social tendencies are liberal it becomes hard to distinguish such a stance from the moderate wing of liberalism. Both positions value reason and experience and try to keep close to social reality. The difference is that simple conservatism is less interested in abstract ideals and more inclined to accept settled habits and expectations as the guide to what is reasonable, even when they carry forward nonliberal understandings. If dogmatic religion and authoritative aspects of family life are socially accepted, it accepts and supports them.

However, such an outlook is not self-sustaining and cannot be relied on to keep liberal tendencies from going to extremes. Its lack of definite principles is its downfall. Simple conservatism is not seriously concerned with truth. It treats all social understandings, even the most basic, as negotiable interests. Adherence to what is established means it must rely on principles that are not seriously in dispute, and it cannot defend those principles against attack because the fact of their being attacked makes them useless to it. Liberalism constantly calls particular traditions into question. If a tradition cannot defend itself by liberal standards—and the point of tradition is that it gives us what liberal standards cannot justify—it will eventually come under attack and lose the sanction of general unquestioned acceptance.

In an age generally sympathetic to liberalism, tradition will become unable to function unless its defenders can put forward definite arguments of their own that appeal to something transcending social agreement. Simple conservatism cannot do so, because social agreement is its final standard. The simple conservative is not impressed by philosophical claims. He reduces religion to a combination of traditional observances and optional private belief. In the end, religious belief that is only private evaporates, because it has no functional relation to reality. Traditional observances become socially unacceptable because their public element comes to seem a violation of the equal standing of irreligion. Simple conservatism is therefore unable to find a place to make a stand. It always retreats, like the derided God-of-the-gaps, and in time liberalism remakes it in its own image by forcing it to give up everything distinctive for the sake of consensus.

Simple conservatism has been unable to prevent the triumph of increasingly radical forms of liberalism. It has accepted the creation of a radically secular public order that treats substantive appeals to anything other than human will and scientific reason as irrational and oppressive. That development, which came to maturity in the sixties, has made simple conservatism, which assumes a social order defined in basic ways by openly accepted nonliberal attitudes and practices, an empty position. It can no longer think or act coherently, because it cannot sustain substantive arguments at odds with those of its opponents. A desire to seem experienced and thoughtful and an awareness of the thinness of liberal ideology may lead public men to use the language of conservatism, but the substance is gone. Simple conservatism grumbles, drags its feet, and tries to moderate the disruption caused by implementing liberal demands, but it cannot argue against the justice of those demands or deny them ultimate victory. The most it can do is to try to delay and cushion its own defeat.

The failure of simple conservatism has not kept thinkers such as Roger Scruton from proposing a more philosophical version of the same thing in the form of a reflective conservatism that refers to nothing beyond everyday life and treats human goods simply as human things that arise over time out of the life and experience of men living together.[2] To preserve such goods, it is said, all that is needed is an attitude of natural piety toward those who have gone before, together with the ordinary decencies that make possible the continuity of generations and a tolerable life in common. To support that piety and decency no transcendent reference is needed, only the reflection that they have a social function and correspond to the untutored feelings of ordinary men, and so have a presumptive claim to acceptance. In a postmodern age, skeptical objections can then be dissolved by the same skepticism that they employ themselves, leaving piety and tradition in possession of the field.[3]

In support of the practicality of the proposal, Scruton mentions the imperial Romans and Chinese, whose official religions had more to do with ritual, respect for ancestral ways, and the ordinary duties of life than any very definite conception of something metaphysically transcending the quotidian. These examples are not encouraging. Neither stoicism, formalistic Roman rituals, nor imperial Chinese Confucianism—which was indeed sometimes atheistic—sustained the social order as a whole. They were specialized affairs mainly of interest to a small official class ruling over an illiterate and superstitious populace without much involvement in public life or day-to-day contact with the state. Something else—the family system, local civic loyalties, ethnic attachments, popular cults and superstitions—provided the practical basis of everyday social cohesion and order. A system based on an imperial cult and particular local attachments that combines superstition for the masses with austere philosophy for the classes seems unlikely to be of much use today or in any foreseeable future. Neither class distinctions nor local and popular attachments have anywhere near the strength and stability among us that they had among the Romans and Chinese. Nor, given the power and pervasiveness of mass communications and mass society generally, is that situation likely ever to change.

CONSERVATISM IN AMERICA

The fundamental weakness of simple conservatism has deeply affected American political life, since it has been difficult for any more explicit and substantive form of attachment to tradition to maintain itself among us. America began as an overseas extension of England, and thus as part of European and Christian civilization. National independence, followed by enormous territorial, economic, and demographic growth in new lands far from Europe, largely obscured the original sources of American order and made it seem something novel and self-generated. As a consequence, our country today has little attachment to blood and soil, and no memory of an ancien régime of throne, altar, and sword. The inherited and unspoken habits and attachments that are the basis of our conservatism often have an uneasy relationship to national symbols that liberals can claim more easily than conservatives, such as the Revolution, the Founding, the Statue of Liberty, and the building of a new country by settlers and immigrants from all over the world.

The Classic Compromise

Our Revolution, the first of the liberal revolutions, ended by making liberty and equality the ground of our political creed. It was followed by a Constitution that set up a supreme political authority based on agreement and without reliance on any definite law higher than human purposes. Amendments and interpretations, together with the need for some highest principle to guide decision, have greatly strengthened the hold of the principles of the federal Constitution on American society as a whole.

The effect of those principles has not been limited to national politics but has come to extend to social life in general. The federal government has legal supremacy and ultimate responsibility for ensuring peace. It has the right to ask men to kill and die for it, and the loyalty it demands normally takes precedence over all others. The principles for which it stands—liberty, equality, security, prosperity, and the like—are understood as supremely authoritative and worth the sacrifice of all other considerations. In accordance with their limited, practical, and contractual orientation, those principles make men's material interests and the purposes they happen to have the supreme standards. As a result, American political society has been largely understood as an arrangement constructed to advance goals such as security, prosperity, and the freedom of the individual to do as he chooses. Liberty is viewed as an ideal that ennobles the whole arrangement, but in the absence of an authoritative conception of the good life that includes a definite transcendent component, its practical content has tended toward the individual material interests summed up in the "American Dream."

Despite such tendencies, America has been in many ways the most conservative of Western countries. It has been the most anticommunist, the most resistant to the welfare state, the most visibly religious, the most vocally concerned with traditional moral values. It has also been unusually stable, politically. That stability was based on a compromise between liberalism and tradition that reflected American pragmatism in its most non-theoretical form. Before the decline and collapse of that compromise, American government neither defined transcendent goods nor ignored them categorically. Government functions were limited, especially at the national level, and in practice government policy respected transcendent goods. America had an unspoken established religion, a sort of moralistic but otherwise minimalist Protestantism that knit together the public order with popular understandings of ultimate things. As the Supreme Court could observe as recently as 1952, "we are a religious people whose institutions presuppose a Supreme Being."[4]

While logically weak, the compromise between liberalism and nonliberal tradition worked. It held up remarkably well in the face of expansion, social change, Lincoln's war to preserve the Union, Roosevelt's New Deal, and the foreign wars of twentieth-century internationalists. It depended on the practical success of American institutions and the national habit of avoiding systematic thought, both of which slowed manifestation of the implications of stated American principles. Everyone gained from it. Conservatives needed liberalism as an aid to the integration of new populations and territories, and liberals needed tradition for survival and stability. The result was a political order that could satisfy both liberal and conservative impulses as long as neither went too far.

In recent decades the great compromise at the heart of American political life has unraveled. In spite of resistance, liberal principles came to be understood and applied more and more comprehensively, until social unity could no longer be based on vague Protestant moralism and religiosity and on the moral authority and halfway liberalism of those long-dead white male propertied slave owners, the Founding Fathers. A destructively pure form of liberalism became authoritative in American public life. Ruling elites came to understand conservatism as simple resistance to the plain demands of public morality and therefore as a threat to any tolerable public order.

The key period in the transformation was the sixties, which brought the school prayer decisions, the sexual and gender revolutions, and comprehensive antidiscrimination legislation. The first made the social order utterly this-worldly, the second made family life a purely voluntary and private affair, and the third abolished historical in favor of constructed community. The new status of liberalism as a comprehensive rational system, and the end of any need to take nonliberal attitudes, practices, and institutions seriously except as injustices to be eradicated, was signaled by the publication of John Rawls's *A Theory of Justice* (1971), and by the growing tendency among ruling elites to treat accepted habits and understandings as presumptively wrong.

With that breakdown of the American compromise, the link was snapped between government and American tradition as a whole—and between government and the people. The American public order has consequently entered an enduring state of crisis that features a combination of anarchy and soft totalitarianism. Politics has become definitively an affair of interest groups and ideologized elites whose relationship to popular concerns, which have tended to become more purely those of self-seeking individuals, is decisively manipulative rather than organic.

The Rise of Conservatism

The result of such developments was the appearance of a broad-based explicitly conservative movement for the first time in America. The post-fifties conservative movement has attempted to resolve or at least mitigate the crisis of American politics, generally in as moderate a way as possible. The issues agitating that movement have been diverse, from abortion to welfare. What has united it has been opposition to the growth of increasingly radical and centralized government and defense of decentralized traditional institutions. Since American conservatives have naturally believed they should affirm the traditions of their own country, they have accepted the ideals of freedom and equality while attempting, in the manner once customary in America, to accommodate necessary illiberal principles and practices through tacit limitations on stated ideals. In effect, the point of the conservative movement has been the renewal of the historic American compromise.

A reverence for the Founding Fathers has given American conservatism much of its focus and coherence. The point of this reverence has been to preserve the features that made liberalism initially attractive while providing a way to slow its development and minimize the harm it does in its more extreme forms. American conservatives have emphasized the particular arrangements that were a prominent feature of the historic American regime and tend to make popular habits and customs independent of the state: family, local community, church, and the responsibility of ordinary people for their own well-being and the maintenance of social order. Conservatives have advocated limited government, federalism, private property, local democracy, gun rights, and informal social control through a combination of nondoctrinal Protestantism, moralism, and traditional habits and prejudices.

Yet the attempt to restore a conservative form of liberalism has met with severe difficulties. It is difficult to bring back or even argue for an illogical compromise that has fallen apart. Furthermore, few among the educated and articulate have supported the attempted restoration. Our elites quite naturally favor the formal public institutions that they dominate, especially the national ones, and the liberal principles on which they are based. Most of American political thought has been concerned with the development and application of those principles. With the growth and centralization of formal education and the mass media, and the increasing centralization of social life generally, liberal principles have become ever more dominant.

In the absence of a nobility or hierarchical church we have no widespread and well-developed tradition of nonliberal thought to provide a counterweight. The absence of antiliberal symbols and traditions of discussion has made it difficult to articulate what is wrong with liberal demands and to present contrary views in a way that makes sense in American public discussion. That situation has made our conservatism even less articulate than conservatism elsewhere. It has generally been anti-elitist and often anti-intellectual. William F. Buckley Jr., himself an intellectual elitist, struck a chord when he remarked that he would rather be governed by the first few hundred people in the phone book than by the Harvard faculty.[5]

Such qualities have been serious weaknesses. Lacking both an inside understanding of politics and an adequate theoretical grasp of tradition and society, conservatives have been simple-minded, shortsighted, and easily manipulated. Politicians may want conservative votes and be willing on occasion to take symbolic stands in favor of popular traditions and prejudices, but the serious business of governing has been carried on by national elites, who are always liberal.[6]

Failure and Regrouping

The American conservative movement has achieved very little that has been constructive. In the absence of a coherent grasp of history and politics it has attended too much to particular hot-button issues and too little to basic factors. The dominant liberal order has been able to absorb and neutralize conservatives who attained positions of influence and to quash movements that would not play along.[7] No attempt to reverse the New Deal, affirmative action, feminism, the sexual revolution, or the secularization of public life has had the slightest chance of success. While the evident failure of socialism has inhibited and sometimes reversed direct government participation in economic life, the regulation of social life to advance the goals of liberalism has expanded. Periods of Republican Party ascendancy, supposedly times of reaction, have in fact been marked by the consolidation and extension of liberal initiatives—in the fifties of the New Deal welfare state, and in the eighties and the first years of the twenty-first century of affirmative action, political correctness, mass Third World immigration, open-ended internationalism, and libertinism in popular culture. In recent years, much of the national conservative movement has abandoned anything recognizable as conservatism, effectively accepting radical secularism and other advances of the social Left and signing on to the Bush program of big-government multiculturalism and neo-Jacobin interventionism.

Varieties of Conservatism

Nonetheless, the American conservative movement has slowed liberal advances, especially in comparison with other Western countries. And it has raised issues and initiated organized tradition-based resistance to liberalism. The inability of simple conservatism to hold any particular line and its consequent repeated surrender have led to a variety of somewhat more principled proposals for moderating liberalism. Each proposal has emphasized different aspects of the traditional American order as the key to renewal. Some have argued for radical restrictions on government action that would limit the compulsory application of liberal principles to a small part of social life. Others have emphasized regionalism and local control. Still others have urged state support for traditional virtues and family arrangements. On the whole, the proposals have failed to deal effectively with basic issues. Instead, they have accepted fundamental liberal principles while laying hold of one aspect or another of the American compromise and emphasizing it as a general restraint. Such a strategy effectively concedes the battle because of the social dominance and clear logic of liberalism.

Constitutionalism

Constitutionalism—the attempt to limit the development of liberalism by an appeal to the constitutional text and original understandings—is a constantly recurring theme of conservatism in America. It is an attractive position in some ways. It combines an appeal to principle with reliance on actual civic agreement, and it provides an apparently neutral, nondogmatic, and mutually respectful way of maintaining the public authority of the classic American compromise. It can also draw on the general American and conservative reverence for the Founding Fathers. Yet it has not held up. It retains considerable grassroots backing but has few serious adherents among politically aware and connected conservatives.

Decades of failure and retreat suggest fundamental weaknesses in constitutionalism. Something more substantive than respect for prior agreement and written law is needed to maintain a somewhat traditional order. A document can help articulate an order, but it cannot serve as its basis. Written constitutions have to be interpreted in a way that seems sensible to those who govern through them: they cannot stand against general trends in political thought and practice. Interpretive agencies eventually follow whatever view of politics and political reason is dominant among articulate elites, and they interpret a constitution accordingly. A written constitution is very likely to be captured by the dominant view and made its tool; indeed, it is very likely to serve as a means of putting that view into effect all the more thoroughly. If the readings needed to yield results that seem right are improbable, they will nevertheless be adopted.

That has happened in America, so much so that the federal judiciary became the institutional spearhead of the sixties revolution. Efforts by conservatives in recent decades to change the direction of the judiciary have been ineffective, on the whole. They have gone against the grain, because judges measure themselves by the views of legal, scholarly, and journalistic elites rather than those of the politicians who appoint them or the people to whom the politicians appeal for votes. As elite views have grown more liberal, judicial attitudes and assumptions have followed. Enormous expenditures of time and effort by the Right have therefore failed to yield solid gains. The Supreme Court, which is now dominated by justices appointed by supposedly conservative Republican administrations, has recently constitutionalized racial quotas in *Grutter v. Bollinger*,[8] removed concern for traditional morality from the police power of the state in *Lawrence v. Texas*,[9] and reaffirmed a virtually unlimited right to abortion in *Planned Parenthood v. Casey* and subsequent cases.[10] The stated grounds for the *Casey* decision were that an individual right to define the meaning of the universe is basic to liberty, and a reversal of *Roe v. Wade* would undercut the position of the Supreme Court as constitutional oracle. Such reasoning underlined the current status of the Supreme Court as an institutional prophet of the established liberal faith.

Neoconservatism

Neoconservatism is a slightly more substantive form of conservatism that in recent years has been the most influential version of the tendency. The term covers a variety of moderately conservative forms of liberalism that have tended to emphasize supporting the liberal order by helping it retain enough traditional moral substance to function and endure. Neoconservative domination of the conservative movement should come as no surprise. The post-sixties public world unreservedly accepts liberal modernity, and in such a setting the only conservatism that can appear at all reasonable is a minimally substantive viewpoint like neoconservatism. A movement must be able to explain itself in terms that media gatekeepers and the politically influential find rational, and other forms of conservatism cannot easily do so today.

Most neoconservatives began as former leftists or moderately conservative liberals who worried that liberalism is at odds with the loyalties to God, country, and family that sustain a free society. They were aware that liberal goals like freedom, equality, and prosperity would not be advanced unless people have understandings and habits—honesty, diligence, restraint, public spirit—that make it possible for markets, bureaucracies, and institutions of self-government to work properly. Those understandings and habits need support from things that cannot be bought, manufactured, or administered, such as religious faith, stable family life, and standards of respectable conduct. They must be part of a settled authoritative tradition by which men live. A practically minded liberal, if such a thing is possible in the long run, would have to be at least somewhat traditionalist.

Neoconservatives want, on the whole, to save liberalism through ad hoc adjustments and restrictions on its further development. They look for ways to promote necessary nonliberal loyalties while keeping them subordinate to the liberal order. They preach respect for the religious beliefs and moral habits of the people, to the extent that they can be domesticated to the needs of a liberal society, although they often do not share those beliefs and habits themselves. Beyond that, they look for ways to generate orderly habits and loyalties out of liberal institutions like the market. A classic neoconservative strategy has been to try to base moral and social order on habits of enterprise, restraint, and reasoned loyalty that successful families and groups develop and pass on to their children in a market economy. Such an approach supplements liberalism and helps preserve it by limiting the state somewhat and by promoting ways in which liberal institutions themselves can support needed moral restraints.

In line with their basically liberal outlook and acceptance of existing arrangements, neoconservatives treat freedom and equality as supreme values but define them in less ambitious ways than do more advanced liberals so that they will be more consistent with a stable and orderly society. They praise Martin Luther King Jr. unqualifiedly as a hero of equal freedom, but their MLK is one dedicated to patriotism, moral restraint, and the merit standard, because they believe long-term social well-being requires such a Martin Luther King. Their project depends on their ability to determine the content and meaning of accepted political slogans and symbols so that they are interpreted in a way most people are not likely to adopt if left to themselves. Neoconservatism therefore requires centralization of intellectual and cultural life and of education, so that the necessary principles can be correctly determined, explained, and inculcated. For ambitious intellectuals, neoconservatism has a special appeal, because it gives them a crucial role in engineering the meaning of our national symbols and beliefs.

But more is needed to motivate and maintain traditional virtues than the neoconservative strategy assumes. Virtue does not arise out of a system of this-worldly self-interest, ultimate loyalties cannot be used as a means, and the development of liberalism is difficult to stop. An analogy to free markets and socialism may be helpful. When the socialists became convinced that markets were necessary they tried to invent a "social market" consistent with their ideals. It turned out to be impossible. If the principle of central control comes first, the market suffers severely. If the principle of contract rules, socialism must be given up. A similar result seems likely in the case of an attempt to create a usable conservatism that is subordinate to a liberal order.

Liberalism emphasizes equality and the satisfaction of individual goals within an orderly framework that facilitates those things. As neoconservatives recognize, maintenance of a social framework sometimes requires sacrifice of personal interest. When self-sacrifice is needed, a desire to promote equal satisfaction of preferences is not likely to be enough to motivate it. Something more demanding is required that proposes more substantive goods than equality and hedonism. To survive, the liberal framework must be subordinate to a larger and more authoritative system of obligations capable of grounding commitments such as patriotism and family loyalty. Freedom cannot itself be a final standard justifying loyalty. That is why Americans have wanted so much to see "the cause of freedom" as God's cause.

The issue is difficult to get around. Liberalism puts freedom first, which means it cannot be subordinate to other goods but must remain open-ended and self-defining. As time goes by, its demands grow and erode inherited restraints. It is hard to see how the process can be reversed without explicitly rejecting the primacy of freedom and thus liberalism. Neoconservatives have sometimes expected that problems with the social-services state and the absurdities of political correctness will lead to renewed acceptance by chastened liberals of the decencies and moralities that order informal private institutions like the family and local community. After all, the failure of socialism has meant that private property and the market are recognized as social necessities and tolerated even by one-time Communists. Why should traditional distinctions, connections, and moral views not receive the same benefit?

A difficulty with such pragmatic arguments for limiting liberalism is that decencies and moralities—unlike private property and the market—cannot flourish if they are merely tolerated as necessities. Once they have been put seriously in question and influential people have come to see them as irrational and oppressive, something more substantive is needed before they can once again be relied on. They have to be understood as positively good and even ultimately binding in conscience or they will not be able to restrain desire. To understand them in such a way, however, requires a common recognition of goods beyond those accepted by liberalism even in its neoconservative form.

In addition, settled patterns of decency and morality are likely to involve prerational loyalties attached to concepts of identity—concepts such as "people like us" as opposed to "those other people"—that are decisively illiberal. Without the distinctions on which such loyalties depend, it seems unlikely that the ethical standards of a family or group will be able to define themselves, maintain their coherence, and endure. Such distinctions are unacceptable to neoconservatives, who often started as civil-rights-era liberals and in any case reject the presumed bigotry of particularism. They are forced to take the view that a functional social and moral system can survive based on universal considerations without the assistance of particular cultural habits, attachments, and boundaries.

One way neoconservatives have attempted to attach universalistic concepts of freedom and equality to concrete understandings of identity has been to identify those concepts with America and its institutions. Liberal universalism finds a concrete object of loyalty in the American state. America, it is said, is a "proposition nation," with liberty and equality as the universally valid propositions and mass immigration and right-liberal imperialism as the corollaries. That tendency has grown as it has become more apparent that the Left has won the culture war, at least among the respectable, and the traditional values and standards of an increasingly poorly defined people have accordingly become less usable as a reference point.

It seems unlikely, however, that such an arrangement will be able to maintain itself. How rewarding can it be to say *civis Americanus sum* when "America" is a universal order continually redefined by political operatives in accordance with current needs, and when everyone who wants to be is equally an American? Previous universal empires, like Rome and China, relied on a divine emperor, on genuine local particularities like family, class, and local civic attachment, and on the threat of outer barbarians. Each had generally stable boundaries and a particular classic culture. Why should future universal empires not also depend on truly particular identities, boundaries, loyalties, and antipathies? To the extent America succeeds in making itself truly universal, it seems likely to emulate international institutions like the UN or EU, which are incapable of generating loyalty and have disabled themselves through inefficiency and corruption. There is also, of course, the difficulty that not everyone may want to be a citizen or subject of world-America.

For some, neoconservatism has served as an initial step out of liberalism. On the whole, however, it has functioned more as a way of lining up conservative impulses in the service of the established public order. It has confused the loyalties it tries to promote by subordinating them to liberal goals and by sapping resistance to the direction of events. It follows simple conservatism in recognizing no ultimate authority other than social practice, and in the end it concedes every issue to whatever positive beliefs have become dominant. Neoconservatives have been ready to follow the development of liberalism wherever it might go, distancing themselves from the center of ideological power as it moves to the left only to the degree needed to establish their position as necessary participants in the mainstream political discussion. That approach to politics can claim the virtue of immediate practicality, but it is often difficult to distinguish from careerism.

Libertarianism

As their name suggests, libertarians treat individual freedom as the supreme political good. They argue that discretionary state power is the great threat to enterprise, prosperity, and idiosyncratic ways of life. They identify those things with freedom and believe they will be best protected if law is reduced to property rights. Although from one point of view libertarians are fundamentalist liberals, their insistence on basing public order on strict theoretical principles means that they reject existing institutions as a standard. They are therefore more principled, if less well-connected, than neoconservatives and are able to provide a somewhat stronger challenge to the advanced liberal order.

At their best, libertarians try to make liberalism less imperialistic than either advanced liberals or neoconservatives do. Although they are strongly attached to markets, they need not argue that markets can do everything. The more intelligent among them are careful to distinguish the principles authoritative in law, which they say should be property, contract, and freedom, from the principles that apply in other aspects of life, which can be whatever people find good and worthy of attachment. The attachment to small government makes that distinction more meaningful among them than among more advanced liberals.

Many libertarians expect that the attitudes and customs found worthy of attachment in libertarian society will largely be those found so in traditional society. They claim that the best way to let human life develop and flourish in accordance with its own principles, which conservatives believe to be those known through tradition, is to set it free of the administrative state that advanced liberalism makes all but omnipotent. They point out that the activist state disrupts arrangements like family, historical community, inherited culture, and religion that enable people to live productively and cooperate voluntarily without bureaucratic supervision. Among other things, government intervention to reduce inequality means taxes on arrangements that work and subsidies for arrangements that do not. If traditional arrangements are truly better, libertarians say, a less active government would likely lead people to rely on them to order their lives and provide the security the market cannot give. Traditional values arose without state intervention to answer the needs of life, so why would they not reappear if the state that suppresses and supplants them is downsized?

Such views are likely correct to an extent. Nonetheless, libertarianism is a form of liberalism and suffers from many of the same defects. Like liberalism in general, it is not adequate to the needs of public life. Freedom as an ultimate standard can only mean the untrammeled self-defining will, but politics and social life have to do with limitations on the will. Contract can only bind if it is part of a larger order of things that is fundamentally non-contractual. What moral reason is there not to cheat if there is no moral principle superior to the will that forbids cheating?

Like other liberals, libertarians try to do without transcendent authority and to construct society on rational hedonistic lines. The point of government and law, they say, is to enable men to pursue what they want. That approach to government makes opposition to government intervention and the special position accorded property rights seem more a matter of preference and policy than principle. Furthermore, their radically individualistic outlook disposes most libertarians to reject traditional understandings of human connection and obligation in favor of something based on purely contractual principles, even though in theory they are willing to let entirely different principles apply in public and private life.

Since it is very hard to maintain an absolute separation between the two, institutions such as the family are likely to find it difficult to maintain their authority in a society that establishes individual freedom as its supreme public standard. And to the extent such institutions weaken, government inevitably will be called in to pick up the pieces.

It is hard to get the big government genie back in the bottle. A political order based on will as the standard of value naturally develops into one based on an ever more comprehensive approach to maximizing the satisfaction of preferences. Why must property be respected if doing so makes people less satisfied overall? Why allow suffering that could easily be prevented by a violation of libertarian principles? In other words, why would a classicizing version of liberalism not lead once again to the advanced politically correct welfare state? Libertarianism aims to re-create nineteenth-century liberalism, which proved unstable. Why expect the history of liberalism to reverse when liberalism emphasizes clear principles and progress and lacks self-restoring features?

Libertarians propose to subordinate the claims of equal freedom to limitations on government action. That proposal is reminiscent of the arguments of old-fashioned liberals in favor of free speech, and it appears impossible to make such arguments in a way that will stand up over time. If equal freedom comes first, demands that government authority protect it against some concrete threat from private actors will easily override concerns about the benefits of institutional autonomy in civil society. The latter always seem too indirect and speculative to worry about in the face of a specific abuse. Besides, such concerns always look like special pleading on behalf of unjustified private power. What sort of person, liberals ask, would put the rights of property first when the poor and marginalized are being victimized?

The weaknesses of libertarian arguments within the basic liberal framework they accept make it doubtful that libertarianism can stabilize that framework and prevent its collapse. In the eyes of contemporary liberals, the great inequalities libertarians are ready to permit, and the apparent mindlessness of what liberals view as property worship, overwhelm libertarian arguments. Liberals have trouble taking such arguments seriously. They tend to view libertarianism as a hobby for computer programmers and science-fiction fans, or as a front for either yuppie nihilism and greed or backwoods obstinacy and bigotry.

Yet the popular and intellectual appeal of libertarianism is growing, due in part to the degeneration of liberalism and in part to technological changes that extend markets and improve their efficiency. Its adherents have established an intellectual presence and influence far beyond their numbers, aided by the clarity and force of their arguments and the obvious failures of bureaucratic management. They have been very effective in deflating statist claims by demonstrating the necessity of markets for freedom, prosperity, and other good things, and by dressing up their arguments with romantic images of opportunity, choice, and creativity. They are optimists. They believe that long-term trends favor markets and informal institutions over the state. They argue that easy connectivity allows more and more activity to elude supervision, thus weakening bureaucracy and allowing free development of nonmarket and nonstate institutions, so that whatever arrangements are found necessary for the good life can once again establish themselves. They feel justified in claiming the future.

The future of classicizing versions of liberalism will depend to some extent on the direction of future economic and technological developments, and whether they give the advantage to markets or bureaucracy. However, recent history shows that it is extraordinarily difficult to reduce the size and activity of government. The active distrust of government that is at the root of libertarianism is hard to maintain at a time when the security and livelihood of many people, and most intellectual life, depend on government money. It seems likely that libertarianism will remain the special cause of a small but vocal minority, although it will retain influence as part of the shifting compromise between bureaucratic and market institutions that now constitutes liberalism. It is conceivable, however, that by challenging at least some established pieties it may play a part in bringing about a renovated understanding of social order that emphasizes the self-organization of institutions other than the state and thereby makes room for tradition.

Populism

Observers such as Paul Gottfried and others associated with the journal *Telos* have seen populist movements as the main challenge today to the advanced liberal state.[11] In a sense, that view is correct almost by definition: if comprehensive management by experts is the problem, the solution must involve more participation by the people, and therefore a populist element. In itself, however, an appeal to the habits and desires of the people cannot serve as the basis for a serious challenge to contemporary liberalism. By its nature, populism lacks a stable elite. Without one, it cannot define and limit itself, establish coherent principles, and become the foundation of a stable political configuration.

Populism, like modern political ideologies generally, turns the triumph of the will into the ultimate political standard. However, the will of the people cannot substitute for principles that transcend will and make political rationality possible. Lack of settled principles has made populist leaders opportunistic in their approach to issues and populist movements unstable, easily diverted, and unable to make enduring changes that advance their fundamental goals. In America, such movements have attracted sporadic support, perhaps because of the continuing vitality of the notion that the people ought to rule as directly as possible, but media opposition and the individualism to which the movements appeal soon causes them to dissipate. The Wallace and Perot movements were one-election wonders of little long-term importance. Populist movements have been more lasting and more significant electorally in European countries where popular traditions support familial and communal institutions, especially in nations such as Italy, Austria, and Belgium, in which the state has weak historical credentials. Even in such circumstances, however, they have remained minority protest movements, more successful in making popular discontent visible than in doing anything about it.

For political commentators, populism has often been less a serious belief backed by theory and analysis than an attempt to avoid the necessity of dealing with troublesome issues by appealing to the people as a sort of *deus ex machina*. Progressives have expected the people to do away with class society and its oppressions, while conservatives have expected them to save traditional ways from liberal relativists and social planners. Both have hoped that the people would save thinkers the trouble of defining an alternative to technocracy and explaining how the alternative can be known to be better and made to work. The hope has always failed, and with the growing incoherence of "the people" it looks less promising than ever.

Nonetheless, populist movements direct attention toward the need for a certain diffusion of power and for institutions other than global markets and the administrative state. Like libertarianism, populism may in the end contribute to a more articulate and comprehensive challenge to managerial liberal society.

Religious Conservatism

Especially at the popular level, American conservatism has always had a strong religious element. That is not likely to change. The American order was founded on religion as well as liberalism, and in any event secular conservatism is never likely to be more than the private view of a few comfortable intellectuals. Conservatism involves an understanding that in basic ways life cannot be understood or controlled. Such a sober and disenchanted outlook will not endure unless men are willing to accept reality and give it their allegiance. In the long run, they will do so only if they believe the world makes sense and at bottom is good. The mystery of life then becomes something positive to which they can submit without degradation rather than mindless contingency that crushes them when they cannot outwit or escape it. To view the world in such a way is to be religious. Apart from such a view, we look for a substitute for the goodness of reality in intoxication or in fantasies of this-worldly redemption.

However, religious conservatism has shared the weaknesses of American conservatism generally. The liberal tendencies of American intellectuals and academics have deprived Christian conservatives of intellectual leadership. They have often been either vague and inarticulate or anti-intellectual and one-sidedly concrete about their faith and its connection to public life. It is difficult to rise above accepted ideas, and they have too often attempted to explain and defend their views on their opponents' assumptions. The connection between religion and the classic American order can distort religion as well as support it. Christian conservatives have identified Christianity too often with the details of the American order and even its antitraditional elements. America is God's country, they have thought, and the cause of freedom, equality, and prosperity is God's cause. Even among Christian conservative intellectuals there can be found a liberal American nationalism that idealizes American institutions, emphasizes the universal obligatory validity of freedom, equality, capitalism, and American military power, and easily connects to a neoconservative attempt to put religion and culture at the service of power and prosperity and to make America a universal nation destined to bring a conservative form of liberalism to the whole world.

Such a religiously tinged right-liberalism cannot go deep enough to fit our needs. A better future does not lie in promoting conventional pieties and giving established understandings a religious flavoring, but in transforming a society and culture that are growing inhuman in a direction more worthy of human life. If conservatism is to be relevant to our needs it must show how that transformation can grow out of our past. American conservatism must draw on what is most fundamental and enduringly valuable in American religious tradition. That tradition can help put America in a larger setting in which she is neither a demon nor an object of religious devotion but a human society worthy of our loyalty— although containing evil as well as good. Since America has sprung from the West, and the West from Catholic Christendom, it is no surprise that Catholic writers now provide much of the intellectual support for principled conservatism among us, even though they are rarely well known to the general public, and even though conservatives whose loyalties and interests attach them first of all to the established order often hold them at arm's length.[12]

WHAT IS NEEDED

Conservative resistance to liberalism has repeatedly stumbled. The strength of liberal trends and the innate reluctance of conservatives to break with accepted habits and views has made conservatism shortsighted and unable to respond adequately to events. A conservatism that relies only on social practice, legal forms, popular will, or fundamentally liberal principles cannot overcome liberal arguments that are founded in modern ways of thinking. It must constantly give way and in the end abolish itself.

The crisis of liberalism is a civilizational crisis having to do with the nature of reason and reality, so the response must go equally deep. The increasing radicalism of liberalism has estranged many conservatives from the ruling order and is forcing them to clarify their position and broaden their understanding of events. That process will continue and is likely eventually to bear fruit. The project of developing and propagating an adequate response to liberalism nonetheless faces serious practical difficulties. Conservative thinkers have been too few and conservatism too much at odds with the interests of experts as a class and expertise as an institution for a comprehensively conservative view to define and develop itself, achieve stability, and attract adherents. Among intellectuals today, conservative impulses generally lead at most to suggestions for how liberalism might be moderated. Theoreticians with a more comprehensive view of our present situation and what is needed have had little influence. Popular religious and social conservatism has often been ready to contest basic issues, but it is cut off from intellectual culture and public responsibilities and displays the weaknesses of populism and American conservatism in general.

One attempt to refound American conservatism on a deeper and more comprehensive basis was that of Russell Kirk, who discovered, with the aid of imagination and piety, a "conservative mind" that had previously gone largely unnoticed among us.[13] He attempted to describe that mind and give it renewed life and substance through his writings and lectures, the periodicals he founded and edited, and his work as a teacher and mentor. His invocation of a restored conservatism has inspired writers and scholars, but today he is more admired than followed. His limited success suggests the difficulty of reformulating conservatism in America.

Conservatism treats public life as a meeting place between the concerns of the day and transcendent principle mediated through tradition. Tradition cannot be created by imagination and goodwill but must grow out of a particular history. A conservative is a man of particular attachments who cares less for tradition and the transcendent in general than in particular. Prewar writers, such as T. S. Eliot, who moved to England to find a tradition, and the Southern Agrarians, who were faithful to the one they inherited in the American South,[14] took the particularity of tradition very much to heart. They also felt somewhat weakly connected to American nationality.

There is much good in America and her history and national ideals, but attachment to America is not enough to sustain tradition and culture. Our national institutions are mostly based on commerce, national defense, material well-being, and pragmatically ordered freedom to pursue what one chooses. Much of our history as a nation has been one of consolidation, economic and territorial expansion, technical rationalization, and assimilation of immigrants to the national enterprise. The potentially universal implications of that history and those institutions have given them an aura of transcendent importance and even made them, for some people, a sort of religion.[15] However, a tradition and culture cannot look primarily to such things and remain traditional, cultured, or coherent. Their scope of concern is too limited. From a conservative perspective, our tradition and culture have become too much entangled with universalistic dreams, material concerns, and legal institutions. That entanglement has made even conservatives unable to respond effectively to something as obtrusive and destructive as the dissolution of what remains of our country as a particular substantive society through official multiculturalism and mass Third World immigration.

A serious American conservatism must be at once more universal and more local. It must emphasize federalism, localism, and limited government, because life and loyalties have less to do with comprehensive legal structures and grand disembodied ideals than with concrete religious and historical communities and the goods attained through them. Nor can an effective American conservatism stop with worldly goods or at water's edge. Since our national institutions are established for limited and practical ends, they must be connected to something larger, so that security, prosperity, and the arbitrary freedom of the individual do not take on the quality of ultimate principles. For their own health our institutions and principles need correction and guidance from a deeper grasp of the traditions and understandings that have implicitly ordered our life as a people. America is not a religion, but a particular form that the civilization of the West has taken in special circumstances. She was not founded in 1787 or 1776 but existed long before then as a complex political society with roots in Europe. Her institutions are a variation on inherited English and European arrangements. Our loyalty and support for them, like the institutions themselves, must be placed in a broader civilizational setting in order to make sense.

CHAPTER EIGHT

Putting It Back Together

THE POLITICAL CATASTROPHES OF THE LAST CENTURY SHOW THAT POLITICS overreaches and fails disastrously when it is cut off from its natural and transcendent setting and made a pure matter of will and technique. Technocratic liberalism is more cautious and less brutal than other modern systems, but it suffers from some of the same defects and is likely also to end in failure. For its health and our safety, politics must once again connect to things beyond content-free abstractions and this-worldly techniques and goals.

REASON

The fatal flaw of liberalism is its defective view of reason and the good. Liberals claim that there is no way to resolve disputes as to relative goods. They promise to avoid such disputes by making government a system for advancing the goals of each man equally. Choice among goals becomes a strictly personal matter, and the question of the good is eliminated from public life.

The project cannot succeed. Goals cannot be favored equally because they conflict. To be dealt with rationally they must be placed within a larger system of understandings that tells us what things are, how they relate to each other, and what they are worth. We discover and do not create that system. Liberalism denies that there is a system to discover, and by doing so makes itself unable to discuss questions of the good. It tries to make up for this deficiency by extracting, from its claim of moral ignorance, a system of morality and public life that it calls tolerance but is nevertheless compulsory. Such a sleight of hand is accepted not because it is persuasive but because it is useful: by confusing issues and avoiding difficult questions, it allows the established order to maintain itself through obfuscation.

Beyond Scientism

We need something better. However, complaints that liberalism is irrational and based on obfuscation will get nowhere unless a constructive alternative is offered. Equal freedom will remain the ultimate standard for social life until there is a public source of knowledge regarding substantive goods that justifies favoring some goals over others.

But what is that source to be, and how can we agree on it? How can views that reject equal freedom as a standard be made rational, moderate, solid, and useful? We have seen that the solutions offered for the pathologies of liberalism that stay within the worldview defined by liberalism and modern natural science are not workable. Something fundamentally different is needed: a different and broader understanding of reason, knowledge, and reality that will enable us to make sense of society, morality, and human life and live together rationally as human beings.

Going beyond the understanding of reason that has led to both liberalism and modern natural science does not mean rejecting reason, science, or even all aspects of liberalism. It means recognizing the need for
something more. Freedom and equality are good things in their place, but
we have seen that they cannot serve as ultimate standards for public life.
Similarly, modern natural science is rational and extremely useful, but it
does not give us the whole truth about the world. It is a limited enterprise,
an effort to discover principles that enable us to predict and control nature. That enterprise must be guided and justified by considerations that
go beyond it, and it must recognize a rationality larger than its own.

It is evident that we are able to know ultimate truths to a degree.
Otherwise, we could not know anything, since all things are interdepen-
dent. The question, then, is how we do it. That question seems especially
puzzling in connection with our knowledge of society, politics, ethics, and
aesthetics. Our knowledge of those things cannot conform to the modern
aspiration toward neutral impersonal universality, because it depends on
evaluations and judgments that inevitably have a personal and cultural
element. Whether something is good or bad, wise or unwise, is something
that in a sense we perceive: we call those who are good judges of such
things "perceptive." But the perception is less discrete and quantifiable,
less reproducible, and more dependent on the personal qualities, history,
and situation of the perceiver than is reading a meter or identifying the
species to which a plant belongs.

Since evaluative statements do not seem scientific, and science is
notably rational, many infer that such statements are not rational but are
mere statements of nonrational preference. This inference is perverse.
"Rationality" is an evaluative term, since to say a proposition is rational is
to say that one evaluates it as worthy of belief. Someone might object that
a term like "rational" can be used merely descriptively, so that a preference for the principled, coherent, and reliable is no more rational in itself

than any other subjective preference. Nonetheless, we cannot have such a preference unless we can recognize when something is principled, coherent, and reliable, and we cannot do that, or indeed recognize and classify anything whatever, without making evaluations and accepting the standards on which they are based as correct. However good our evidence for a classification, evidence does not interpret itself. Interpretation requires evaluation.

Interpretations and evaluations, although not scientifically demonstrable, are basic to rationality. Modern natural science depends on them, so that science itself is not scientific through and through. It rests, for example, on assumptions of the continuity of the present with the past, the existence of a community of inquirers able to choose the most reasonable interpretation of evidence, and the ability of that community's members to recognize each other, understand each other's results, and rely on each other's judgments. Such assumptions are not demonstrated scientifically but must be accepted before scientific investigation can go forward.

Scientism—the belief that modern natural science is the whole of knowledge—is at odds with science, because the latter depends on judgments of good and bad that are never altogether impersonal. It depends upon a not fully articulable human rationality that never exists in pure form, separated from substantive judgments of value, the practices and traditions of particular societies, or indeed the qualities, habits, orientations, and connections of particular men.[1] The importance of the personal element in science is suggested by the importance scientists place on the senior scientists under whom they have trained and with whom they have worked.[2] Since an open-ended version of rationality is necessary even in science, it must be legitimate to rely on it in moral and political reasoning.

Transcendence

Human rationality involves making sense of our thoughts and actions by relating them to an overall understanding of reality: that is, to an overarching and all-inclusive system, never fully grasped, that is ordered by ultimate principles which determine truth and goodness and do not depend on what we think or want. When we find things worth doing and believing, we recognize something in them that brings them into relation with that system. Without it we are lost, quite literally, and cannot begin to make sense of our situation and actions. Maintaining the relation between that system of ultimate understandings and our thoughts and actions—bringing the latter in line with rational standards so that we can judge them true and right—is among our most comprehensive, enduring, and authoritative goals.

No one simply wants what he wants. Man is rational. He judges his own goals and actions by reference to general schemes. The willingness to sacrifice particular goods like pleasure to meaning, to the demands of a more inclusive system that gives sense to particulars, shows up in low ways—for example, the sacrifice of practical interests to prestige or revenge—but also in higher ones, and when it does it is altogether reasonable. When a man identifies himself and his thoughts and actions by reference to something larger than himself—say, to his family, country, or understanding of what is noble and good—it becomes rational for him to sacrifice seemingly more concrete interests to higher ones. By doing so he is sacrificing the lesser to the greater, giving up peripheral goods for the sake of things that touch him more closely and make him more truly what he is. In short, he is living in accordance with reason. To disrupt such a system of understandings and deprive it of social reality, as liberalism does when it reduces all goals to subjective preferences, is to discredit goods worth sacrifice and freedoms worth having. Beyond that, it is to make reason impossible by destroying the overall order of thought on which it depends.

Too much reason destroys reason. Liberals, and rationalizing moderns generally, insist on discussing, defining, and demonstrating, but such activities are difficult in connection with ultimate goods and truths. It has always been recognized that there is something elusive about ultimates,[3] and their elusiveness is essential to what they are. To state a principle fully and to demonstrate its truth subordinates it to what defines and proves it. It shows it to be secondary. A principle that is secondary, however, can always be preempted by some other principle and cannot serve as a final measure. Ultimate goods are paradoxical. We need them to resolve conflicts and decide questions rationally but cannot fully know them. To choose anything over them would be unreasonable, but to attempt to demonstrate them or define too comprehensively what they are would compromise their ultimacy. All of this is part of what it means to say that ultimate principles are transcendent.

To approach the matter from another quarter, recognition of the highest goods is a prepolitical and in a sense prerational act, because it is part of what constitutes politics, rationality, and even personal identity. We cannot stand aside from something so basic, grasp it from outside, and bring it in line with our preconceptions and goals. The independent liberal ego that chooses its values is an impossible fiction. The necessity of ultimate goods, and their transcendence of all our understandings, show once again that man cannot be understood as the measure. The measure is something we need but cannot know completely, if only because it measures our knowledge and commitments along with everything else. It is that situation which makes humility, faith, and consciousness of sin lasting aspects of human life.

The Liberalism of Fear

The impossibility of defining ultimate goods is one of the strongest motives for the belief that freedom should be the goal of social order. Any goal that can be fully stated seems limiting, oppressive, and mindless when treated as ultimate. We can always look beyond it to other and higher goods it would deny us. A society that believes in human dignity and rationality, and insists on defining all things explicitly and comprehensively, is likely to adopt liberalism—which attempts to deny that there is any good which can be viewed as ultimate—as its governing outlook.

It does not escape the danger of tyranny by doing so. The attempt to make final principles of government fully explicit always ends in bullying and obscurantism. Fascist and communist societies, which explicitly make some definite this-worldly thing such as "will" the ultimate measure, are obvious examples. Theocracies also become tyrannical by attempting to reduce the transcendent too much to a specific set of prescriptions applicable here and now. And in the end, liberal societies become tyrannical as well, because to define freedom as the final standard is still to define an ultimate standard that is concrete, this-worldly, and fully knowable.

A state based on such a standard will eventually feel compelled to silence objectors and force the standard on everyone. Since the standard is perfectly clear, and what has to be done is obvious, why do otherwise? How can it be right to allow any violation of what is clearly known to be just? Why not, for example, establish a legal requirement of zero tolerance for discrimination, define the offense as broadly as possible, and use whatever means are necessary to enforce it in all situations? The collapse into tyranny will likely be slower in the case of liberalism than in the case of fascism or fundamentalist theocracy. Because the ultimate standard is stated in a negative and formal way, the oppressive consequences of taking something fully articulable and limited as the standard take longer to develop. The collapse is just as certain, however, and its careful pace makes it all the more thorough.

Liberal values are not self-sufficient. Like other large human undertakings, government does not make sense unless it is ordered toward a system of goods that precedes our purposes, goes beyond our knowledge, and integrates actions in their moral quality with the order of the world. Even legitimate liberal goals like personal and political freedom require standards that transcend desire, because without them whatever goals government sets for itself become absolutes. Even freedom is interpreted in such a way as to become tyrannical.

TRADITION

But how can we hope to determine a standard that is better than equal freedom and man-the-measure, especially when the standard cannot be fully grasped in any event? The intellectual presuppositions of liberal society make that a very difficult question. Those presuppositions lead men to consider assertions rational if they are (1) purely formal, like mathematical truths; (2) immediately obvious, like sense perception and elementary logical principles; or (3) verifiable in accordance with settled public procedures that have been found reliable, like the findings of the modern natural sciences. In such cases people think they have a reliable grasp of the assertion and its basis. They feel justified in accepting its authority.

Nothing of the sort seems possible in the case of ultimate standards. Men disagree on them, so they are not immediately obvious. Furthermore, there is no well-defined procedure for determining what they should be, since a procedure for judging has to be based on understandings of the good and true already accepted. While ultimate goods and truths may be a matter of natural law and reason, natural law and reason are discernible mainly to those who have already come to accept their teachings. They cannot be counted on without support by something beyond pure rationality.

Growth

The process through which we come to recognize ultimate standards is complex and relies essentially on tradition. We order our lives by reference to the world as a whole, but we cannot fully grasp it. We can, however, recognize its ultimate principles in part and act on them in specific cases. We learn about goodness by observing good deeds and good men and imitating them. As we do so repeatedly, good principles become encoded in habits and attitudes that seem right to us, to which we attach ourselves, and by which we and others find it good to live. Practice, with the help of observation and reflection, makes perfect.

That step-by-step process is the way in which tradition develops, and it gives it its coherence and reliability. Tradition starts with basic functional patterns that establish themselves because they work. Those patterns grow and extend themselves through the strengthening and development of what is helpful and through the rejection of what leads to conflict and failure. Beliefs, attitudes, and practices that work are extended and refined. Those that do not wither and die. Each pattern is associated with a variety of specific situations and traditions. Those situations and traditions all matter, but each in a different way and to a different degree. Family dinner at six is a tradition; so are representative government and Christianity. It might be a tradition for a family to combine the three by saying grace before dinner and arguing politics over the meatloaf. Such traditions can conflict, and when we choose among them we show which we value most. The practical demands of life and conflicts among particular traditions force us to bring them, and the goods to which they relate, into a system that distinguishes greater from lesser and enables each to contribute to the others.

Tradition comes to form a mutually supporting system that reflects our thought and experience as a whole. The deeper, stronger, more widespread, and durable our experience of the goodness of some traditional practice, attitude, or belief, and the more support it draws from other particular traditions, the more settled and central it becomes to our way of life. Tradition thus comprises an ordered system of habits and understandings that have proved useful in a huge variety of practical affairs, and a comprehensive and generally coherent point of view that reflects very extensive thought and experience. That system has the reliability that comes with vast experience and reflection and enables us to understand it as descriptive of realities it does not exhaust.

Necessity

We can only live a human life. The ultimate standards that help make us what we are can neither be dispensed with nor subordinated to arm's-length neutrality and impartial expertise. The overall tradition we follow—the crystallized experience of the society to which we belong—is a necessary source of the knowledge we need to live in accordance with reason. To accept the authority of tradition is to accept the basic features of our situation and to live as well as we can in the world as we find it. To reject that authority is to part with the network of practices and understandings that make a human life possible. There is no other workable way to organize our lives.

The most common alternative to acceptance of tradition is a simple sort of rationalism that relies exclusively on explicit rules and formal institutions. That alternative can be made to seem plausible, at least verbally, but it cannot sustain itself. Rules require common sense and informal traditional understandings to be understood and made usable. Formal institutions such as markets, bureaucracies, and expertise must be able to call on habits and attitudes that can only arise informally, in ways that cannot be planned or controlled, among people who live and deal with each other for a long time. Otherwise they will not work as intended.

Complex human activities could not exist without tradition. Practical arts are learned mostly by experience and imitation because most of what we need to know about them consists in habits, attitudes, and implicit presumptions that we could not begin to put into words. We have no means other than tradition to accumulate, conserve, and hand on such things. Without participation in the traditions that constitute our social world we would be like children fostered by wolves—dumb animals with no conception of who we are, and no goals other than immediate gratification of crude impulse. We cannot even engage in human speech without accepting the definitions and rules that constitute a particular language—that is, without obediently accepting a particular tradition.

In the case of higher-order activities, such as politics, religion, and the conduct of life generally, individual inventiveness and expertise that are not integrated with the practice of the activity itself and subordinated to its tradition become wholly subsidiary. The statesman and saint are not those who have studied political and religious systems and become expert technicians who can do with them what they want. They are those who live the life of religion or politics as they exist in a particular tradition supremely well. How could it be otherwise, when such activities are so complex and subtle that no one could hope to state all their principles, and so comprehensive that an external perspective is impossible?

The innovations of those enduringly remembered as great men, even when contestable or wrong, have been attempts to fulfill what was there in their tradition already. Otherwise their innovations would have failed for lack of connection to the existing system and its tendencies. Washington and Lincoln acted out of their best understandings of the traditions of their country and what was needed to secure goods long possessed. Christ based his teaching on the Law and Prophets and aimed to fulfill them.

Even in the eyes of opponents who believe they misapplied the traditions they inherited there is an evident difference between such men and men like Robespierre, Lenin, and Hitler who rejected and destroyed societies they hated in the name of a radical new order of their own invention.

There are of course bad traditions. But we know they are bad with the aid of other traditions more than we do through disembodied reason. Loyalty to tradition is necessary to its reform, since we cannot jump over our need for tradition to a self-contained rational grasp of the good, beautiful, and true. If it is experience that has led us astray, it will most likely be more experience that corrects us. Even to convert from one tradition to another is most often to build on what our original tradition taught us and turn to one that better achieves the ends we have already come (with the aid of our upbringing and experience) to know as good.

Particularity

Tradition must grow up and be passed on mostly implicitly, through stable relationships and concrete personal contacts. It therefore differs by time, place, and connection. We must take it largely as it is. We cannot lay hold of it from outside, reconstruct it, and make it scientific and universal. Nor can we simply pick and choose among particular traditions. Since tradition deals with things we cannot quite grasp, and its parts are related in ways that cannot be altogether untangled, we must largely accept a particular tradition as a gift from those who have come before. Our social and moral life has an essential element of loyalty to the particular society of which we are part, and to our own section of that society. It is through love of a particular tradition accepted as authoritative that we go beyond self-centered desires, learn to be social, participate in common goods, and learn to think, choose, and act intelligently.

Our tradition is rightfully part of what we understand ourselves to be. For that reason our basic loyalties cannot be altogether universal.

While we owe something to all men simply because we are human, pure generalized solidarity is too vague in its demands to establish moral order. A "universal nation" could exist if liberal universalism were an adequate social philosophy, or if there were a shari'a that could adequately capture the transcendent. Neither condition holds. We must be guided by what we are, and we know what we are in part by contrast with what we are not. Our self-understanding and even reason depend on particularity. Sources of guidance that profess lucid universality, such as philosophy and social science, are far too fragmentary to create a general point of view by which anyone could live. Nor are those sources more rational and reliable than tradition when they pretend to give answers adequate to carrying on life as a whole. They give complete answers only by cheating.

While reliance on particular tradition is unavoidable and irreducible, our loyalty to tradition cannot be absolute. Our grasp of the good and true is not merely social and traditional. Tradition is about something other than itself, and it invokes universals as well as particularities. There is a sort of family resemblance among the great and enduring traditions. Each aspires to the transcendent and universal, and deals with how moral and spiritual order can be made concrete in human life. Each orients itself toward stability, deals with the enduring conditions of life in ways that have proven themselves workable in the long run, and seeks what might be called the rooted and enduring midpoint of human nature and experience. The universal element in tradition cannot be fully grasped: if it could, tradition would be far less necessary. Nonetheless, that universal element is tradition's goal and ultimate standard, and it must somehow take precedence. If loyalty to Brooklyn conflicts with loyalty to truth or the human race—for example, if an unnecessary war would bring prosperity to the Brooklyn Naval Yard but disaster elsewhere—it is the former that should give way. When and how it does so cannot be stated categorically, however, but must be left to tradition and a judgment of the particular case.

The partial arbitrariness of tradition reminds us that tradition is not our ultimate concern. Since our ultimate orientation is toward the world as a whole, which transcends the social order and its traditions, our particular loyalties must have at least a residual element of contingency and choice. That is the enduring element of truth in such notions as religious freedom and the social contract, although not one that should be exaggerated. Man is social but not simply social. The social order must reflect the absolute but not be mistaken for it. If tradition were not particular and self-limiting it would not point us toward something beyond itself. To avoid national self-worship, a national tradition must have local and class variations and rivalries, and connections that cut across national borders. A religious tradition must have local cults, rites, and devotions, a choice of personal observances, and a history of development to make it evident that there is no single form that fully captures the reality toward which it points. A global society that established one single particularism as universal—like the one to which Islam and liberalism each aspire—would necessarily be totalitarian.

TRADITION AND REASON

Traditionalism is the recognition that tradition has its own authority and is not merely a default position or set of suggestions to be judged on other grounds.[4] It accepts that knowledge is indispensable with regard to things that do not lend themselves to the methods of the modern natural sciences. If such knowledge is not available through systematic observation and measurement, then we get it through something like Pascal's *esprit de finesse*[5] or Newman's illative sense,[6] through the coming into focus of obscure realities by way of the concurrence of innumerable considerations that cannot be individually picked out and may have been known directly only to those who came before us. Tradition is a social version of that process. It is the making concrete of what seems too vague to talk about.

Pluralism and Rationality

Traditionalism is more concerned with truth, however partial and however attained and expressed, than with clear justification. It rejects the modern dream of a purified scientific procedure applicable to everything and giving rise to universal propositions stating all knowable truth. Tradition's basic assumption is that there is no single method for attaining the good and true, no Archimedean point available to us from which we can know everything knowable. It accepts limits and dogma, because almost any comprehensive system of social cooperation needs them, but is not itself narrow or dogmatic, and it more commonly tolerates a variety of principles.

Tradition has a somewhat incomplete and pluralistic aspect. It is against its genius to present itself as self-sufficient. It presumes that traditions that endure and reflect extended experience should change only in response to something weighty, but it does accept the need for some change. Since traditionalism recognizes no master key to all knowledge, it looks at life in society from within, and it accepts practices basically as they are, in accordance with their internal standards, rather than attempting to impose an external standard of universal applicability. Traditionalists find it natural for each major aspect of life to run on its own principles while accommodating other spheres of activity. They do not try to make all institutions democratic, for example. They let family life, religion, and politics be family life, religion, and politics, each with its own value, way of being, and scope of action, rather than treating them as instruments of some master principle like efficiency, social welfare, or the liberation of the individual. To the extent that traditionalists try to unify tradition by reference to an ultimate principle, it is a principle that is transcendent, like God or the good, and therefore incapable of full implementation through any clear standards or specifiable line of conduct.

In accordance with such an approach, traditionalists do not deny reason but only recognize that like other departments of human life it has conditions and limitations. Neither reason nor tradition can be altogether subordinate to the other, if only because they help constitute each other. Tradition relies on rationality, because it is an inheritance of knowledge accumulated, ordered, and refined from sources that include reason, and because its comprehension and development make use of rational ordering and insight. Similarly, rationality must be traditionalist, because to find application it requires concepts, connections, and judgments provided by experience and tradition. Both are necessary to politics, moral life, and every activity that is at all complex and comprehensive, including the activity of knowing.

A rational traditionalist accepts both tradition and reason as basic to what he is, knows, and does. What distinguishes his position from that of the rationalist, irrationalist, or fideist is that he is willing to criticize and adjust his beliefs, loyalties, and way of life as necessary in order that his acceptance of both tradition and reason makes sense. Some obvious alternatives to his position are commonsense liberalism, simple rationalism, simple conservatism, and postmodern irony. A brief explanation of each may help clarify issues:

- The commonsense liberal is the ordinary educated participant in public affairs today who accepts the traditions of liberal modernity as the settled background of legitimate discussion and practice. Those traditions call for acceptance of reason, observation, and will as the sole ultimate authorities. Such a view contradicts itself by making it impossible to accept its own authority as a tradition. If the commonsense liberal sees the conflict and wants to make his outlook more coherent he will reorient his views in some way.

- The simple rationalist aspires to more rigor. He adopts the modernist perspective that views tradition as extrinsic to our grasp of the good and true, and he believes that ultimate standards can be known by purely rational means. The problem with such a position is that human reason is not a perspicuous self-contained system. It depends on tradition for the concepts it applies and for basic understandings that often cannot be articulated but are necessary to make sense of particulars.

- The simple conservative response to the failure of simple rationalism is to accept whatever practices and attitudes have grown up and become authoritative in one's environment. Simple conservatism rejects reason as a standard in favor of pure social fact—of tradition treated as something self-contained and absolute. In contrast, rational traditionalists believe that tradition and reason should accept, support, and limit each other. The difference is illustrated by attitudes toward liberalism. Once liberalism has become socially authoritative, simple conservatives cannot help but accept it, because it is established, while rational traditionalists continue to reject it, because it is incoherent and at odds with the needs of human life and thought.

- The postmodern ironist agrees with the conservative that we rely on tradition, but he clings to the rationalist ideal of transparently justified knowledge. He rejects tradition as a road to truth, because it is contingent and bound up with particular perspectives. He is forced to claim that none of our beliefs are justifiable, and that he holds his own beliefs "ironically"—that is, at arm's length. He refuses to doubt his own skepticism. Rather than presenting a position, he attempts rhetorically to elude the intellectual risks and difficulties involved in defending one. Traditionalists recognize, to the contrary, that it is a brute necessity to have things we understand as simply true. We believe our beliefs, and it is point-less to tell ourselves that we are not justified in doing so. The sensible course is to try to understand how what we understand as true and justified can rationally be seen as such in spite of its dependence on particular traditions.

Concepts and Tradition

Postmodern irony arises because we are limited and social and, in a sense, do not fully possess our own knowledge. We need tradition to give our thoughts distinctness and stability and bring them into a definite or-der. We rely on it to tell us what things are and what they mean, and to connect reason to the world. That situation is too paradoxical for literal-minded moderns. So they rebel against the basis of knowledge, the union of thought and object through reason and tradition, and call the resulting state of permanent unresolved rebellion *irony*.

The proper response to our situation is acceptance rather than rebel-lion. Without tradition reason empties out and goes mad. We make sense of things as best we can. The rationalized insanity of the present day is the result of a way of thinking that rejects commonsense understandings of the identity and meaning of things and treats concepts of the kind used in physics as the only ones rational enough to take seriously. The distinc-tion between an electron and proton, and the properties of each, are abso-lutely clear and always the same, and it is assumed that all characteristics and distinctions worth bothering with must be of that kind. On such a view, concepts that have always ordered human life become irrational ste-reotypes that should be avoided as much as possible. Such concepts can-not be defined and applied with the universality and rigor of physics, and so are viewed as a matter of subjective bias.

The result is that it becomes impossible to draw commonsense conclusions regarding persons and actions. Everything must be made exact, a demand that makes it impossible to apply substantive standards and forces us to rely on default assumptions like equality. Hence the liberal understanding of "prejudice": it is assumed that if you distinguish men and women, or Americans and Frenchmen, you must mean something absolutely simple, categorical, and unbending. It follows that it is irrational and wrong to distinguish them. Similarly, the two possible attitudes toward people and actions become zero tolerance on the one hand, and total acceptance on the other. If conduct is not acceptable, the rejection has to be total and equal for everything in the class. If the conduct *is* acceptable, then it must be treated as a pursuit on a par with all others, and indeed given special protection against social prejudice if some people doubt the point.

To the contrary, human rationality has to reflect the world and our way of understanding and acting in it. The world is not—at least for us—a single lucid system of objects and forces with demonstrable properties and relationships. We can think effectively only with the aid of intelligent discriminations and inferences that cannot be altogether reduced to rules. The concepts that have been found useful in ordering human life and thereby become traditional reflect that situation. They have a complexity and subtlety that makes them difficult to define in the abstract. Such concepts—we, they, friend, enemy, promise, favor, offense, man, woman, marriage, family—relate more to the identity of things and what they are for us than to demonstrable properties. They have a functional significance that makes them basic to our understanding of how the world works, but they cannot be reduced to specific consequences in particular settings. That makes them incomprehensible from the technocratic standpoint liberalism favors, a standpoint that cannot deal with human life as it is.

To pick social belonging as an example, human life is carried on through membership in particular societies. To be a member of a particular society, such as a nation, ties a man to a definite people and way of life and enables him to live as the social being he is. Without the coherence of thought and action that comes from such connections, a life in accordance with reason would be impossible. In the case of nationality, such a connection means, among other things, that I should obey the laws, do my part to promote the common good, defend my society against its enemies, and so on.

The relation between nationality and function is not, however, a simple one. It does not depend on actual performance or even ability to perform the duties in question. I had the same nationality when I was a newborn, and would continue to have it if I were insane or on my deathbed or became a traitor. In contrast, our allies during wartime do not become American even when they protect America from her enemies at the risk of their lives. Nationality does not mean that we do this or have that quality but that we are people who *should* do this or be that—conditions permitting—because of what we are. We are entitled to certain rights for that same reason. Indeed, the fact that nationality defines what we are without any very specific regard to our actual qualities and actions is the reason it can join whole populations together in a functioning social order.

Sex provides other examples of traditional essentialist concepts upon which rationally ordered life depends. Those concepts are of special interest today because many people now find traditional standards regarding sex incomprehensible, even though they have nothing very helpful to put in their place. Traditional sexual morality is traditional because in the long run it has worked in a way that seems right in actual experience. It depends on a sense that sexual conduct should have a strong connection to its natural reproductive function. Otherwise, it becomes an unconnected dynamo, an agent of disorder rather than a support to basic relationships and obligations. The required connection is not a simple matter, though. If the connection to function is absolute, so that sexual relations become no more than a reproductive technique, they become dehumanized and will be either rare or constantly abused. If the connection is looser, however, it becomes easy to point to cases in which sexual conduct traditionally considered moral is nonreproductive, and a modern man will ask why other nonreproductive sexual conduct is so different.

The answer is that traditional sexual morality is based on the identity and not the specific consequences of actions. It relies on commonsense concepts having to do with what things are, not technological concepts having to do with measurable properties and results in particular cases. At bottom, traditional morality holds that sexual relations are right when the nature of the act, through its relationship with reproduction, points beyond itself and the particular goals and interests of the participants to enact an enduring objective union, one that defines what the participants are and connects them to the life of humanity throughout time.

Someone might ask why "gay marriage" is so different from marriage between two sixty-year-olds, when both unions will be infertile. The answer is that an attempted union of two men is sterile by what it is—by the identity of the parties and the actions of which a pair of men as men are capable—while a union of a sixty-year-old man and woman is sterile by particular circumstances—their age and physical condition. In the latter case, the marital acts are still acts of a kind that by their natural unhindered design and functioning create a permanent connection carrying profoundly serious obligations that trump self-interest and join the two with the whole human community throughout time, even though they do not happen to have that practical result in the particular case because of factors that do not have to do with the identity of the participants or their acts.

The distinction depends on several points: (1) persons and acts have an essential nature that is not determined by happenstance attributes or specific effects; (2) one's nature as a man or woman is essential to who one is and one's connections to others, at least in specifically sexual matters, so that violating it violates oneself and those connections; and (3) the nature of sex includes a procreative aspect that must be respected, and that aspect is violated when we intentionally do something that defeats it, but not when it fails to go to completion because of abstention or circumstance.

In the past, such points have generally been accepted without analysis or dispute simply because they seemed part of what constitutes the human world in which we live, but recently the technocratic outlook has made them incomprehensible to many people. Indeed, commonsense essentialist thinking relating to matters of sexuality and human identity is now viewed as simple bigotry.[7] That change in outlook has resulted in a collapse of social understandings regarding sex that has been catastrophic for family stability and relations between the sexes and generations, which depend, like human actions and relations in general, not on a technical analysis of cause and effect in particular cases but on what the parties understand themselves and their connections and actions to be.

In the traditional view, being a man or woman, and being married, are matters that, like nationality or friendship, involve certain functions and obligations but cannot be reduced to them. One's sex is basic to what one is. By natural design, the sexual union of man and woman produces children—though not in every case. It follows that such a union should be permanent, transcend particular desires and interests, and be connected to the social realm. Those implications, because of their importance, become integral to the very nature and meaning of the act. To engage in the act is to enact the union with all its attributes.

The institution of marriage as traditionally understood expresses natural functional understandings of what things are, mean, and should be that tie them to the strongest impulses and very identities of the parties. It promotes an orderly, reliable, stable, and generally satisfying system for the relations between the sexes and the continuation of the human race. Such things are far too important to the pattern of our lives and how we understand ourselves to ignore or treat as an ignorant way of dealing with matters that should be handled in a purely technical fashion. To say that marriage could as easily involve two men or two women is to say that the importance of sex has nothing to do with its natural life-giving function, and that either marriage or being a man or woman is fundamentally irrelevant to who one is. If such views were accepted, marriage would reduce to a private contract based on idiosyncratic purposes. How could such a contract have enough purchase on human life to serve anything like the function marriage traditionally—and necessarily—has served?

Sexual morality is the part of morality that relates to our closest and most basic connections to others. Traditionalist concern with it is not at all narrow or obsessive. It is a consequence of the importance of the particular person, and of the habits and attachments that make him what he is and connect him durably and productively to others. A view of morality that slights family and sexual life and fails to interpret them to us is inadequate and inhuman.

TRADITION AND TYRANNY

Many people object to the authority of tradition on the grounds that traditions are sometimes wrong or mask self-interest. That happens, of course, but something similar could be said of any authority. Tradition favors traditional elites and errors, but other social authorities—law, democratic politics, money, consumer taste, TV personalities, therapists, government regulators, social scientists, diversity consultants, academic political theorists—favor other persons, classes, and illusions. Tradition is not a cure-all, and it will not function adequately unless those involved are at least somewhat oriented toward the good and true. The same is true of any source of guidance. Discussions of ethics and knowledge are pointless without the right orientation. In discussing the relative merits of authorities, we must assume that a proper orientation is present at least to some degree. The question then becomes which system of authority and cooperation makes the best use of whatever good tendencies are available.

Compared with other authorities, tradition has obvious advantages with regard to the risk of tyranny, corruption, and general mindlessness. It is a decentralizing principle that tells those in power to look to something other than personal and party views. It is independent of particular persons, exists through the enduring tacit consent of those involved, and takes into account all considerations believed to be relevant, even if these are difficult or impossible to articulate. It is an indispensable stabilizing and moderating influence. Indeed, moderation and prudence would be impossible without the accumulated experience and the sense of things that are difficult to articulate which is socially available only through tradition.

Traditionalism starts with an acceptance of our limitations. But it also accepts the fundamental goodness of what exists, especially what is common and enduring. It respects particular men and peoples as they actually are. It recognizes that we cannot impose order on them but must largely accept whatever order is present or implicit, and that renewed order must be realized indirectly, through an acceptance of practices, attitudes, and symbols that make up a concrete way of life oriented toward realities confessedly beyond our grasp. Traditionalism recognizes the necessity of continuity, the limitations of human knowledge and power, and the importance of things—such as mutual personal obligation and standards of right and wrong not reducible to desire—for which modern ideologies have trouble finding a place.

Such recognitions make traditionalists more reliable opponents of oppression than progressives. Traditionalism fundamentally rejects totalitarianism, the attempt to transform the world by force in accordance with absolutes claimed to be fully possessed. It recognizes that we cannot force our schemes on recalcitrant realities but must most often respond to specific problems by making improvements here and there or doing something that fosters what seems good or protects what seems threatened. In particular cases—for example, in opposition to a totalitarian government—we can act in ways that seem quite radical and call for overthrow of the established order so that more natural modes of human functioning can reassert themselves. What we cannot do is to provide a method for determining in advance just how society should be organized and what the results of social life should be. In each case we act under circumstances that cannot be altogether understood, by reference to concerns that often cannot be clearly formulated, and toward results that in many respects cannot be predicted.

Concreteness and Transcendence

Freedom and reason must find embodiment in a developed public understanding of what the world is and what goals make sense. Many people nonetheless believe that freedom and reason are at odds with any particular official understanding of the world, man's place in it, and the good. After all, if the authorities understand those things, why not forget freedom and reason and force everyone to accept whatever is already known to be good and true using whatever means seem effective? On that line of thought, freedom and reason would depend on skepticism, a paradox since they are also thought to impose clear universal requirements that obligate everyone everywhere.

Such difficulties can be avoided by understanding what is ultimately good and true as transcendent—as incapable of being fully known by us, but nonetheless accessible through practices and understandings that orient our lives toward something beyond social fact. If the good and true transcend social fact, then no system of discipline and doctrine can fully embody them. They can only be realized in ways that cannot be altogether specified by authority and depend on local and personal initiative to relate them to particulars. That necessity gives local knowledge and decision, and thus conscience, a definite function, and so makes necessary a certain freedom for individuals, communities, and traditions.

An understanding of the good and true as knowable but only in part and from particular perspectives fits the needs of a free and rational society. The same understanding makes it impossible, however, for social order to be totally logical and transparent. Man is an in-between creature, and neither life nor government can be understood completely or reduced to rules. It cannot be demonstrated beyond objection what things public authority should insist on, what it should support or encourage, and what it should leave up to the choice or conviction of individuals and local communities. Those determinations must still be made, and to avoid arbitrariness and tyranny they should be made with the aid of some relatively public and objective standard that complies with the unforced expectations of those involved. The standard most readily available, and the one most likely to avoid oppressiveness, is the tradition of the particular community.

The need for freedom to exist concretely through a definite relationship to a particular tradition and culture has pervasive implications that are at odds with a multiculturalist liberalism that insistently opposes any particular cultural grounding for public life.[8] Freedom that matters must be part of a system of common goods and meanings that provides a setting in which choice makes sense. For the system to be concrete and comprehensive it must reflect a particular culture; for it to be stable and effective it must include definite institutional forms that define social meanings and understandings. Freedom worth having thus requires things that function like ethnic cohesion and established religion. In the absence of such things, which enable a common understanding of transcendent goods to gain concrete and authoritative public reality, goods are reduced to personal prejudices, and particular desires become the only possible standard. The result is liberalism and its familiar pathologies.

Nor will freedom be effectively defended unless it is integrated with the identity and social position of its defenders. Without stable personal identity and social position to anchor freedom and make its exercise a continuous course of conduct integrated with what I am and my connections to others, it cannot be distinguished from random whim. Freedom requires serious social distinctions and roles and is impossible in a radically egalitarian setting. It was the distinction between Christ and Caesar that made Europe free, the freedom of the church and aristocracy that limited royal dominion, the freedom of heads of households that established the sanctity of the home, and the freedom of the well-to-do and respectable that established the republican freedoms on which ideals such as the rule of law depend. If there is nothing that gives us each a definite place in the world independent of state and money, society becomes an aggregate ordered solely by numerical or abstract hierarchical principles. The alternatives become the simple domination of the weak by the strong that liberalism fears, and the impotence, mutual isolation, and comprehensive system of controls that it imposes as a remedy.

Rights we can live by are not universal human rights. They are the rights of Englishmen, of Americans, of any people whose way of life defines freedom and gives it a function with respect to a guiding understanding of the good. To deprive such ways of life of concreteness and authority in the interest of universality, rationality, multiculturalism, and so on is not to generalize and perfect the freedom they secure but to destroy it by turning it from a possession of the people into something defined for them by their betters. To make freedom truly universal and equal is to make it featureless and without connection to anyone in particular. It becomes an abstraction defined and redefined without limit by government officials, whether welfare administrators or Supreme Court justices, who will inevitably tailor their definitions to favor the survival, dominance, and efficient operation of the system they manage.[9] It is for that reason that the contemporary liberal state makes freedom from traditional strictures absolute, thereby disrupting the traditional institutions those strictures support, while passing off state power as therapy or a defense of the disadvantaged against oppression.

Freedom requires a fundamental rejection of "political correctness" and an acceptance of some things now denounced as parochialism, patriotism, classism, sexism, role stereotyping, and the like. It should not be surprising that rejecting advanced liberalism requires rejecting a moral view that distinguishes it from all previous understandings of good human relations. The current view treats distinctions—such as those relating to sex—that have been basic to all societies as irrational, oppressive, and fit only for extirpation by all means necessary. That view is thought to mark a decisive and permanent advance in moral understanding. To the contrary, the inability to make sense of enduring and indeed universal features of human life shows a cramped rather than enlightened view of things. It is even self-contradictory. To consider the whole of the past stupid and evil just because it was discriminatory is no less bigoted than to consider all foreigners stupid and evil just because they reject some of our odder customs.

Universals

Opposition to tradition today often goes far beyond opposition to particular bad traditions. Tradition itself is held to be oppressive. It restricts human conduct in ways that are not determined by neutral rational procedures, so that whatever distinguishes it from liberalism is, from a liberal standpoint, prejudice and oppression. Traditional attachment to particular culture and historical community is considered racist, because it is attachment to the ways and identities of particular peoples. Traditional religion that says something distinctive is thought fundamentalist, because it appeals to authorities liberalism does not recognize. An acceptance of traditional relations between the sexes that recognizes their distinctiveness and complementarity is understood as sexist and homophobic. To say something is traditional—that it is a matter of deeply ingrained social stereotype—is, for many people today, to refute it.

Tradition is accused of an essentialist tyranny. It forces us to comply with an ideal image that has nothing to do with what we are in ourselves. Such accusations reflect a problem not with tradition but with modern thought, which has difficulty relating particulars to universals and to stable conceptions of identity. Such conceptions suggest limitations that are now felt as tyrannical. If all men are mortal and Socrates is a man, then Socrates is mortal whether he likes it or not. If I am Socrates, then I am stuck being Socrates and cannot equally be Alcibiades or Diotima.[10] Modern man hates to be classified and given a particular identity. Rather than submit to such indignities he would rather have the power to define arbitrarily what he and other things are. He wants to do away with universals and settled identities so that everything can be a law unto itself. That is "tolerance" as now understood.

Yet we cannot do away with universals and identities. Life forces us to recognize that we are a small and limited part of a world we did not make. A life of reason requires principles that make the world a whole and make things what they are, principles that do not depend on us. Those principles allow the world to make sense in some reliable way and enable us to say what things are and mean. Stable limitations, distinctions, and classifications are necessary, and when driven out in the name of modern reason they return in a less worthy form. A man who turns his back on traditional classifications must still rely on categories in order to think at all. In the absence of tradition, he will turn to a scheme constructed by taking some particular abstraction or thing—race, class, party, or system of thought, or a particular goal such as money, power, pleasure, or equality—and treating it as the ultimate standard to which all others must be referred. The result is the imposition of a mindless scheme on complex and adverse reality—that is, tyranny.

The alternative to such an obsessive and tyrannical universalism is not a denial of universals and distinctions but traditions that give us concrete connections and ideals of life based on standards which we cannot fully understand but are known through experience to order life in ways worthy of attachment. Such connections, ideals, and standards are necessary for any tolerable existence. Objections that assume that they are wrong are pointless, because they ignore the conditions of human life. Tradition is the natural state of man. It can be weakened or disordered but never abandoned. We always classify, and we always pick up by far the greater part of our habits and understandings informally from those around us. To object to that situation or to avoid thinking about its implications is to refuse to deal with life as it is.

STEREOTYPES

It is difficult for many people today to accept the distinctions and limitations on which traditional ways and institutions depend. The modern mind believes that discrimination—classifying people and applying stereotypes to them—is wrong, because to categorize and limit the individual violates the right to self-determination that is the essence of his dignity. It is thought that distinctions and discriminations are arbitrary acts of will that have no natural limit and typically go to extremes. Even to suggest that they are legitimate requires an enormous break with attitudes that now seem fundamental. How, after all, could one have a public forum today on the *benefits* of discrimination?

In addition, advanced liberal society makes the point of traditional distinctions and discriminations difficult to see. It discredits, disguises, and, to the extent possible, destroys the conditions that enable significant social functions to be performed outside neutral bureaucracies and the market. It becomes hard to imagine a legitimate alternative to the advanced liberal state or interpret opposition to its indefinite extension as anything but a mindless or crudely self-interested attack on fundamental decency. The family, for example, is necessary to social functioning and political freedom, and sex roles to the family, but if the functions of the family are hidden and discredited then the meaning of sex roles is obscured, and they appear to be simply arbitrary and oppressive inequalities.

In Concept

In advanced liberal society, "family" loses all content and becomes a sentimental name for any collection of people more or less living together. More specific conceptions of the family are regarded as bigoted and oppressive. The deconstruction of the family is one example of a more general process by which all local and particular forms of social organization come to seem illegitimate because they depend on inequalities. Any distribution of power from the center increases the strength of some more than others, and to tie the distribution to human nature and accepted habits and understandings, as is necessary to make it self-sustaining, is to reproduce traditional power relationships. Irresponsible centralized government comes to seem a fundamental moral necessity in a comprehensive system of social justice. The taboo on traditional distinctions leads to tyranny.

A truly human life requires institutions other than bureaucratic and market arrangements to play a serious role in ordering social relations. It requires allowing those distinctions which such institutions find relevant but which bureaucracies and markets do not—such as sex, class, nation, culture, and particular community—to affect attitudes and conduct. To do so is not to reject justice, because there is nothing specially just or equal about the liberal view. Liberalism allows sharp social distinctions as long as they are justified on grounds of efficiency and based on things that can be measured and controlled from above, like money, formal education, and bureaucratic position. Allowing such distinctions and no others makes sense if they are sufficient for the needs of life. But they are not.

They might be sufficient if all significant social goods were transferable commodities that could be subjected to external control. However, life involves participation in things that transcend us. Our most basic goods include things like religion, culture, and the other connections and commitments that make us what we are. Our participation in such goods differs from person to person in ways that cannot be controlled externally. Knowledge, good sense, human relatedness, and religion cannot be administered, and the state cannot parcel out identity and fulfillment in equal portions.

For that reason, it is absurd to accept a guiding principle of government and social morality that tries single-mindedly to force goods to conform to an egalitarian system of distributive justice. Any serious attempt to create a scheme of rationally administered equality with respect to social goods will suppress the things that matter most to us. Goods that cannot be controlled from above need a social setting that allows them to develop and affect human life in their own way. That setting is always unequal in ways that make no sense from a liberal standpoint. If honor and mutual trust are allowed to follow their own laws, they will result in inequalities. If they are allowed to affect conduct only to the extent that these inequalities can be justified on liberal grounds, they will disappear.[11]

In Practice

Stereotypes are absolutely necessary to any form of society. The most abstract and universal social principles must somehow come down to earth and establish their presence in particular persons and things if they are to affect human life. In liberal as in other forms of society, some sort of authority present in particular places and embodied in particular men, and the stereotypes that define and support it, are necessities. There must at least be policemen, for example, and the policeman's role rests on immensely powerful social stereotypes.

No one treats a policeman like another man. The response is elemental: we cannot help but feel the force he represents. Our attitude is not simple fear of consequences, which rationally would often lead to less cooperation rather than more (as a criminal defense lawyer would tell us). Nor is it personal regard: police officers are not high in the class system, and respect for them individually is beside the point. Rather, it is a matter of a social stereotype fundamental to our kind of society. To deal with a policeman is to deal with government power; to view him as just another man would be radically to separate oneself from the social order in which one lives.

The role of the policeman shows the necessity and power of stereotype-based discrimination: of understanding and dealing with people in accordance with their place in a social scheme. The rules through which modern government exists must make themselves felt as authoritative. By making plain their demands and the *ultima ratio* for compliance policemen make it possible for them to do so. A policeman is The Law—it is he who makes the law manifest. That function requires suppression of an officer's individual and human qualities. His demeanor, his uniform, and the public expectations that constitute his stereotype keep those qualities firmly in the background. The supremacy of the policeman's stereotype—what he is, simply as a police officer—over everything else about him is a necessary part of a system of government as pervasive, complex, and artificial as our own. Whatever happens to other instances of stereotyping, this one will remain as long as anything like modern government exists.

Nor is the policeman the only one whose role requires such emphasis and clarity. Judges, doctors, and clergymen, those whose acts give concrete form and presence to the abstractions of law, science, and religion, are also set apart by the observances that surround them. We are meant to feel differently about them. That is why they dress differently, and why they, along with college professors, high officials, and other custodians of specially important functions, are entitled to special forms of address. Such men are not to be treated like others.

The point of the different treatment is not to give some an unjust advantage over others, although it often has that effect, but to integrate human acts with social and symbolic functions. We are social beings, and stereotypes construct our social world. They are part of applying any system of thought and feeling to concrete affairs. As such, they serve a critical social and moral function. Without stereotypes to make men represent a larger system of things, human acts would have no public quality, and government would be reduced to mere personal domination. It is because of the attitudes and customs that set policemen apart and make them special that an arrest by a policeman is the exercise of state power and not simply one man overpowering another by force. Without such attitudes and customs there could be no effective division of function and responsibility. Society would become a mere aggregate, no more capable of intelligent collective action than a herd of cattle.

Stereotypes such as "father," "citizen," "friend," and the like lead us out of the chaotic war of all against all. They tell us what we are, how we should act, and what we can expect of others. By establishing a network of accepted expectations and duties, stereotypes make possible the self-government of men in society, and the personal responsibility, mutual respect, and moral aspiration that depend on it. By tying personal identity to social order, stereotypes give us a home in the world and a reason to live by the rules. They make us comprehensible to ourselves and each other, and enable us to have characters with moral content. It is through stereotypes that we become fully human. Without them, human life would be mindless sensation, impulse, and fantasy, and human relations a battle of egos arbitrated by money, cunning, chance agreement, and force.

To eliminate "the stereotypes that divide us" makes no sense. It would be either to eliminate stereotypes altogether or to insist on a single stereotype for everyone. The former would end our ability to think, which depends on our ability to categorize. The latter would make pigeonholing worse by forcing everyone into a single slot. Multiple complex stereotypes are a necessity. One-size-fits-all does not work for human beings any more than for shoes.

Justice

Nonetheless, in the case of race, sex, and similar qualities the call to eliminate stereotypes is taken with great seriousness. It is not obvious why viewing women differently from men or Trinidadians from Sicilians is so much worse than viewing civilians differently from policemen or mothers from brothers. If stereotyping is bad because it sets some decisively apart from others and denies individual differences and equal treatment, they all seem bad. Certainly stereotypes, like all other social institutions, give rise to oddities and abuses that might be weighed against their social function. Policemen, officials, and managers sometimes take advantage of their roles to act badly, for example, and the same could be said of the sexes in their dealings with each other.

It seems unreasonable to propose that all stereotypes should therefore be abolished, and no one seriously wants to do so.[12] The usual claim is that stereotypes are more objectionable—more "invidious"—when based on qualities about which one can do little or nothing, and when they have extensive consequences not immediately justifiable by reference to rationally ordered functions. Being a policeman is voluntary and temporary, unlike being black or female. Also, functional stereotypes such as "police officer" have a clear justification and definite limits because they have a direct and rational relation to particular social goals. In contrast, stereotypes based on race, sex, and the like, because of their supposed irrationality, seem to have no clear limits, and so threaten oppression. Moreover, qualities that enduringly characterize a man, and are pervasively important for reasons that are not strictly functional, are understood to constitute his identity. Treatment based on those qualities is seen as a comment on the worth of the man himself, which can be highly offensive.

Such answers overestimate the differences among stereotypes and underestimate the complexity of human life. No stereotype is completely voluntary, rational, and situational, and if there are aspects of human life that cannot be turned into transparently logical functions then the stereotypes that grow up to deal with those aspects will also be somewhat opaque. Like society, which they articulate and make possible, and like human beings themselves, stereotypes are complex, varying, and very mixed in nature. Those who think attitudes toward policemen are rational and not visceral should deal with the police more often.

All stereotypes determine what a person is far more comprehensively than a narrowly functional analysis would justify. A civilian does not get time off from being a civilian, nor a policeman from being a policeman: an off-duty cop is still a cop. An off-duty or retired judge is not just another man; he retains his title and is treated with special consideration. If you have a doctorate you can insist on being addressed as "doctor" in all possible settings. The advantages of being a Nobel Prize–winning author or CEO of a major corporation are not limited to those necessary to a particular rationally defined function. Otherwise, people would not fight so hard to get to the top. The effect of stereotypes like "clerk" is not narrowly functional in a technological sense, and it is not chosen by clerks. If I am a clerk, and a clerk is inferior to an assistant vice president, then I am inferior. Stereotypes determine what someone is so that we can deal with him accordingly. "Clerk" tells us who a man is just as "darkie" once did, and both are oppressive in manifold ways. In contrast, a Harvard diploma—let alone a Harvard professorship—is the present-day equivalent of a patent of nobility. It means that you are a superior person. Why else would people treat getting into Harvard as they do?

Nor does being black, white, male, female, or the like determine one's life comprehensively. Numerous are the settings in modern society in which it does not much matter who or what you are. As the *New Yorker* cartoon tells us, "On the internet, nobody knows you're a dog."[13] Even where such aspects of identity are felt to matter, what they mean varies by setting and who is involved. Among family and friends, race and sex matter to the extent those involved—who likely have the same background themselves—feel appropriate. If the parties disagree, the connection usually falls apart and one can form that is more congenial. Among strangers the situation varies widely. If unfavorable prejudice were as widespread and effectual as sometimes claimed, it is hard to see how antidiscrimination laws could ever have been adopted. And to the extent large numbers of blacks or women do not like the effect of race and sex distinctions, and find the matter pressing, both are numerous enough to step largely out of any system of inequality by choosing to deal preferentially with those like themselves. With 35 million blacks in the United States, with urban black communities that stretch on for miles, and with economic life increasingly independent of locality, blacks need very little white cooperation to arrange their lives so as to minimize racial issues if any large number of them wished to do so.

Such possibilities radically limit dangers of the kind people fear from stereotyping.[14]

Stereotypes, including functional stereotypes like "police officer," can be abusive, but fighting abuses may be a better remedy than a campaign of forcible stereotype extirpation. Man is a social animal, so a campaign to make social treatment and position irrelevant to identity is absurd and gets nowhere. Who I am is inevitably connected with what I do and what others think of me, and all those things are necessarily intertwined with social stereotypes. Even in the most liberal society, we do not make the world in which we find ourselves. Nor, beyond a point, do we make our position in it. If you are tired of being a private you cannot simply choose to be a general. Since few are always on top and many are down below, it is not clear why social justice should depend so strongly on just how each is assigned his place. It is hardly satisfactory to say that what justifies inequality in liberal society is that the many down below choose and deserve to be there. The issue should rather be whether the distinctions have enough of a function in human life to make them worth retaining. The current antidiscrimination crusade does little or nothing to reduce the evils associated with these human necessities. It has not made people get along better in daily life but has rather multiplied points of dispute.

It is clear that stereotypes based on characteristics like sex and ethnicity have crucial functions that cannot otherwise be carried out. For example, stable and functional family life depends on justified, concrete, and complementary expectations about sex roles—in other words, sex-role stereotypes. Men and women need to be able to rely on each other and know what to expect. The innate qualities and inclinations of the sexes normally differ somewhat. By making possible an accepted division of responsibility that mostly corresponds to natural tendencies, sex roles promote the functional and stable families necessary for decent child-rearing. They provide an objective standard in relationships in which subjectivity and often manipulation and distrust would otherwise reign. Weaker families and increased misery have been the predictable consequences of recent attacks on sex roles. Why should a man feel responsible for his family if his wife is presumptively an autonomous breadwinner as much as he is, if she is told she should not rely on him and he is ridiculed for feelings of protectiveness, and if having the children in the first place was her choice alone?

Ethnic stereotypes and discriminations also serve a necessary function. A way of life human beings find tolerable must be based on definite cultural ideals backed by expectations regarding conduct and at least informal sanctions for those who fall short. Young people, for example, need to have complex concrete traditions before them that offer ways of living which are better and more interesting than careerism, hedonism, aggression, victimization, or depression.[15] Such ideals, expectations, sanctions, and traditions differ by time and place, and the differences are necessarily connected to stereotypes as to how people of one group or another act. If the French emphasize style, formal correctness, and certain refinements more than most, they and others will be aware of it. That emphasis and awareness will take the form of a complex of stereotypes that identify the French as French and enable them to make their standards concrete and hold themselves and their compatriots to them. Such an arrangement will be impossible unless the French are able to establish settings ruled by their own hierarchies of consideration. Culture exists by being authoritative, and when reduced to private taste it ceases to exist. If there is no setting anywhere dominated by Frenchmen who feel entitled to run things in accordance with their own views, then there can be no French culture.

The existence of such a setting evidently requires discrimination between those who are French and those who are not French. Culture always requires boundaries, and it almost invariably has an ethnic connection. The eradication of ethnic discrimination means the abolition of boundaries and therefore particular culture. It is hard to believe that the abolition through multiculturalism of varying communal practices and ideals—of all distinctive French, Japanese, and Brazilian culture—would lead to universal or purely individual practices and ideals of remotely equal value. A level of culture consisting only in things that the whole world has in common and understands the same way would be a low level indeed. Even ordinary honesty has a cultural component—for example, the distinction between situations in which truth is strictly required and those which allow some leeway—so in a truly multicultural world it could not exist for lack of coherent habits and expectations to define and enforce it.

Conclusions

The recognition of ethnic and similar distinctions is regarded as extraordinarily dangerous. Those who would abolish them envision no problems should they succeed, as though they served no function and without them people would find nothing to fight over. It should be clear, however, that it is not universal human tendencies like ethnocentrism that are dangerous, but the failure to integrate them with other aspects of life and to restrain them by other considerations. The lesson of the events following the collapse of communism is that the attempt to create a utopia based on eradication of a fundamental impulse—even greed, which some have called the root of all evil—is supremely destructive.

If we destroy sexual and ethnic stereotypes, something else will replace them as a source of identity and point of contention. As traditional stereotypes weaken, identity and social discrimination will come to be based more on functional stereotypes like "policeman" or "CEO." Most men today end up, largely against their will, as low-level subordinates in large organizations established for no very elevated purpose. To make functional stereotypes and identities the only ones that matter is to deprive the great majority of any basis for pride in what they are, and to make position and wealth an obsession for the talented and energetic minority. Such a situation deprives the majority of all dignity and makes them defenseless against upper classes who jockey for advancement while denying human ties that would make them responsible for others.

Why is that a good thing? Its natural consequences are envy, snobbishness, resentment, subservience, self-seeking, apathy, and brutality. A ruling class whose members define themselves by wealth, power, formal education, and bureaucratic position may see "affirmative action" as a necessary attack on irrational bigotry, but the majority, who lack the particular advantages on which their rulers pride themselves, and to whom kinship, gender, ethnicity, religion, and the like continue to matter, are necessarily injured by comprehensive programs aimed at destroying the significance of basic aspects of their lives.

Impulses relating to family, kinship, religion, private property, and various particular loyalties will remain with us, but the influences that refine and civilize them can be degraded or destroyed. The Soviet Union spent seventy years and tens of millions of lives trying to abolish the profit motive. The ultimate result was kleptocracy and mafia rule. It tried to abolish the alienation of man from man; it created a nation of men drinking themselves to death. The purpose of current antidiscrimination efforts is to break all connection between practical affairs and the human feeling that things like sex and ties of history, blood, and common culture matter. Those efforts weaken the habits and institutions which tie such feelings to other concerns and so moderate their effects, enabling them to play a civilizing function of their own. The consequences so far have been sexual chaos and victimization, the fantasies of identity politics, nepotism and cronyism in high places, suppression of free speech and other freedoms for fear the people will tear each other to pieces, and communal war in failed multi-ethnic states. We will undoubtedly see much worse. Ethnic discrimination has killed millions, but the discrimination between policemen and prisoners in utopian tyrannies has killed scores of millions. Why does no one worry about the latter?

The rational and obvious response to such considerations is abandonment of the attempt to eradicate stereotypes and discrimination based on factors men have always believed relevant to their mutual relations. Such things may often be oppressive, just as government, taxes, the police, armies, private property, lawyers, courts, etiquette, and all other social institutions are often oppressive, but in one form or another they are inevitable and necessary. Treating a judge with special consideration, treating women as different from men, taking historical and cultural connections into account in dealing with organizations and individuals—all should be acceptable as legitimate aspects of social life. Abuses—which are always present and often severe in all human arrangements—can be dealt with piecemeal and as possible. To reject stereotypes and discrimination in principle is pointless, however, since in some form they will always exist and order social life. The question is whether the considerations habitually and legitimately taken into account in social life through their incorporation into social stereotypes will include only money, bureaucratic position, and formal certifications, or whether more complex, subtle, and humanly important concerns will be allowed to play a role as well.

Society cannot be reformed and made transparently rational and equal in the way liberalism demands. Nor should we wish to make it so. The individuals and institutions that compose it, by reason of their intrinsic dignity and their relationship to an order of things transcending human purposes, have an innate manner of functioning that should not be violated for the sake of something as abstract and all-consuming as equality. Other ideals are needed, and tradition is needed to define them and their relationships. In opposition to a rationalism that flattens, traditionalism insists on making room for the diverse and sometimes contradictory principles that constitute human life: universal principles, the individual soul, and ordered diversity—including sexual distinctions, historical and cultural particularities, civic and occupational groupings, and hierarchies of various kinds. Those things make life comprehensible and human. They should not be suppressed.

What allows such things to come together in a social and moral order worthy of attachment are the principles of tradition and of subsidiarity—genuine particularity within transcendent unity. Tradition puts things that we cannot fully grasp in order; subsidiarity gives full credit to the local and particular while recognizing that their dignity comes from their connection to larger things that none of them fully embodies and none of us can fully grasp. In America, subsidiarity has been made concrete through a genuine though vague recognition of the divine as a principle underlying social and political life, and through federalism, states' rights, local government, private property, family values, and other principles that limit and distribute power. The advanced liberal order rejects all such principles as reactionary and oppressive. It insists on a unitary order based on simple principles that facilitate social management in the interest of maximum equal satisfaction. That order is an attack on any world in which human life can have a home. It is an expression of the fundamental inhumanity of liberalism. It must be opposed.

CHAPTER NINE

Faith and Authority

To say that knowledge and reason depend on tradition is to say that they depend on faith. As Anselm said, *credo ut intelligam*—I believe that I may know. It is faith that tells us that tradition is not only a practical necessity but a guide to truth, that through it the bits, pieces, and glimmerings that are immediately available to us have grown into attitudes, practices, beliefs, and symbols that show us how the world is and make truths available we could not otherwise attain. Without faith we could not trust the thoughts that enable us to identify experiences and come to grips with them. Nor could we rely on the conditions reason needs to function: the accuracy of memory, the validity of first principles, and the reliability of the linguistic, cultural, and social setting thought needs to operate. To abandon faith is to abandon knowledge, reason, and life itself. Without it, without acceptance of the mystery at the heart of things, everything becomes incomprehensible.

Faith Seeks a Footing

Faith is "the evidence of things not seen."[1] It ties thought, action, and experience together and gives them a stable and comprehensive unity justifiable by reference to something beyond them and beyond our grasp. We need it to understand the world, simply because our thought has objects outside itself and cannot be self-contained.

Rationalists complain that faith overreaches because it goes beyond what we fully grasp, and that it is bigoted because it is particular and denies other possible faiths. Such objections are pointless, since faith is necessary for knowledge and reason, and perverse, since it is basic to the sense of limits that tells us our place and enables us to avoid overreaching. To accept faith is to recognize concretely that which exceeds us: to reject it is not humility but hubris. Without some concrete sense of what exceeds us, our limitations become too abstract to seem relevant. We cannot say anything about them, so they stop existing for us.

Knowledge Naturalized

The dependence of thought and knowledge on faith is paradoxical, so there is always a temptation to ignore our situation or explain it away. Some have proposed theories that reduce knowledge to a natural process to be understood like other natural processes. It is said, for example, that trust in our knowledge is justified by the reflection that our species and society would not have lasted as long as they have unless our traditions of knowledge were in touch with reality. We always have some beliefs or other, and people with true beliefs no doubt prosper more than others, so their beliefs can be expected to prosper as well. Hence the practical persuasiveness of long life and prosperity. Those who attain them are generally quite satisfied with their beliefs.

Nonetheless, it is unlikely that our knowledge can be explained and justified by the Darwinian standard that it promoted reproduction and survival in the past, whether we are talking about the survival of the species or the survival of a culture. Our knowledge is not limited to survival needs. It reflects our orientation and interests, which go beyond reproduction and survival and are sometimes at odds with them. It is discontinuous with the knowledge of the lower animals and so with evolutionary history. Most importantly, it has to do with what is true, which is not the same as what is advantageous. Our theories regarding knowledge should be consistent with what knowledge is for us; a Darwinian theory that explains usefulness but not meaning or truth ignores the things that give knowledge the place it actually holds in human life.

In its most comprehensive form, Darwinian thought purports to give a simple and self-contained explanation of everything: what exists is what has arisen by chance and thereafter survived. Whatever seems to fall outside the closed circle of mechanistic explanation—consciousness, rational justification, existence as such, or peculiarities of the world that appear designed—it denies, tries to explain away, or refuses to discuss. It would show a lack of good sense to accept, without better arguments than seem to be available, a view that combines such extreme ambition, such conceptual and ontological minimalism, and such suitability to the needs of the social institutions now dominant. And in any event, to say that something has been helpful to survival is not to explain what it is, why it works, or whether it is justified. Electric eels may be electric because of natural selection, but that does not explain what electricity is, why it is useful to eels, or exactly how they produce it. The same is true of human knowledge.

Some thinkers—John Dewey, for example—have suggested that we can dispense with truth as a concept. One might treat modern natural science, which for many people sets the standard for all knowledge, as simply a collection of models and methods of prediction that have been found useful. But this suggestion does not survive questioning. Is it true that scientific models and predictions have been found useful, and that our experience of their usefulness is a good guide to the future? If so, they get their importance as part of a larger system of thought and knowledge that enables us to recognize that importance. If not, we have no reason to bother with them.

At bottom, the question is whether knowledge is a concoction of human experience, desire, and functioning, or whether it points beyond those things to something that does not depend on us. We inevitably believe that the latter is the case. Knowledge has its uses, and usefulness is a sign of truth, but the useful is not the same as the true, and our basic concern is with the latter. Knowledge must place usefulness and experience in a larger setting so that we can make sense of them. The things we know and their uses depend on the whole of which they are part, and the nature of that whole is a matter neither of usefulness nor of scientific demonstration. It is a matter of faith as well as truth. Our knowledge remains a mystery.

Faith Threatened

Our connection to a world larger and more permanent than our transitory thoughts and experiences draws on traditions and faith that are so thoroughly integrated with how we look at things that they normally pass without notice. However, issues sometimes arise that disrupt the informal habits and understandings that ordinarily maintain our orientation to an enduring order of things.

A tradition is a composite of symbols, practices, and beliefs, the meanings of which are largely unstated and understandings of which differ. To the extent it is necessary, it is concerned with things that cannot be articulated clearly and the exact meaning of which can wander. It is the way of life of a people as it actually is, and as such it always incorporates conflict, confusion, abuse, vagueness, and a great deal of arbitrariness. It must be passed down informally to exist at all, a necessity that introduces additional uncertainty. Both the weakness of tradition as a human thing and its concern with the inarticulable make it easy for it to lose coherence. Under stress and uncertainty, the unspoken faith implicit in it may not be enough to give human thought and action a stable reference and orientation. Divisive questions may arise that cannot be settled, and the result will be confusion, disruption, and dissolution.

When such questions arise they must somehow be resolved for tradition to remain coherent. If there is no authoritative way to do so, then the accepted principles of the tradition will eventually lose their grip and the possibility of productive thought and discussion will disappear. The collapse of liberal modernity into nihilism, dogmatism, and manipulative rhetoric—like that of ancient philosophy into skepticism, superstition, and wandering speculation—demonstrates its inability to settle ultimate disputes, especially with regard to good and evil, which in turn demonstrates the inability of human reason and experience by themselves to fix truth and meaning.[2]

Perfect unity within a tradition is not possible or desirable, since it would deny the necessary imperfection of our grasp of things, but there must be *something* that keeps the tradition oriented toward a stable understanding of the good and true and restores it when it strays. The importance of features capable of maintaining the coherence of tradition is difficult to overstate. Rational thought would not be possible if we did not have principles we are entitled to rely on as true. Without a coherent tradition, such principles cannot be distinct or coherent. Even the language needed to express and develop our thoughts would lose its meaning, since language takes on distinct meaning by reference to a tradition that fixes common truths, references, and understandings. You cannot philosophize in a multicultural pidgin.

Externals can aid the stability and coherence of tradition. For example, geographic isolation or social and political boundaries can provide it with a stable setting in which to exist, protecting it from disruption. Government and other authorities can support it, or at least avoid undermining it, by recognizing and cooperating with it, by restricting the range of their own activities to avoid disrupting it, and perhaps by penalizing direct attacks on its fundamentals. Nonetheless, the main safeguard of tradition must be internal. Since we need tradition to make sense of our world, it is too encompassing for us to stand outside it and keep it in line. To manipulate tradition is to destroy it as tradition. It must largely stand up for itself.

Faith Formalized

Like language, tradition has an innate tendency toward system. It has more substantive moral and religious content than language, and it has an implicit orientation toward enduring and transcendent principles. Its centrality in human life lends an additional element of self-restoring stability. We all have an interest in keeping it together. The more coherent the tradition and the more adequate it is to human life and the world, the stronger its self-restoring elements will be. Whether such implicit self-regulating influences are sufficient for the requirements of life and thought depends on circumstances. In the comparatively isolated and undifferentiated societies that preceded the rise of cosmopolitan empires in antiquity, they were enough to maintain the stability and coherence of tradition. The order of human affairs could be identified with that of the cosmos, and the world was assumed without argument to be as tradition said it was.

New circumstances bring new needs. As society became more complex, communications improved, and political and social relations came to embrace many peoples and cultures, questions multiplied. Everything became debatable. The truth of tradition could no longer be assumed. Trade and empire, technological advances, and written records made it easier to identify and describe the technological, mechanical, and amoral aspects of the world and see that they formed a system that had to be taken very seriously. Once that had happened, it became possible to see the world as an extension of that system, as random or mechanistic and therefore amoral. Hence the views of Democritus and the ancient Chinese Legalists, as well as modern physicalists: the world is composed of elementary particles in space, and what we do with them is a matter of will and power.

Such views do not describe the world as we experience it. Very few if any persons have accepted them thoroughly as the final truth of things. To all appearances the world includes principles that are incorrigibly nonrandom and nonmechanical: good, evil, subjective experience, the necessity of rational decision. We need to make sense of such principles to make sense of our lives. Mechanism and randomness do not let us do that. To understand the world in which we actually live we need a dimension beyond the material here and now.

Hence (humanly speaking) the higher religions that accompanied the rise of cosmopolitan civilization.[3] Those religions told men that in addition to the secular and pragmatic world around them there was another, more important and transcendent world. Special practices and understandings arose to maintain the coherence, stability, and authority of the social understanding of that world. Those practices and understandings made the manner of dealing with the transcendent—with principles that precede and condition everyday life, but are easier to symbolize than to identify and discuss—more explicit and formal. They gave a greater role to institutions and practices that are not purely customary. In effect, they formalized the aspects of tradition that relate to the transcendent as religion and made them a specialized field of doctrine and discipline.

Such developments became part not only of religious tradition but of reason, in the sense that they became necessary to understand oneself and the world. Every society not in the process of dissolution has some shared unspoken sense of the world and our place in it, as well as corresponding beliefs and habits that order the society in accordance with stable, common understandings. Organized religion gives those things a form and structure which make them able to defend themselves and insist on their irreplaceable role in human life. When human society is no longer identified with cosmic order but becomes a collection of specialized and relatively autonomous pursuits, the transcendent must also become a specialty so that it can assert itself and avoid displacement by this-worldly interests and techniques.

The need for formalization has differed in various times and places. Until not long ago, the need was less acute in India and China than in the West. The former are comparatively compact land masses of subcontinental scale, separated from other major civilizations by natural barriers. They lack the complexity of internal obstacles, such as seas and mountains, that made possible the development of an enduring diversity of political, cultural, and religious centers in Europe, the Mediterranean basin, and the Middle East.[4] Outsiders could more often be held at arm's length and fought off or absorbed. Cultural imports could be dealt with from a position of superiority and either rejected or informally reinterpreted and integrated with the established system. As a result, cosmological understandings and cultural cohesion were challenged less in India and China than in the West.

Fewer threats to the unity of tradition and culture meant less need for explicit rational unity of thought and less emphasis on the specific authority of revelation. The Confucians could put cultural heritage where the West put philosophy and religion, the Chinese emperor could remain the Son of Heaven until 1912, and "Hinduism" could mean the acceptance of any somewhat mainstream form of Indian religious tradition. In addition, the common tendency in the East to view ultimate reality as impersonal, and human goals and the world around us as indifferent and illusory, led men to downplay the possibility of ordering human life by reference to substantive goods and truths. The practical consequence was a tendency to turn away from public life and free inquiry and toward dynastic despotisms in which the greater part of social life is carried on in inward-turning groups, such as Indian castes and Chinese extended families.

In contrast, the Eastern Mediterranean was a crossroads, a marketplace and arena that favored scientific rigor, philosophical argument aimed at universal truth, and monotheism. Multiple enduring centers of social life and culture meant continuing confrontation of opposing understandings of human life and the world. The great age of Chinese philosophy was the Warring States period (480–221 B.C.). Almost the whole history of the Mediterranean basin and the West has been a warring states period. To survive in such a setting, a way of life had to establish defenses and put its case in an explicit, focused, and universalizable form. When ancient Israel settled, urbanized, and became part of that cosmopolitan world, the Israelites preserved the integrity of their way of life by filling out their informal, domestic, and pre-Mosaic tribal traditions with sacred Scriptures, a comprehensive code of sacred law, purity rules that required ethnic separation, lawyers, and a temple and its priesthood.

Since that time, Scripture, law, scholarship, and purity rules have been sufficient to maintain the coherence of Jewish identity and tradition, at least among observant Jews. Islam, a movement of simplification that arose on the fringe of the civilized world, has had similar ordering principles, although it emphasizes political domination rather than ethnic separation as a means of maintaining the practical authority of the faith and the way of life it commands among those who have accepted it. So armed and guarded, Judaism and Islam have survived in the heartland of ancient civilization, while pagan communities and religious or philosophical sects lacking principles and institutions sufficient to establish stable practices and beliefs, and to preserve them from disruption, disappeared long ago.

From the outside, the departure from the informal, anonymous, and flexible aspects of tradition induced by authority based on explicit revelation may look like a sort of noble lie, an artifice that maintains the coherence and apparent intelligibility of life and the world at the expense of responsiveness to further needs and experiences and, ultimately, of truthfulness. The formalization of implicit faith as dogmatic religion even appears to be circular, since it attempts to explain particular features of the world and maintain their coherence by appeal to a system of superparticulars: God, sacred texts, particular doctrines, and so on. Why not leave the inexplicable inexplicable, some might ask, instead of providing an incomprehensible explanation?

From within, however, such developments can only appear as an intervention from above that gives knowledge of a scope, reliability, and concreteness that is required for human life but surpasses human capacities. To deal with the mysterious we must name it and say what it is, to some extent, and that project requires a system of religious symbolism and dogma that can only be attributed to revelation.

Rejecting revelation has the usual advantages of skepticism: it seems to risk nothing and avoid all possibility of a false move. Trying to avoid risk can itself be a false move, however. Man is social, and reason is common to all. We cannot live reasonably unless we can view the principles by which we live as public and stable. To make sense in the long run, a rejection of revelation must, like any other complex decision, be part of a stable and coherent tradition of thought that constitutes the public truth of an enduring community. Otherwise it becomes a personal gesture without definite or lasting significance.

Once cosmopolitan civilization has arisen, the truth implicit in culture can no longer be self-supporting without some concrete transcendent reference. Its public stability and coherence require acceptance of some definite authority based on revelation. To reject all revelation is to be left with nothing that can be relied on as truth, apart possibly from the natural sciences. These, however, cannot answer necessary questions. They also must depend on broader traditions of knowledge that the rejection of revelation leaves fatally unmoored. Under such circumstances we are left to choose among cynical rhetoric, narrow specialization, the radical privatization of reality, bullying attempts to create truth by force, and the decline of discourse into an increasingly incoherent association of words. None of those choices offers hope of a way of life in accordance with reason.

For a long time, then, to live a life of reason has been, in the Western world, to orient oneself by reference to the authority of some revelation. Even skeptics have depended on the habits and attitudes of non-skeptics, since skepticism is of necessity parasitic. Nothing has happened to change that situation. To the contrary: the spread of Christianity in China, Korea, and Africa, the growth of Islam in Africa and its radicalization in Muslim countries, the appearance of the false gods of ideology everywhere, and even the decline of a de-Christianized and post-Marxist Europe, indicate that men are as dependent on revelation as ever. The need for public, systematic, and comprehensive thought that comes to stable and reliable conclusions based on some concrete authority above reason is unavoidable. The choice today is not between faith and reason, or between reason and chaos (by whatever name)—for chaos is not something we will live with—but among faiths anchored in revelation and capable of sustaining reason.

THE CHURCH

The development of revelation as a response to an increasingly cosmo-politan and differentiated social world did not stop with Judaism. Both Judaism and Islam are valid only for a single people—Islam intends to be universal, but its universality consists in the merging of all human-ity into a single nation—and their very detailed codes of law maintain coherence and stability by resisting change even on minor points. Their textual bases make them appear to possess the divine word fully here and now, and so deprive them of adaptability. Those who fall away from strict legalism have difficulty finding a place to stop. They tend toward either this-worldly radicalism or a mysticism that soon becomes unorthodox. They lack the comprehensive and flexible rationality needed to support public order in a post-Hellenic world that encompasses large populations with diverse national and local traditions and also accepts the advantages of free public life, including free inquiry on a broad range of issues.

Freedom and Authority

The more cosmopolitan and diverse a society the greater the necessity of an authority that can bring inquiry to a conclusion and draw a reliable line between truth and error. Modern natural science, an institution represen-tative of a world of free public discussion, views theories that do not allow for public confirmation or refutation as empty speculation. The diversity and contentiousness of cosmopolitan civilization create a similar situation with regard to ethical and religious belief. For a belief to seem worth tak-ing seriously it must be possible to test it by some objective standard, at least indirectly, as through the testing of beliefs with which it bears a nec-essary connection. Otherwise, a proposed resolution of the fundamental conflicts that will inevitably arise can only be the opinion of one man or faction, which anyone can rationally accept or reject at will. The result is that free public life will eventually fall apart. The traditions sustaining it will either disintegrate, split into warring factions, freeze and forbid discussion, or become specialized pursuits incapable of ordering life as a whole. The unhappy results will be rigidity and sectarian narrowness, as in orthodox Islam and Judaism and fundamentalist Protestantism; restriction to particular social classes and aspects of life, as in Confucianism; disappearance of the usable common understandings necessary for public life and objective inquiry, as in much of the non-Western world; or triviality, manipulation, and dissolution, as in the West generally today.

For a religious tradition to deal authoritatively with ultimate issues without engaging in the wholesale suppression of valuable aspects of human life, something at once more focused and more supple than textual, scholarly, ritual, or prophetic authority is needed. Since human reason and experience are not enough to resolve all unavoidable issues, the method of interpreting fundamental principles must be understood as embodying an intelligence with special insight into truth, and thus as equivalent to continuing divine guidance. Otherwise the tradition suffers from an inner weakness that will predictably lead to irrationality and collapse. But if we know in advance that a tradition of life and thought is doomed to incoherence, what it tells us can no longer be viewed as a tolerable approximation to the truth upon which we can confidently rely. It is only a practical stopgap, something we do not believe but find useful in pursuing particular ends we happen to have. It loses its authority, and therefore its ability to define reality for us. It is no longer our tradition.

Truth and Personality

Since reason and truth are self-consistent, the basis and method of decision should complement tradition and other aspects of the way in which we come to know the world. Tradition is necessary because realities that concern us often cannot be known in a fully explicit and propositional way. The traditions that point to those realities do not fix their own meaning beyond all doubt but must be interpreted. That can be difficult. Attitudes, practices, events, and propositions can be construed to have very different meanings without violating formal criteria. Impartial expertise can develop possibilities and cast light on details, but it cannot by itself settle much of practical importance, especially outside the hard sciences.

Access to truth that cannot be unambiguously formulated and proven depends on orientation and commitment. Knowledge has a necessary personal element. Tradition, the common mind of a community, also has a personal aspect. It depends essentially on attachments and loyalties. It embodies preferences and beliefs, and it makes decisions. To believe as a member of a community—as we must, if our beliefs are to be stable and coherent—is to put our trust in its common mind, and to let ourselves be formed by it. That is what it means to accept the authority of a tradition.

For that acceptance to be rational, and to maintain our commitment to truth, we must accept that our community of belief has a relationship to ultimate things that makes it capable of knowing them truly. The Christian account of God become man and still active in his church makes comprehensible, in the most complete and direct way, how a community can have such a quality. It makes reasonable the love, loyalty, and trust toward one's community and tradition that in the long run is necessary for coherent thought. Since God is understood as a living presence in the community here and now, it becomes comprehensible that an authoritative decision of the community on disputed matters should rightly constitute our understanding of how those things stand. The Christian account has no visible competitor in that regard. It is the view that best suits those who believe that knowledge is possible and recognize that it depends on tradition and thus on the mind of a particular community.

Structure and Decision

When a specific question is to be resolved, the mind of the community must be brought down to earth and made concrete through a human authority that is its representative or guardian. How to do so has caused controversies in the church and led to the divisions that plague Christendom. Those divisions have enabled the triumph of radical modernity, a movement that possesses if not ultimate coherence then at least apparent clarity and the practical advantage, in unsettled times, of single-minded concentration on pragmatic success.

The problem is long-standing and cannot be solved here. However, some solution must be found if the church is to play its proper role in the renewal of intellectual and social life. It seems likely that a solution will have to draw heavily from Christian tradition. In that tradition, when consensus has been lost and disputes cannot be resolved through discussion, doctrine has normally been determined by some combination of hierarchy and church councils and by taking Scripture, tradition, and reason as ultimate reference points. The largest, most stable, and most influential Christian communion has added to that mix the ultimate responsibility of a single man, the pope.

In the present day, many people object to such modes of authority as obscurantist and authoritarian. Nonetheless, some sort of traditional hierarchy is necessary in religion. Individual judgment notoriously needs correction. A democratic assembly, other than an extraordinary meeting called to deal with a specific crisis that overwhelms particular interests, tends to draw authority from the groups and interests its members represent. It serves as a vehicle for the ambitions of its members and their backers. And for a large and diverse body dealing with something as difficult and specialized as doctrine to act at all coherently, it must be dominated by a small, cohesive, and continuing group. To insist on the appearance of democracy in such a situation is to encourage manipulation and guarantee obfuscation. Democracy has strong claims in the case of contingent decisions that reflect relative personal interests, but in doctrinal determinations such concerns are irrelevant.

The point of tradition (and still more of revelation) is that it relates to matters beyond the competence of popular opinion and formalized expertise. It tells us something that as social beings we need to be able to recognize collectively as reliable and true. A small group that is independent and responsible for a broad range of ecclesiastical affairs while lacking means of physical coercion seems most likely to deal with doctrine coherently and intelligently. The authority of such a group rests on its claim to stand for correct doctrine. The ambitions of its members are often moderated by the circumstance that they are likely to be rather aged and by the reflection that there is little further to which they can reasonably aspire. They cannot do as much or enforce their will as easily as a larger group, they are more dependent on voluntary cooperation, and as a practical matter they must point to reason, tradition as a whole, and understandings they cannot create by themselves to justify their actions.

Some such arrangement is consistent with the genius of tradition, because it is personal as well as universal, concrete as well as flexible. Only Christianity understands the community as the earthly body of a divine person. Only some definite way of settling contested issues enables the visible church to speak and act in a definite and authoritative way. And only if that method of settling disputes maintains considerable independence from other centers of social power—as it does in Christianity through the distinction between Christ and Caesar—will the necessary concern for the integrity and persuasiveness of the conclusions be maintained.

The traditional Christian arrangement displays the natural form for a system of truth to take in a world of free public life. It is altogether in character that Christian culture has been so fruitful for so long; that Christianity—especially Western Christianity, which has most emphasized the need for a final decision-maker—has fostered learning, philosophy, and the arts; and that its distinctive institutions have included universities, free political bodies, and modern natural science. The recent decisive rejection of Christianity in much of Western society, and with it the rejection of a principle of transcendent public truth tied to some distinct representative, has been accompanied by irrationalism, a radical decline of nontechnological culture, and the attempt to reduce politics and public life to purely technical functions, thereby abolishing them in theory while making them tyrannical in practice.[5]

Extra ecclesiam nulla salus ("Outside the church there is no salvation") is not a contingent feature added to an arbitrary doctrinal system for self-interested purposes. It expresses a necessity of the post-Alexandrian situation that makes coherent thought and meaning with regard to the world as a whole impossible in the long run—at least in a cosmopolitan society with Western traditions of public life and rational inquiry—without something very much like an authoritative church. Other religions cannot fill the gap. Islam, to the extent it can resolve issues, is unbending and tyrannical, Judaism lacks universality, and Eastern religions have too little to say about the things of this world. Those Protestants who have rejected an authoritative church, while trying to maintain and even expand Christian traditions of self-government and free inquiry, have had difficulty maintaining the coherence and relevance of their outlooks. Most of their churches are ending either in fundamentalist rigidity or liberal dissolution. Such considerations do not prove the truth of Christianity or any particular form of it. They do suggest, however, that it is unlikely that a system of truth satisfactory especially to Westerners will be found outside Christendom.

CHURCH AND STATE

The dominant view in the West today is that religion has no place in public life and should be kept strictly private. There are reasons for the dominance of that view. Modern thought makes all authority seem utterly external to the individual and so at bottom illegitimate. Religious authority is especially frightening, even regarding purely ecclesiastical matters, because it seems to represent an external tyranny over the soul itself that is not based on the understanding of reason currently dominant and so seems irrational. However, the problem is with modern thought and not religious authority. The current view is extremely unusual historically, far from unanimously held in the world at large, and of doubtful practicality and coherence. Even where it is accepted, it is far better established among governing elites than among the people at large, so much so as to raise suspicion that it has more to do with the needs of power than with the demands of reason and justice.

In fact, the authority of the church is not primarily that of a ruler, let alone a tyrant, but that of a custodian of something passed down. The church must have internal discipline to function, but its primary purpose is to present, not to enforce. Like other intellectual authorities, it should have substantial independence but no direct political power. The good, beautiful, and true need to be institutionally separate from political power to be seen as superior to it. A believer would no more give the state authority in religious matters than a physicist, sculptor, or moral philosopher would give it authority in science, aesthetics, or morals. Conversely, rule by priests has many of the same disadvantages as rule by philosophers or law professors. Few people want it.

Government is organized force. There are many goods it cannot promote effectively, and its legitimate respect for the highest goods does not require it to enforce them directly or to define them beyond what practicality demands. The single most important political function of the church is to relativize the state by placing it in a larger setting. It can do that only if church and state have substantial mutual independence.

That is not to say, however, that there should be no connection between church and state. A "wall of separation" between them is no more possible than between government and physics, economics, morality, or architecture. Knowledge and aesthetic and moral merit are public goods. The government encourages them and when necessary makes practical decisions on disputed points, as when it decides how it will define and punish offenses, design public monuments, and draw up curricula for public schools. An attempt to make public life neutral in such respects would be absurd, even though those who deal most authoritatively with the concerns in question must maintain a certain independence from politics if they are to keep their integrity.

Much the same applies to religion. The government is obligated to act by reference to the public good, and it cannot do so without taking goods connected to religion into account. Government involves itself comprehensively in moral issues. It must deal with ultimate questions of life and death, as when it must decide issues such as the nature of marriage: whether it is a contract people enter into for their own purposes that they can define as they wish, or rather a moral reality that transcends desire. It educates the young, telling them what life and the world are like, what they owe themselves and others, and whether God, their country, or their own desires are at the center of things. It takes positions on symbolic issues such as those involved in the punishment of crime and the ceremonies and holidays through which it establishes the nature of its authority and of the social world it rules. And it takes on very broad responsibility for the well-being of the people. Its concern with equality and tolerance has recently made it responsible for the spirit in which the people deal with each other. How can such matters be dealt with rationally in abstraction from a comprehensive view of ultimate issues?

Government must take a position on questions that depend on the nature of man and the moral world and are therefore religious. It must try to get people to agree with its answers. Every government inculcates and enforces the understandings on which it is based, including the religious ones, in a variety of ways. At present a favorite method of enforcing the official view is stealth: excluding other religious views from public affairs while claiming that the official view is not religious. The exclusion is passed off as necessary for political freedom, but it destroys it. Politics is the interplay between the traditions of a community, which establish the general order of its life, and public decisions backed by force. To suppress the religious aspects of community tradition in public affairs is to make it impossible for the community to carry on its business in the way it finds natural and comprehensible. It is to cripple popular participation in government.

Where absolute separation between government and religion is demanded, the demand should be recognized as a screen for the suppression of one scheme of attitudes, loyalties, and beliefs in favor of another that also functions as a religion. In a society that accepts self-government as an ideal and views the state as subordinate to society, the accepted public religion should be based on the understandings accepted in society generally. Religion should become established in the same way other basic constitutional understandings become established. If that were allowed, religious authorities would influence the decision of issues on which they have something special to say, just as economists, medical researchers, or constitutional scholars do now. When issues that touch on religion come up in practical politics they must be decided somehow. The alternative to recognizing the views and authorities most generally accepted among the people is to take guidance from some other source. What is that other source to be?

The view that liberal society is uniquely rational, free, tolerant, popular, and nondogmatic is mistaken. The effect of the increasingly radical insistence on church-state separation is that government no longer defers or accommodates itself to popular, traditional, or ecclesiastical answers to religious questions but instead makes up its own answers with its own goals in mind. The new official orthodoxy idealizes "choice" but is not itself optional, and the way it is formulated and applied is often tyrannical. It is taught in school, dramatized on television, and inculcated by all respectable social authorities. It extends its authority even into private life. Dissenters are treated as divisive and extremist, as bigoted fundamentalists whose views pose a threat to society and must be excluded from public discussion.

Extremism is dangerous, but its dangers cannot be avoided by intolerantly driving religion out of public life and replacing it by a view that presents itself as nonreligious. The dangers of ideological bigotry are always present, even among secularists, and they will more likely be reduced by recognizing them as a permanent part of political life and finding less simple-minded ways to moderate them. While religion has sometimes led to bloody persecutions and wars, the same can be said about movements that claim to be secular, including (as demonstrated by the French Revolution and recent wars in Serbia and Iraq) liberalism itself. The last century saw butchery in the name of secularism and social progress that dwarfed any cruelty ever perpetrated in the name of religion.

What is needed is an outlook that recognizes the complexity of the world and human society; leaves room for Christ, Caesar, and dissenting views; and lets the paradoxes of their mutual recognition, conflict, and accommodation work themselves out differently in different settings. It needs, in short, a rule of reason in religious matters. A rule of reason takes into account prudence and the need to maintain cooperative relations among those who differ. It cannot be a rule of religious neutrality, since on basic issues neutrality is impossible. Nor can it be a rule that pretends to solve all serious issues in advance. The question is not what principle guarantees peace and justice in every possible setting but how as a practical matter people can live together in a particular time and place on the best terms possible. Sloganeering about separation of church and state is useless as an answer to that question, since every society has a governing understanding that functions as a religion. What is needed is an approach to religion and politics that accords with both reason and the moral and religious habits of the people and so makes political freedom and good government possible.

CHAPTER TEN

Bringing It All Back Home

BUT WHAT IS TO BE DONE? FROM A TRADITIONALIST POINT OF VIEW, THE modern world looks doomed. The insistence on rooting out all social institutions not based on administration, money, formalized expertise, or free-floating choice leaves little room for the complex informal connections and understandings needed for decent human relations or even ordinary rationality. We appear headed for tyranny, chaos, and neoprimitivism as social trust disappears, and as institutions stop functioning in an orderly, rational, and above-board way and come to rely on crude supports such as force, fraud, bribery, and primitive blood and tribal loyalties. The post-liberal future may look rather like post-Soviet Russia, only with less common culture and more varied and numerous Chechens.

IS TRADITIONALISM POSSIBLE?

Such a catastrophe must be averted if possible, but the triumph of liberalism that points to it seems so comprehensive, overwhelming, and bound up with forces that appear irresistible that it is hard to know where to begin. Many people are convinced it is impossible to reverse the triumph of liberalism. They believe that it is an aspect of modernity, and modernity includes a ratchet that only lets it turn one way. "History" remains an absolute in many minds, even for those who imagine that they reject absolutes and no longer believe in progress. Traditionalist theories about normal social functioning or the restoration of Christendom have no political support and are radically at odds with the character of public discussion. Still, historical developments are never unequivocal. Liberalism and modernity have weaknesses and contradictions, and tyranny is never as invincible as it looks. There is always a great deal to do here and now.

Difficulties

Traditionalism is an odd position, so much so that many believe it makes no sense. The more it is needed the less possible it seems. It attempts an articulate defense of what cannot quite be said. It appeals to history but opposes its recent direction, exalts natural growth but denounces what has grown up in the West over the past several hundred years, and in the name of a principle of authority denies the official principles of present-day society.

When tradition becomes argumentative it is evident that something has gone wrong. The problem is not tradition as such, however, but particular traditions. We need tradition. Without it we cannot understand ourselves, our situation, or our actions. Tradition can nonetheless contradict itself and become self-destructive. Not every tendency is a tradition that should be honored. To be recognized as authoritative, tradition must be consistent with its sources: reason, experience, revelation, loyalty to the past, concern for the future, and the human sense of coherence and rightness. It must be part of a coherent way of life that makes sense of human needs and tendencies and joins the natural, social, and transcendent into a livable order. It must show us the how, why, and wherefore of life. In particular, a tradition cannot claim authority if it makes its own authority nonsensical. Liberal tradition says that we make up our own how, why, and wherefore. It demands that social order justify itself demonstratively and do without principles that cannot be made explicit. Whatever cannot be demonstrated and made explicit becomes a matter of individual opinion and choice. Such demands would destroy all tradition, including liberal tradition, and a tradition that presents them cannot be taken seriously however influential it becomes.

The dominance of liberal tradition fails to refute traditionalism. It does, however, make problems for it as a practical matter. How can a man live by inherited understandings when those understandings have become antitraditional? We need tradition because we are social, and we follow it out of loyalty, but for those very reasons we find it hard to buck public consensus. Science and liberal democracy are now thought to have refuted and superseded tradition. The rejection of tradition is taught in the schools, presumed in public discussions, and promoted by all reputable authorities. Its claim of authority seems out of place today, and attachment to it has come to appear willful and self-contradictory.

The very organization of life seems antitraditional today, and attempts to hold to tradition quite generally fail. Tradition is largely habitual and preconscious. It must be learned through contact and example. It is grounded on settled common understandings: what a friend is, what men and women are, what constitutes a Christmas dinner or a well-spent life. In a society based on contract and bureaucracy, the function of such conceptions seems to evaporate. Enduring personal habits and loyalties are replaced by rational self-interest, neutral formal institutions, and universal communications networks. Shifting human purposes and technical considerations become decisive; things come to depend on what men want to make of them rather than anything enduring. Such developments seem to reduce talk of tradition, loyalty, integrity, and the like to sentimentality or obfuscation.

To put the matter in general terms, traditionalism is concerned with essential qualities and connections, while modernity is concerned with technical factors, temporary relationships, and specific purposes. The change from the former to the latter cripples not only traditionalism but any sort of opposition to the spirit of the times. Hence the futility of rebellion today. If things are only what men make of them, and nothing has an essential connection to anything else, everything dissolves into transitory purposes and dependencies. Any sort of independence—economic, social, intellectual, or spiritual—becomes impossible, because it would require a man to have a stable nature of a kind no longer thought to exist. Someone who wants to recognize an authority other than money, ambition, power, or fashion cannot do so today so in a way that appears to make sense, because in the absence of a recognized objective moral order he can appeal to nothing but willfulness. To his fellows he can only appear a rebel without a cause, a man asserting only himself. As a practical matter, he is likely to make his rebellion good by attacking the remnants of traditional order. Attempts to escape the oppressiveness of the modern world exacerbate its disorder. They are trivialized, commercialized, or harnessed to the purposes of the advanced liberal state, and in that way integrated with the liberal enterprise.

Strengths

Yet we need not accept skepticism, secularism, and anti-traditionalism as our historical fate. Claims that we understand our present situation well enough to know that we are stuck with it permanently are not believable. There is no science that predicts future beliefs. A spiritual situation is unlikely to remain compulsory once we understand it well enough to describe it accurately and see what is wrong with it.

The modern understanding of knowledge and reality is not a trap that will endure forever but a human structure of thought with flaws and limitations that eventually will become obvious and destroy its ability to hold our attention. It is too narrow to satisfy the needs of life. Its emphasis on logic and its commitment to progress mean that its deficiencies lead to grosser and grosser malfunctions which its commitment to transparency makes difficult to hide altogether. We are not only modern men but human beings living our lives in a world that does not reduce to the way we explain it. If the stories we tell about our situation mean we cannot carry on our lives in a way that makes sense to us, then we will end by changing the stories.

The absolute triumph of the antitraditional is an illusion. Yes, the weakening of tradition and the corresponding decline of transcendent attachments have profoundly affected life. There are fewer marriages, fewer children, more divorces. Juvenile well-being has declined radically in the face of vastly increased wealth and social expenditures. Manners have become crude, fraud and fraudulence are growing problems in intellectual life, and entertainment has become increasingly stupid, violent, obscene, and boring. Yet much good remains, and the actual attitudes and understandings men live by include many things that cannot be explained by the principles publicly acknowledged.

Life goes on as it must. Liberal institutions are parasitic; a liberal order exists by tempering explicit secular hedonism with a residual implicit orientation to the transcendent. This orientation is needed for social life to be possible at all and it can exist concretely only through tradition. While liberalism is explicit by nature, the virtues inconsistent with it can persist without acknowledgment. In spite of the progress of liberalism, ordinary virtues can still be seen throughout the world around us: in everyday decencies and occasional heroism; in community service, patriotism, and churchgoing; in the nostalgia liberals warn us against; even in the inarticulate, popular cynical view that there is something seriously lacking in current ideals. Honesty and loyalty are still admired. Men and women continue to marry, have children, and make sacrifices for their families. There are still soldiers willing to risk their lives for their country, even though such conduct has become incomprehensible.[1] We do not know how to talk about such things, let alone justify them,[2] but life cannot go on without them and so they remain.

The attitude of elite and populace toward each other sums up the situation today. Elites consider the people ignorant and bigoted. The people think their rulers pretentious, hypocritical, self-seeking, and absurd. The reason for the dislike and suspicion has less to do with personal qualities, with regard to which elite and populace may differ little, than with social position and function. Elites stand for the principles publicly accepted, the people for actual day-to-day life, and their opinions of each other display the opposition between accepted theories and the habits and attitudes that enable life to go forward. The people admire standards not based on desire, and they respect loyalty to one's people and their ways, while those on top view such attitudes as ignorance and bigotry. In contrast, elites insist that the one indispensable virtue is equal acceptance of all ways of life consistent with the efficient rule of bureaucracy and money. The people, depending on mood, may view that insistence either as comical, because of its irrationality, or as an aggressively intolerant attack on the value and coherence of their own identity and way of life.

While liberal elites seem to hold all the cards, no society can be liberal through and through. Social life depends on an unproclaimed attachment to tradition. In the end, the traditionalist outlook has advantages that outweigh its difficulties and must be decisive. It alone can deal adequately with what we cannot fully grasp, measure, and control. It alone connects morality and human life to the rhythms of experience and the nature and tendencies of things. And it alone provides a basis for that trust in the world which is needed to motivate cooperative and effective action. Action in common requires faith in something that transcends and encompasses us, and success goes to those who care about something more substantive than winning. Moderns are afraid to give themselves to such things, because it would mean subjection to an alien power outside themselves.[3] The traditionalist does not share that fear, because he knows he did not create himself and cannot control events. He accepts that man is necessarily part of something larger, and that life and the world follow their own principles. He is willing to accept human limitations and the need—in a world that is neither purely human nor altogether alien—to trust something beyond human knowledge and will.

POLITICAL ENGAGEMENT

We must begin with basics. Our goal is to live well as human beings. We are social, and social goods such as settled common loyalties make our lives what they are. Those goods depend on common understandings on which we believe ourselves entitled to rely. Liberalism makes all goods individual and optional, eliminating the ability to rely on common understandings as to what is good. It destroys the setting many of our most basic goods require in order to exist. Social action of some sort is therefore a necessity.

Some observers argue that the current social order is doomed and that traditionalists are powerless, so their social action should take the form of building up the inner life and defenses of particular communities capable of surviving the current order as it falls apart.[4] Societies that live by their own traditions can exist as associations within a larger and less morally coherent polity. Historical examples include the church before Constantine and the millets of the Ottoman Empire. Modern examples include such self-contained religious groups as the Amish and strictly or-

thodox Jews, and to a considerable extent Mormons and pre–Vatican II
Catholics in non-Catholic countries. The common claim that traditionalist demands are pointless, because history has passed them by, lends support to such strategies. If you can't beat them, and don't want to join them,
then withdraw.

However, traditionalists cannot choose withdrawal. They must
take part in public life at least in self-defense. We live by our setting and
connections as well as by our choices. The world we inhabit is complex
and multi-storied, and it extends without a break from the home and the
individual soul to the highest public affairs. To become a habitat its various levels must be tied together and made coherent through culture and
religion. That process is difficult when the attitudes and practices that
shape public institutions deny what transcends us and disrupt particular
traditions and connections on principle, as a matter of vindicating inclusiveness and tolerance.

Modern life is intrusive and liberalism imperialistic. The "ordinary life" to which we are expected to accommodate ourselves today is
shaped by mass media devoted to commerce and hedonism, by huge impersonal organizations devoted to moneymaking and control, and by an
interventionist state devoted to extirpation of all social authorities other
than markets and neutral expert bureaucracies. Most of us are employees
and must sign on to whatever program the institutions that employ us
see fit to impose. More and more institutions, prodded by antidiscrimination laws and public standards of respectability, are insisting on understandings that are radically opposed to traditional beliefs on such basic
matters as sex and religion. Institutional demands for the acceptance and
indeed celebration of radically antitraditional views has begun to make
it difficult for a traditionalist to accept a responsible job with, or have
his children educated by, a mainstream institution.[5] In the coming years,
such difficulties are likely to affect life more and more, and the situation of

traditionalists seems likely to become rather like that of religious minorities in Europe before nineteenth-century emancipation, though perhaps more difficult because of the intrusive omnipresence of government and commercial culture.

A Traditionalist Movement

Such tendencies must be resisted by all who see what is wrong with them. A traditionalist movement in America would be a practical and mostly informal alliance of those attached to traditional ways and understandings, working together against enemies of tradition as opportunities arise and as common concerns suggest. It would have its strains and limitations, since traditions oppose as well as support each other, but there is common ground as well, for disagreements among the great traditions are much smaller than their common opposition to the technocratic liberalism that threatens them with common destruction.[6]

The immediate practical function of a traditionalist movement would be to make life in accordance with tradition easier and more practical for those inclined to it. It would do what it could to defend the strength and autonomy of families, local communities, and particular institutions against the imperialism of commercial society and the managerial state. More generally, it would try to give a public presence to principles other than those of liberalism, such as respect for inherited ways and local and transcendent attachments. Such a presence would allow those principles to exert whatever public influence good sense suggests and popular understandings permit. At a minimum the presence of the traditionally oriented in public life would open up discussion to a broader range of human goods, extend the scope of what is conceivable, and help relativize liberal modernity and limit its overreaching.

Ideally, each tradition would contribute something distinctive to the movement: for example, Protestantism its connection to American history and talent for local self-organization, Catholicism its ties to the roots of American society in medieval Christendom and natural law, and Judaism its long experience in maintaining group integrity in complex and adverse situations. Each could learn from the others.

Grand Vision

Liberalism is based on the liberal notion of the good life—in theory doing your own thing, in practice a combination of careerism, hedonistic consumerism, and political correctness. In response, traditionalists must put forward their own understanding of the good life. The traditionalist view of the good life varies somewhat by tradition, but it is certainly based less on technology, desire, and purely formal standards like equality than on substantive goods and settled attachments. In particular, it gives a place of honor to God, country, and family, with "God" including transcendent standards generally and "country" and "family" interpreted in an old-fashioned way to include all degrees of kinship and local as well as national community.

The liberal vision of the good life will not be questioned unless public and political discussion puts it in question. Liberals attempt to win the point without discussion by claiming that basic issues are divisive and should be kept out of politics. Each of us, they say, should pursue his own vision of the good life within a common system that facilitates that quest for everyone. The proposal seems evenhanded, but in fact it simply restates liberalism by resolving all disputes over the good life in favor of the individual pursuit of whatever one likes, to the extent that the ability to do so can be made equal. As such the liberal proposal is not at all neutral but favors some goods over others—for example, nonsocial indulgences over enduring human connections. It makes a society oriented toward careerism, consumerism, cautious hedonism, and political correctness the only legitimate possibility, and it places traditionalist understandings out of bounds. It establishes the liberal version of the good life as a public absolute.

"Gay marriage" provides an example of the practical workings of liberal neutrality and tolerance. Until quite recently, marriage has been understood as an institution that is both social and natural, supported by a network of laws, customs, and understandings that guard it as the uniquely legitimate setting for procreation and the rearing of children. It seemed very unlikely that children could be reared properly or that most men and women could find fulfillment outside marriage. Everyone knew what the parties had a right to expect from each other, and those common understandings kept it functional and reliable. Today, such understandings are weakening, and recognition of "gay marriage" would bring the trend to completion by destroying the objective function of marriage. The result would be a decisive rejection of social understandings that give sex a specific meaning, and the concomitant establishment of other understandings as authoritative for everyone who is not a hermit or radical sectarian.

If that happens, we will all have to live with the consequences of the abolition of marriage as an institution with specific natural and social functions that support definite expectations and obligations. It is neither neutral nor good sense to reduce such a fundamental change to a pure question of individual rights. We all find it difficult to avoid the way of life that finds social recognition and support among those with whom we live. That, indeed, is why many claim that homosexual attachments should receive formal social recognition and honor. The question, therefore, is whether the new way of life, in which sexual relationships are thought to have no essential nature but are simply what individuals and positive legislation make of them, will be better or worse than one that recognizes one particular social institution based on a sexual connection—the family—as natural, necessary, and prior to the state.

To impose, as a matter of human rights, the liberal answer to that question without discussion is oppressive. Traditionalist complaints that there is something oppressive about the tendencies leading to "gay marriage" puzzle liberals. It is hard to see why. Basic social principle is always backed by a system of coercion. Rights that matter have teeth. "Gay rights" have already brought us indoctrination in school and workplace and various requirements of public conformity to the new moral doctrine. In Europe, one can be fined or jailed for objecting to it. Presumably we will see much more along the same lines.

More basically, "gay marriage" and similar changes mean that arrangements based on human tendencies that appear of themselves and create patterns and attachments men live by in all societies are replaced by arrangements based on content-free abstractions like preference satisfaction and the liberal understanding of equality. The result is that self-sustaining habits, institutions, and understandings that mostly run by themselves—the sort of thing liberals refer to as "ingrained social biases"—give way to arrangements based on money, formal legal rules, and the coercive apparatus of the state. How, social conservatives ask, can that fail to mean oppression and stunted lives?

A judgment that something is oppressive depends on an overall understanding of how life works and what makes sense. Something that denies free play to things that are worthy of attachment and help constitute human life is rightly viewed as oppressive. The destruction of marriage, which people in almost all times and places have treated as a basic institution necessary to a desirable way of life for most adults and all children, is oppressive if anything is—even if the name is retained and abolition takes the form of marriage's conversion into a revocable contract of subjective content and significance for anyone who wishes it.[7]

Local Action

Political understandings become concrete and comprehensible in institutions. Actuality is persuasive. Traditionalists must offer an alternative to the current order that people can see in operation, join, and help promote, or at least find worthy of tolerance and cooperation. Such an alternative would offer a better life to those who choose it, and if accepted by even a small minority of the articulate would enlarge the world of discussion and help transform a social and political world that has grown dogmatic and narrow.

A renewed traditionalist order would require that arrangements advanced liberalism has destroyed or profoundly weakened grow back and regain their health. That is a complex matter, but it depends on something simpler, a change in fundamental orientation. A tradition is a form of life with ramifications from personal and domestic matters to grand public institutions. Each level depends on the others, but the points that orient and anchor them all are the local and personal at one end, and the metaphysical and religious at the other. The first step for the restoration of tradition is for people to orient their lives toward concerns that transcend the pragmatic here and now and do what is needed to establish the new direction and guard it from disruption.

Some among us have long been engaged in that effort. Anyone can support it by doing what he can close to home. Tradition is never far away. It does not invent but secures and fosters the good everywhere present, at least implicitly and potentially. It has a thousand points of entry and sources of guidance. Natural feelings lead toward right patterns of life. History shows how we got where we are, and the classics put us in touch with what is permanent. Living memory tells us of ways of life more in keeping with substantive goods than those now ascendant. Discussion helps clarify, broaden, and focus our thoughts. And as liberalism destroys itself, the resulting irrationality and chaos bring the opportunity for new growth.

Liberal tyranny is a soft tyranny. It depends on a pervasive system of social control that leaves little room for other ways of life but most often is not quite compulsory. There are many practical ways to fight it. It is bureaucratic, so we strike a blow by carrying on life less bureaucratically. It depends on comprehensive systems of education, training, and propaganda, so we carry on the struggle by giving other ways of thought and learning a place to exist: by homeschooling children, turning away from mass media, and developing independent institutions of knowledge.

Every man who starts his own business, every family that adds to its independence by reducing its expenses, every woman who stays home to run the household and educate her children, every local congregation that takes on more demanding standards of conduct, every independently minded scholar who writes a book, gives a speech, contributes to a little magazine, or sets up a website, establishes a zone of ordered freedom within the anarchic tyranny that is advanced liberalism. Collectively, such people can establish a living alternative to the ways and understandings now dominant. The inhumanity of life within large organizations, and the degradation of journalism, formal education, popular entertainment, and official expert opinion, will make such alternatives increasingly attractive. Eventually we may reach a tipping point, and social life begin to take on a different form.

The success of such efforts will require building up particular local communities in which traditionalist concerns have a home. Such communities cannot regenerate overnight or by detailed plan, but some needed things are evident. Tradition requires boundaries that create settings in which nonliberal forms of social organization can maintain coherence and continuity. It requires concern for education and the institutions that make possible a full community life. The next generation must be brought up to respect tradition and the transcendent more than the commercial, hedonistic, and egalitarian standards now dominant. That will not be possible unless home, school, local community, and alternative media provide a refuge of sanity from which a declining public order can be judged and found wanting. A change in orientation that begins individually and is initially perhaps backed mostly by words and gestures must grow into something far more social and comprehensive.

Public Life

Complementary efforts must extend beyond local communities into politics and public life generally. Those efforts would include practical measures to protect particular traditionalist interests from attack. The battles social conservatives have been fighting for years provide examples: the successful campaigns to defend homeschooling, and the generally less successful struggles to preserve public recognition of religion and marriage as fundamental social institutions. Such battles are necessary, but they are holding actions likely in the end to be lost unless something more basic changes.

More fundamentally, traditionalist political efforts should promote changes in general principle, possibly small in immediate effect, that open a door out of liberalism and make a better world possible. We start where we are: immediate radical change is hard to bring about and never works as intended. Final objectives should nonetheless go to the root of the matter. What is needed is not a new system built to order, which will never come into being anyway, but new fundamental principles that can work out their implications over time just as liberalism did. It took three hundred years to progress from John Locke to John Rawls. Something similar may be needed for a renewal of tradition.

In the public sphere, the single most necessary change is the disestablishment of liberalism. Constitutional adjudication, human-rights guarantees, and the conventions of public discussion must no longer impose the liberal position as the compulsory answer to all basic questions regarding social life. Concerns regarding goods other than equal freedom must be allowed to develop and take effect in accordance with their merits. The fight over the federal courts, which impose liberal standards on us all in the name of the Constitution, is rightly recognized as the single most important issue in our public life. That fight must continue, but it must be supplemented with a far more vigorous and effective campaign to persuade the articulate public that the liberal results imposed by the courts are not only extralegal and at odds with self-government but politically, socially, and morally wrong. Their imposition by judges without popular participation is not a shortcut to a plainly good end but rather a form of self-willed tyranny that rightly discredits the judiciary.

Once the possibility of a more complex public good is accepted in principle, that good can be filled out by whatever social agreements grow up and establish themselves. Politics can become once again a matter of mutual persuasion regarding the good life and the measures that foster it. Traditionalist politics are mostly a matter of shared ultimate commitments and nonideological common sense. The goods that have always been thought relevant to public life include inherited loyalties and a right relationship among social order, inherited tradition, natural law, and the highest human goals. Traditionalists should insist that such concerns once again become part of public life. To the extent that there is general agreement on them, it should be reflected in how people live together and the laws that order their mutual relations. To the extent that there is no agreement, then those involved will have to work out some sort of possibly shifting *modus vivendi*.

Such possibilities are the stuff of self-government, while the liberal solution now in vogue is a utopian and tyrannical fantasy that avoids divisive questions by imposing liberal answers without discussion. The claim that compulsory liberalism guarantees peace and freedom, while allowing other views to exert influence brings war and persecution, rests on the claim that liberalism is uniquely consensual, rational, and safe. We have seen that such claims are unfounded. Peace does not depend on a super-principle like liberal neutrality that claims to solve all basic issues in advance. It depends on habits and conventions that make disputes less frequent and moderate them when they arise. In practice, recognition that agreement cannot always be achieved can be expected to lead to attitudes and practices intended to reduce or mitigate conflict—for example, the devolution of power, a preference for inherited institutions, restraint regarding government interventions, and caution about disturbing factors like large-scale immigration. A more traditionalist system would work by prudence, local self-government, and an attachment to established arrangements rather than by an impossible conceptual perfection alleged to make all basic problems disappear.

The institutional approach suggested here is procedural and does not guarantee any particular outcome. The immediate political goal is not a New Jerusalem but the moderation of technocracy so that concerns other than the equal satisfaction of preferences can once again play a role in public life. By stages, people would develop their common understanding of the good and accept whatever laws and institutions come to seem right under such conditions. How that understanding develops would depend on leadership, experience, mutual persuasion, local traditions, and a great many other circumstances.

For example, the initial public religion in a more traditionalist America would likely be the one America had before the judicial coup of the sixties: an informally established, minimally doctrinal, and basically Protestant Christianity. Such a restored informal establishment, however minimal, would move American public life closer to what most people and traditions (including those which reject the American public religion as such) believe proper than does our current increasingly perfectionistic establishment of advanced liberalism. Such an arrangement would not satisfy everyone, but the same is true of every conceivable arrangement. Anything more specific (such as Catholicism) would lack the necessary public support; anything more abstract (such as "Judaeo-Christianity") would be an artificial construction not taken seriously. An establishment that reflects how most people actually understand the world could be more moderate and could accommodate varying views more easily than could an absolutist principle of disestablishment. Catholics and Jews did not like it when psalms from the King James Bible were read in public schools, but that practice was far more friendly to Catholicism and Judaism than what succeeded it. The nature of the religious establishment might well change as the views of the American people evolve. Such changes have to do with the public sense of what is real. They cannot be forced; their direction and pace cannot be chosen in advance.

The ultimate shape of the resulting polity, like all future things, is difficult to predict. To the extent traditional and transcendent principles answer permanent human needs, they would once again find acceptance and authority. On the other hand, if liberal modernity has led to concrete gains with an easily recognizable human value, those gains could be retained. Many liberal institutions would no doubt stay, since people would remain attached to them, especially in countries where they have long been established. Their meaning and effect would likely change, however, because they would be interpreted and applied by reference to human goods that go beyond freedom, equality, security, and prosperity. They would accommodate nonliberal principles to some degree, in somewhat the manner that American institutions historically accommodated such principles, but with a more explicit acknowledgment that it is right to do so.

Practical Guidelines

Grand visions must be pursued through specific measures. A more traditionalist polity would allow more space for natural human ways of acting than does the current one. It would be more complex and less secular than what we have now. It would recognize that man needs connections to specific individuals and larger social groups, and to an order of things that transcends and includes such things. Those connections must be reliable, substantive, and comprehensive enough to live by. Politics cannot provide them directly, but it can accommodate and facilitate them.

Specifically, a more traditionalist society would feature:

- more responsibility for localities and informal institutions, less for federal and state governments.
- sufficient local coherence and stability to foster enduring loyalties and permit distinct traditions to develop, maintain, and propagate themselves. That would require boundaries to be accepted and authority to be divided and devolved.
- less government responsibility for the material well-being of particular men, so that local and personal connections would gain in importance.
- restriction of antidiscrimination laws to particular needs and settings, for example the necessities of travelers, so that people could establish cooperative connections based on the affinities and commonalities that seem relevant to them.
- protection of rights of local economic regulation to prevent the overextension of rationalized borderless economic relationships.
- an acceptance of genuine authority that is not simply a matter of what people want. If authority is simply what people want, then there is no way to limit it and no reason anyone who disagrees should obey it. The natural consequence is unprincipled tyranny.

- a practical establishment of religion. Both genuine authority and effective free cooperation require respect for goals that transcend choice. That implies at least an informally established religion such as we had in America before the sixties.

Such conditions cannot be created by fiat. They must be intertwined with popular habits and understandings. Their realization depends on time, place, and unpredictable contingencies. Nonetheless, traditional ways have been traditional because by and large they tend to restore themselves. The simplicity, clarity, and abstraction of liberalism make it go to extremes that lead to self-destruction. It is difficult to reverse its course. The same does not apply to the principle of tradition. Political efforts to promote it, remove barriers to it, or, at a minimum, do away with attempts to eradicate it, are by no means hopeless. A reasonably coherent way of life is a practical necessity for human beings, and stable moral community is required for life to be coherent. If that is so, then one way or another what is needed will come back. If government and other social authorities are able to see that development as desirable, then they can accept and cooperate with it.

PERSUASION

Principles and goals must be backed by persuasion. Traditionalists need to articulate and present their concerns to the public so that they can inform discussion. At present those concerns are not understood. The liberal initiatives that are most visible are evidently intended to help people with problems, protect the weak from insult and injury, and allow individuals to follow their inclinations. Apart from affirmative action, which immediately burdens some people, and taxes, which cannot be cut much without cutting social benefits, people do not find that such initiatives interfere with their individual or domestic happiness. They do see problems

with the present state of affairs: public and economic life are overregu-
lated, moral and cultural decline are troubling, and the constant nagging
about health, inclusiveness, and the like is tiresome. But the difficulty of
large comparisons makes it hard to evaluate such issues, people can do
what they want individually and are mostly alright materially, and in any
event a variety of mechanisms have grown up to prevent discontent from
finding a voice and making itself effective.

Traditionalists must change that situation and with it the setting in
which battles are fought. Liberalism is inseparably a method of organizing
society and an understanding of man, knowledge, and reality. The close
connection between theory and practice makes it vulnerable to intellectual attack. The most direct way to get beyond it is to take seriously the
questions—the nature of man and the good life, the relation between the
social and transcendent—that it avoids and cannot answer except through
the imposition of principles whose biggest advantages are the support
they give dominant bureaucratic and market forms of social organization
and their ability to disguise themselves as neutral and purely rational.

Questions regarding such issues are unavoidable, and advanced liberalism cannot survive their full consideration. "Political correctness," the
centralization of intellectual life, and tendencies such as scientism, multiculturalism, and postmodernism obfuscate them and keep them from arising, to some extent. But modern communications, and a principle of free
discussion that retains some cogency in spite of political correctness and
the triumph of the expert, make it difficult to suppress them altogether.

Social Class and Outlook

Present-day political alignments depend on fundamental understandings.[8] If you believe that the social world is self-contained and homoge-
neous and consists solely of individuals and various contractual and legal
arrangements, you are likely to be liberal. If you believe that the social

world is composed of a number of very different things whose overall coherence and functioning depend on a larger setting that finally escapes
our grasp, you are likely to be traditionalist. Where you stand on that
issue is strongly affected by social position. If you are married with children or socially middling, you are likely to be traditionalist.[9] You will recognize that the world is bigger than you and your desires, that it cannot
be altogether understood or controlled, and that it is our personal, local,
and transcendent connections and loyalties that enable us to deal with it.
If you are unmarried, dysfunctional,[10] a celebrity, or a top expert, bureau-
crat, manager, lawyer, or financier, you are likely to be liberal. You will be
less impressed with the solidity of the world and will rely less on personal
and transcendent ties and disciplines.

The classes influential in public discussion today—journalists, policy experts, social scientists, and political operatives—constitute a highly
trained meritocracy. They favor the technocratic liberalism that pays for
their services and makes them important. Their position leads them to
believe that large formal organizations and the ways of thinking that
animate them are adequate to all issues. Education and scholarship provide no corrective for their prejudices, because in their current form those
things are detached from any inherited way of life and subordinate to the
needs of formal public institutions. Their function is to develop perspectives, ideas, and information useful to markets and bureaucracies, and to
train young people so that they are adapted to institutional demands.

Those at home in such a setting base their sense of who they are less
on the things traditionalists care about than on money, academic background, and career. Their affiliations lead them to look at society from
above, as a neutral system to be supervised, controlled, and reconfigured
by experts and functionaries to advance the goals that seem sensible to
them. They think it rational to replace traditional institutions like family, religion, and local community by principles that seem simpler, more

direct, and easier to understand and manage—contract, expertise, individual choice, and bureaucratic regulation. In effect, they favor daycare centers, counseling services, family court, and fast food over the traditional family.

The latter depends for reliable functioning on traditional understandings of sex roles, sexual conduct, and parental authority, none of which can be supervised and managed from above in the interest of efficiency and equality. Accordingly, technocrats reject those understandings. The moral standards they consider objectively valid are formal public rights and obligations. Everything else is personal morality that is strictly private and not a legitimate topic of public concern or comment. Such a view favors their interests, since it suppresses competing principles of social organization; and they also find it personally acceptable, since like most people on top they think they can get what they want in personal relations and will lose more than they gain from a definite system of informal social obligations.

The attempt to simplify, rationalize, and manage social relations seems to many people today as obviously correct as socialism did in the 1930s and 1940s. It seems irrational simply to accept what has been passed down. Furthermore, informal traditional institutions depend on traditional prejudices and stereotypes, which seem unfounded and unjust. People who believe that the point of life is the satisfaction of preferences find an emphasis on what precedes and transcends desire incomprehensible. They see politics and history as a struggle between oppression and liberation. They regard traditionalism as an attempt to bring back old oppressions. The result is that skepticism regarding bureaucratic and contractual solutions is considered equivalent to indifference, irrationality, or worse. Sympathy with traditional moral positions is considered a sort of mental illness.

Making the Case

To make their case, traditionalists must devise ways of presenting their views that are vivid and forceful enough to overcome deep class biases as well as an organization of knowledge and system of intellectual training that excludes their concerns and is backed by everything authoritative and powerful. To make the task harder, it is difficult for traditionalists to be glib. They look at society from within and accept that we cannot fully grasp it but must work with what grows up and attracts the attachment of the people. The lack of a simple theory with a quick answer to all questions fits normal experience but is unhelpful in a time when slogans and sound bites rule, when liberalism permeates accepted beliefs and understandings, and when punchy arguments seem necessary to bounce the discussion out of the rut in which it is stuck.

The position is far from hopeless, however. The goal for traditionalists is less to overcome our fellow citizens than to bring them to realize where their best hopes and fundamental sympathies lie. Traditionalist arguments have staying power. In the end, we all look at life not from above but from within. We are human beings more than members of this class or that, and everyone, no matter what his schooling and position, must confront the same basic problems. A functionary is also a son, brother, husband, and father, a man of particular background, loyalties, and ideals of life who hopes for the good and at some point must face loss and death. When pushed by circumstances, even highly trained people notice when events contradict what the authorities say. At some point, liberals are likely to doubt liberalism and look for something else. Traditionalists must be ready to help them.

What we need is a reappropriation of the whole truth of human life, the loss of which has led to current disorders. Traditionalists can aid that process by insisting on disfavored truths. The intrinsic weaknesses, pragmatic failures, and overwhelming institutional dominance of the liberal and technocratic outlook, together with its emphasis on discussion and clear rationality, make it an easy target in some very important ways if traditionalists can collect their thoughts, find their voices, and go on the offensive. The possibility of breaking the spell of technocratic expertise by the forceful and repeated questioning and presentation of an articulate alternative is within traditionalists' reach.

In spite of New Class dominance, Western polities allow anyone to participate in public discussion. There are ways of channeling and suppressing discussion, but also a thousand forums—dinner-table conversations, local meetings, letters to editors and public officials, radio call-in shows, little magazines, Internet discussions, websites and blogs, campaigns of minor political parties—that permit any of us, at least in America, to present almost any view he thinks right. The expert monopoly on knowledge and discussion has never been absolute, since everyone has his own opinions and points of special knowledge, and the Internet is weakening it by multiplying the possibilities of communication and discussion. A few intelligent, well-informed, and forthright voices in each forum arguing for traditional ways and against the new order could have a powerful effect on the correlation of intellectual forces and eventually on the social order itself.

Those who favor tradition must contest the assumptions and language now dominant. They must insistently pose the most basic questions in every possible setting: What is liberalism? How does it work? What are its strengths and weaknesses? Is liberal rationality rational? Is neutrality neutral? Are we really liberals? Can we live as such? What alternatives are there? Liberal rhetoric must be deflated, the possibility of social technology disputed, the failures of the new order driven home, its Whiggish history debunked, traditional understandings justified, liberal modernity deprived of the appearance of moderation and rationality, and its narrowness and brutal implications displayed. Since liberalism falls short by leaving out too much, the reality of things that cannot be reduced to what we think, see, want, and control must be asserted and emphasized. Man must be shown to be a creature that lives by concrete loyalties and transcendent goods as well as by utilitarian calculations and arbitrary whims. Human life is a compound not only of impulse, appetite, and technology but also of essences and particularities—man and woman, Christian and Confucian, Swiss and Spaniard.

The point of contesting language and assumptions is to force issues to be faced directly. Liberalism calls for turning all social life into a rational system for advancing the pleasure and power of each individual separately. Yet it does not and cannot leave the nature of the social world up to the individual. It says we all have to live in the kind of society it likes, insists that we consent to it, and increasingly tells us that we must celebrate it. If those things are good, then liberalism is good. If they are bad, because they defeat their own purposes, distort the human good, and impose a tyranny of experts, functionaries, and money, then liberalism is bad. To claim that liberalism is entitled to automatic victory because it is neutral and lets everyone live as he likes is an obfuscation that should be exposed so that the real issues can be discussed.

Such discussions matter, for liberalism is not a system of mindless power. It depends on theory, at least in part, and those who live by the word die by the word. Boldness and clarity of statement on basic points are more important than immediate success. Rather than rephrasing their goals in liberal terms for the sake of camouflage and tactical advantage, traditionalists should confront notions like "neutrality," "inclusiveness," and "secularism" directly and vigorously, and with them the belief that liberal goals and standards are unquestionably right.

Above all, traditionalists must claim the high ground. They must keep alive truths that are deeper and more comprehensive than those modernity recognizes. Liberals and the Left have claimed idealism as their own, but the claim is fading. Traditionalism has a different idealism that is more enduring because it is more in line with permanent realities. It accepts the complexity and necessary imperfection of all social arrangements, but it does not treat imperfection as the final word. Evil exists because man is free to go wrong. Without that freedom, and without the transcendent goods that liberalism ignores and suppresses, man would lose his dignity. In opposition to utopian modernity, which ends in inhuman social mechanism, traditionalists' acceptance of both imperfection and transcendence makes it possible to recognize the irreducible freedom and responsibility of each human soul—and the eternal possibilities of hope and action, as well as the unavoidable reality of evil.

Into the Trenches

Concrete arguments presented by a traditionalist movement would be varied and mostly ad hoc. They could include appeals to American traditions of localism, voluntary cooperation, and limited government, which are consistent with the informal institutional autonomy on which tradition depends. Such arguments would make the case that liberalism is oppressive by its own standards, and that traditional ways should be accepted if only for the sake of a less self-defeating interpretation of fairness and tolerance. Traditionalists might, for example, present their own version of the rights that make sense in a diverse and tolerant society:

- The right to resist reprogramming. If school, employer, and government want to turn you and your children into a new kind of person for a new society in which commerce and bureaucracy count for everything and settled ways of life for nothing, the effort is tyrannical and you have the right and duty to resist.
- The right to live in a way with long-standing local backing that is capable of ordering a productive and satisfying way of life. If

an experiment in living[11]—acceptance of traditional sex-role ste-reotypes, for example—has been going on for a long time, does not require the use of force against others, and has enabled many to live in a way they have found good, it is not the job of govern-ment to squash it.

- The right to choose one's associates, especially on grounds long found relevant to the choice. That right is necessary for the au-tonomy and health of local and traditional institutions that de-pend on informal ties and common understandings for their functioning. Forthright assertion of the right is needed to call inclusiveness into question as a good that trumps all others.

- The right to refuse to support social causes one rejects for widely accepted and enduring reasons. The fact that an attitude is deeply rooted in social understandings should count *for* and not against it. Why should a printer, for example, be required to print invita-tions for a "gay wedding" if he objects?

- The right in public life to make the arguments and act (within generally applicable law) on the principles that seem right based on one's best understanding of how the world really is. There is no obligation—in a social order claiming to be based on popular rule and free discussion—to exclude religion from public life.

Such arguments would dramatize liberal intolerance and help limit the ability of the liberal state to pose as the vindicator of live-and-let-live against traditionalist bigotry. They would help start a conversation that does not take the correctness of the liberal position for granted.[12] They should not be pressed too far, however, since the ultimate point is not that tolerance must be perfected but that it is a limited and relative good that becomes destructive when made a final standard. The primary tra-ditionalist argument must be a positive one, that traditionalist positions are right, or at least reasonable and socially beneficial. Complaints that liberal initiatives make life difficult for traditionalists and so deny them equal rights are not likely to get far with those taught to think of tradition as ignorant, obstructive, and dangerous.

The most important goal for traditionalists in politics is to persuade those persons not strongly attached to any definite tradition that they should see tradition as good and its disruption by the politically correct welfare state as bad. Pragmatic success on any large scale is likely to be slow: the traditionalist outlook is deeply at odds with modern public understandings. Nonetheless, traditionalists should develop and live by their best understanding of what is good and present their case as best they can, in season and out of season. The problems are real, the arguments are cogent, time clarifies issues, and the views of even a tiny minority can be influential, especially if they express durable aspects of human life that established views ignore and suppress. Changes in public orientation can be surprisingly fast when suppressed concerns finally reenter public discussion. Nor should expertise be written off: scientists and scholars are interested in how things work, and if there are problems with technocracy they will eventually want to understand them. The truth will out, and when conditions change what seems inconceivable can quickly become reality.

CHAPTER ELEVEN

Looking Forward

THE IMMEDIATE OUTLOOK FOR TRADITIONALISM IS BAD. TRADITION IS what is settled and taken for granted. It is not normally made for combat, and it defends itself awkwardly and too late. Those who deny its authority have apparently swept all before them. They select the facts and create the language, images, and myths current in public discussion. Modern communications turn their views into a universal flood, and it is hard to avoid a soaking. Principled resistance counts as schism and heresy. Those who object have trouble finding their footing, and they often fall back on obstinacy and a refusal to think as means of defense.

The current situation reflects the deep roots of liberal modernity in Western life and thought. It is radically exacerbated by political centralization, huge bureaucracies, world markets, fast and cheap travel, mass commercial culture, instantaneous broadband electronic communications, and radical state-enforced equality. Those things show no sign of abating. Nonetheless, everything comes to an end. Liberalism defeats its own goals of public rationality and private satisfaction, and it even prevents its own social and physical reproduction. What is at odds with human nature cannot last. Man can be disordered, corrupted, and killed but not corrected, neutered, and made manageable. Nor can thought, knowledge, and decision be made altogether explicit, as is demanded by liberalism. Our public life is now based on what is functionally a religion that is hard to make sense of, harder to believe, and relies on deceiving both ourselves and others about the most basic things.

While history is not over, a particular history—the progressive development of Western society toward a particular ideal of rational order—appears finished. Signs that liberal modernity has reached the end of its possibilities include diminishing birthrates; the disappearance of hope and idealism; the growing ignorance and hatred of what the West has been; the decline and suppression of free and rational public life; and the absorption of art, literature, and philosophy into ideology, careerism, publicity, sensation, and perversion. If such conditions persist—and it is hard to see what within liberalism can stop them—they mean the end of liberal society.

It is impossible to predict the specific effect of future contingencies, such as changes in populations, loss of social and moral cohesion, environmental catastrophe, terrorism, and war. Basic principles suggest general probabilities. There is no social machine that runs of itself, and it seems unlikely that the current regime can manage administratively, through incentives, training, therapy, and warehousing, the organizational and behavioral problems that result from the destruction of informal social ties and traditional standards of behavior. Furthermore, the replacement of aging First World populations by Third World immigrants may well make continuation of the liberal state impossible.[1] It seems likely that the demands emergencies make on social systems that are becoming less and less able to rely on settled loyalties and informal connections will make politics increasingly unprincipled and brutal. Recent tendencies toward terrorism, torture, and preemptive war may be only the beginning. Liberalism is likely to become little more than a perfunctory justification for societies that work in a far more primitive way. What we look forward to is less "history" as continued meaningful development than incoherence, arbitrariness, and the reign of brute fact and cynical propaganda, moderated or exacerbated by eternal human virtues, vices, and limitations.

However, disorder is not final. The particular and prerational are the raw material of social life. They become civil through tradition, and civility attracts us more than does chaos. It therefore seems certain that in some way trends toward radical individualism, egalitarianism, and hedonism will be reversed, and that the moral and social future will resemble the past more than the present. Man needs a life in common with his fellows, and common life requires common understandings of the world and our place in it. Society depends on authority, and authority depends on an acceptance of principles that precede particular goals. Tradition and religion answer such needs. They are never lost altogether, and they always restore themselves. Even today they permeate the fine texture of social life if not public doctrine.

The more the present order destroys coherent traditions of life the more it destroys its own future. If current understandings of reason are too narrow for our needs then others will develop. The best hope is that evident inadequacies and antistatist trends will limit reliance on the advanced liberalism that now dominates public life and that they will allow it to weaken as its deficiencies become more obvious, so that liberal society can transform itself into something fundamentally different. Suppressed traditions may find their voice and reassert themselves, sustaining principles may sprout and take root. A comparatively smooth transition to something better is possible, and we should do what we can to promote it.

Man proposes, but God disposes. A common understanding of reason and the good cannot be forced on people or made to order. It is difficult for us to do more than refine and reconfigure what already exists. We will undoubtedly continue to see repeated attempts to find a way out of our difficulties that amount either to reinventing liberalism or bringing back earlier modes of life and thought. I have argued that the former leads nowhere, because liberalism is based so much on clear, simple principles that leave little room for new growth. Most observers consider the latter impossible as well, although the possibility remains that liberal modernity in its current form is an extreme deviation within the Christian civilization of the West rather than its ultimate fate. If Christianity provides the most complete form of life possible, as its adherents believe, then a reversion of Western civilization to type and thus to Christendom remains a possibility. Only time will tell.

Even a bad system is unlikely to be abandoned unless there is something definite to replace it that people are ready to accept. Until that happens, life bumps on, held together by anything available, even by dreams that cannot be realized. For the immediate future we are likely to remain stuck within liberal modernity, at least in public life, except to the extent that individuals and small groups can make their way to something more hopeful.

One possible outcome of present tendencies is a Soviet-style implosion. If all social order becomes dependent on the administrative state, when that becomes terminally corrupt and nonfunctional everything goes. Another possibility is the growth of sectarian religious communities, leading either to a new Constantinism, as one community comes to set the tone for society at large, or to a neo-Levantine form of society made up of a loose assemblage of ethnoreligious groups under unprincipled military or dynastic rule. The growth of religious communities seems likely, since people have to organize their lives somehow, and consumerism, careerism, and political correctness are evidently inadequate for that purpose. They cannot motivate reproduction, for example, and in the end Darwin is likely to prevail—whatever the consequences for Darwinians.[2] Whether such religious communities will lead to a rebirth of public life on a newly substantive basis or to its final disappearance cannot be predicted. The former development would require a general recognition of concrete public spiritual authority of the type that once made Christendom possible, and it is possible that recognition of that necessity will guide developments.

However these things may be, the crisis will eventually resolve itself. Faith is necessary to knowledge, tradition is necessary for human beings to order their lives reasonably, and what is fundamental is resilient and eventually finds its place in the world. The task of those persons who recognize the defects of the current order is to understand it for what it is, to resist it, to keep alive what they can for better days, to take advantage of the rights or favors it grants, to ask the questions from which all religion and tradition spring, to pursue what answers seem best, and to make the case, in season and out, for something more worthy of humanity.

The answer to today's confusions, in other words, lies in faith, the realization that we do not make the world, that we recognize rather than create the good, beautiful, and true, and that to do so adequately we must draw on a wisdom greater than our own. Our acts can make sense and be fruitful only as part of an order for good founded in the nature of things. In spite of its apparent strength, liberalism is based on a refusal to face obvious human limitations and on a fear of anything greater than ourselves. Unable to deal with suffering, death, or the transcendent goods that give life its order and meaning, liberalism must fail. The world belongs to tradition, because only tradition connects us to the world as it is.

Notes

––––––––

Chapter One: Liberal Tyranny

1. John R. Lott Jr., "More Gun Controls? They Haven't Worked in the Past," *Wall Street Journal*, June 19, 1999, Eastern ed.; Daniel Patrick Moynihan, "Toward a New Intolerance," *Public Interest* (Summer 1993): 119–22.

2. For a general discussion of the current regime upon which I draw here and elsewhere in this book, see Paul Edward Gottfried's trilogy: *After Liberalism: Mass Democracy in the Managerial State* (Princeton, NJ: Princeton University Press 1999), *Multiculturalism and the Politics of Guilt: Toward a Secular Theocracy* (Columbia, MO: University of Missouri Press 2002), and *The Strange Death of Marxism: The European Left in the New Millennium* (Columbia, MO: University of Missouri Press 2005). For a review and discussion of the three books, see James Kalb, "Stalking the Therapeutic State," *Political Science Reviewer* 35 (2006): 380–415.

3. See, e.g., Frederick R. Lynch, *Invisible Victims: White Males and the Crisis of Affirmative Action* (New York: Greenwood Press, 1989).

Chapter Two: Principles

1. See Francis Fukuyama, *The End of History and the Last Man* (New York: Free Press, 1992).

2. See, e.g., chapter 1 of Gottfried, *After Liberalism*, 3–29

3. See, e.g., chapter 4 of John Stuart Mill, *Utilitarianism* (Indianapolis: Hackett Publishing Com-

pany, 2001), 35–41, where he argues that the desirable cannot be distinguished from the desired.

4. Judith Shklar, "The Liberalism of Fear," in Nancy L. Rosenblum, ed., *Liberalism and the Moral Life* (Cambridge, MA: Harvard University Press, 1989): 21–38, 21.

5. See Chapter 8 for a general discussion of tradition.

6. Tony Blair's speech to the Labour Party conference on September 28, 1999 provides an example of the integration of economism with liberal standards for freedom and equality. "UK Politics: Tony Blair's Speech in Full," *BBC News*, September 28, 1999, http://news.bbc.co.uk/1/hi/uk_politics/460009.stm (accessed December 6, 2007).

7. Germany, in which prostitution is now officially treated like other occupations, has recently been a leader in this movement of rationalization. Human nature persists, though, so problems have surfaced: prostitutes and their associates are reluctant to join the legal economy, and unemployed women are alarmed by the suggestion that they might lose benefits if they turn down a job at a brothel. Isabelle de Pommereau, "Rethinking a Legal Sex Trade," *Christian Science Monitor*, May 11, 2005.

8. Alternatively, the demand for the effective abolition of marriage can be put in multiculturalist terms: marital customs differ somewhat from community to community, so it would be oppressive and indeed racist to treat any particular ones as authoritative. It follows that all must be made a matter of private taste and thereby deprived of their public function.

9. For an account of certain differences between Japanese and Western modes of social and economic organization, see Robert Locke, "Japan, Refutation of Neoliberalism," *Post-Autistic Economics Review* 23 (January 5, 2004), http://www.paecon.net/PAEReview/issue23/Locke23.htm (accessed December 6, 2007).

10. Francis Bacon, *The Advancement of Learning* (Sioux Falls, SD: NuVision Publications, 2005), 41.

11. See Victor Davis Hanson, *Carnage and Culture: Landmark Battles in the Rise to Western Power* (New York: Doubleday, 2001), on Western distinctives in general, and the author's introduction to Alexis de Tocqueville, *Democracy in America*, vol. 1 (New York: Vintage Books, 1945): 3–17, on the long-term Western tendency toward freedom and equality.

12. *Planned Parenthood v. Casey*, 505 U.S. 833, 851 (1992).

13. Since animals also have preferences, "animal rights" are a major issue for contemporary liberalism.

14. A variety of considerations, including the difficulty of measuring subjective satisfaction, has led many liberal thinkers to favor equalizing resources rather than equalizing satisfactions. Most would also follow John Rawls in permitting inequalities that have the effect of increasing the satisfactions of the worst off. See John Rawls, *A Theory of Justice* (Cambridge, MA: The Belknap Press of Harvard University Press, 1971).

15. The First World War, together with developments such as the atomic bomb and environmental degradation, have sometimes led many liberals, at least rhetorically, to question the goodness of modern natural science. However, concerns such as the dangers of "fundamentalism" seem largely to have brought back the older progressivist view.

16. According to Leo Strauss, "Hobbes reduced virtue to the social virtue of peaceableness." *Natu-*

ral Right and History (Chicago: The University of Chicago Press, 1953), 187. See Strauss's comments on John Locke: "By building civil society on the 'low but solid ground' of selfishness or of certain 'private vices,' one will achieve much greater 'public benefits' than by futilely appealing to virtue, which is by nature 'unendowed.'" Ibid., 247. Also see Albert O. Hirschman, *The Passions and the Interests: Arguments for Capitalism Before Its Triumph* (Princeton, NJ: Princeton University Press, 1977), for an analysis of how capitalist productivity was seen in the early-modern era as a way to get rid of the feudal warrior ethos.

17. The Legalists in ancient China made similar use of Taoist concepts on behalf of unlimited state tyranny. See Vitaly A. Rubin, *Individual and State in Ancient China: Essays on Four Chinese Philosophers*, trans. Steven I. Levine (New York: Columbia University Press, 1976).

Chapter Three: Institutions

1. See James Madison, *The Federalist*, No. 10, in James Madison, Alexander Hamilton, John Jay, and James Madison, *The Federalist* (New York: The Modern Library, 1941): 53–62, for a classic exposition of the view that free and rational government is best secured in an extensive republic with numerous factions none of which is in a position to impose its will.

2. Examples include the almost total failure to enforce sanctions against employers of illegal aliens and the massive official resistance to California's Proposition 209, which supposedly put an end to state-sponsored racial preferences. On the latter point, see Heather Mac Donald, "Elites to Anti–Affirmative Action Voters: Drop Dead," *City Journal* (Winter 2007): 14–29, and Harold Johnson, "California's Quota Commandoes Are Still Winning Victories," FrontPageMagazine.com (October 17, 2002), http://www.frontpagemag.com/Articles/Printable.asp?ID=3937 (accessed December 6, 2007). More generally, see John Leo, "Officeholders Favoring Diversity Ignore Laws They Don't Like," Universal Press Syndicate syndicated column (June 25, 2006).

3. For an account of the political benefits to governing elites of mass immigration, see Fredo Arias-King, "Immigration and Usurpation: Elites, Power, and the People's Will," Center for Immigration Studies Backgrounder (July 2006), http://www.cis.org/articles/2006/back706.html (accessed December 6, 2007).

4. For an account of the deception and technocratic fantasy at the heart of what is called the European project, see Christopher Booker and Richard North, *The Great Deception: Can the European Union Survive?*, 2nd ed. (London: Continuum International Publishing Group, 2005). As the authors point out, supranational political integration and technocratic rule has always been the goal of the project, with the ostensible practical economic goals as a pretext.

5. Theodor W. Adorno, Else Frenkel-Brunswik, Daniel J. Levinson, and R. Nevitt Sanford, *The Authoritarian Personality* (New York: Harper & Row, 1950). For an analysis of the political tendentiousness of that book see Gottfried, *After Liberalism*, 91–95.

6. Richard Hofstadter, "The Paranoid Style in American Politics," *Harper's Magazine* (November, 1964): 77–86.

7. A recent academic example of the medicalization of dissent is John T. Jost, Jack Glaser, Arie W. Kruglanski, and Frank J. Sulloway, "Political Conservatism as Motivated Social Cognition," *Psychological Bulletin*, 129:3 (2003): 339–75, which finds that the core of political conservatism is resistance to change and tolerance for inequality, with common psychological factors including fear and aggression, dogmatism and intolerance of ambiguity, uncertainty avoidance, need for cognitive closure, and "terror management" (concern with fear and threat).

8. See Gerard Alexander, "Illiberal Europe," *Weekly Standard* (April 10, 2006): 32–36, and the many resources available from Eugene Volokh's website "Freedom of Speech vs. Workplace Harassment Law—A Growing Conflict," http://www.law.ucla.edu/volokh/harass/ (accessed December 6, 2007). Examples of criminal convictions for criticizing homosexuality include the following:

- The High Court in Britain upheld the conviction and fining of an elderly preacher who held up a sign in a town square calling for an end to homosexuality, lesbianism, and immorality and was thrown to the ground and pelted with dirt and water by an angry crowd. Richard Savill, "Preacher's Conviction over Anti-Gay Sign Upheld," *Telegraph*, January 14, 2004.

- French philosophy professor and politician Christian Vanneste was required to pay fines, damages, and other costs totaling several thousand euros for saying "homosexual behavior endangers the survival of humanity" and "heterosexuality is morally superior to homosexuality." Anne Chemin, "Le député UMP Christian Vanneste condamné pour injures homophobes," *Le Monde*, January 26, 2006; Colin Randall, "MP Faces Jail over Anti-Gay Comments," *Telegraph*, December 15, 2005.

- Four Swedish men were fined and given suspended prison sentences or probation (the trial court had imposed actual prison time in two cases but the Supreme Court suspended the sentences) for passing out leaflets that claimed, among other things, that "HIV and AIDS appeared early in homosexuals, and their promiscuous lifestyles have been one of the main reasons for this modern plague gaining a foothold." "Far-Right Group Convicted for Gay Hate Pamphlets," *Local*, July 6, 2006, http://www.thelocal.se/article.php?ID=4266&date=20060706 (accessed December 6, 2007).

9. Responses to research findings on human differences provides an example of the political management of science. See Bernard D. Davis, "Neo-Lysenkoism, IQ, and the Press," *Public Interest* 74 (Fall 1983): 41–59, for a discussion of a specific example that was remarkably successful among the educated public: Stephen Jay Gould's *The Mismeasure of Man* (New York: Norton, 1981). For a specific instance of the response to inconvenient research findings, see the symposium on Richard J. Herrnstein and Charles Murray, *The Bell Curve: Intelligence and Class Structure in American Life* (New York: Free Press, 1994), in the October 31, 1994, issue of the *New Republic*. More generally, see Steven Pinker, *The Blank Slate: The Modern Denial of Human Nature* (New York: Viking, 2002). It is worth noting that while politically correct science, or what is claimed to be science, usually

denies innate differences, it can reverse itself opportunistically, as with claims that science has demonstrated that homosexuality is innate and therefore beyond criticism.

10. See Tocqueville: "No vice of the human heart is so acceptable to [despotism] as selfishness: a despot easily forgives his subjects for not loving him, provided they do not love one another. He does not ask them to assist him in governing the state; it is enough that they do not aspire to govern it themselves. He stigmatizes as turbulent and unruly spirits those who would combine their exertions to promote the prosperity of the community; and, perverting the natural meaning of words, he applauds as good citizens those who have no sympathy for any but themselves." *Democracy in America*, vol. 2, 109.

11. For the effect of advanced liberalism on small-scale local human connections, see Robert D. Putnam, *Bowling Alone: The Collapse and Revival of American Community* (New York: Simon & Schuster, 2000), 352: "In small-town America in the 1950s people were deeply engaged in community life, but to many this surfeit of social capital seemed to impose conformity. Then in the sixties tolerance and diversity blossomed, matching almost precisely the decline in social capital." Also see Lynn Smith-Lovin, Miller McPherson, and Matthew Brashears, "Social Isolation in America: Changes in Core Discussion Networks over Two Decades," *American Sociological Review* 71:3 (2006): 353–375, finding that Americans have notably fewer close friends than in the past.

Putnam tries to save the day for tolerance and diversity by pointing out that "joiners" like to meet more kinds of people than stay-at-homes, and that places like Vermont, which are notable for cultural coherence and economic equality, have more civic engagement and social capital and also more tolerance than deeply divided places like Mississippi. It is of course not surprising that places where social coherence can be taken for granted should consequently feature tolerant social engagement. To say that is not to say that increasing diversity and making tolerance a legal requirement will increase social engagement.

12. Special rules apply to the illiberal views and practices of minority communities, such as Muslims in the West, which are generally somewhat favored. One German court, for example, declined to treat wife-beating as a hardship justifying an accelerated divorce proceeding because of Koranic justification of the practice. Veit Medick and Anna Reimann, "A German Judge Cites Koran in Divorce Case," *Spiegel Online*, March 21, 2007, http://www.spiegel.de/international/germany/0,1518,473017,00.html (accessed December 6, 2007). Giving such views and practices favorable treatment makes the informal traditional arrangements of the once-dominant majority less authoritative. That in turn makes state and expert guidance more necessary for peaceful and efficient social functioning.

13. James Tooley, *The Miseducation of Women* (Chicago: Ivan R. Dee, 2003), xi.

14. See, e.g., Allan C. Carlson, *The Swedish Experiment in Family Politics: The Myrdals and the Interwar Population Crisis* (New Brunswick, NJ: Transaction Press, 1990).

15. For a general discussion of the nature and development of human rights, see Asbjorn Eide, "The Historical Significance of the Universal Declaration," *International Social Science Journal* 50:3

(December 1998): 475–98. For a discussion of the relation between human-rights theory and local particularities, see Heiner Bielefeldt, "Muslim Voices in the Human Rights Debate," *Human Rights Quarterly* 17:4 (1995): 587–617. Both essays are written from the standard point of view favoring the current official understanding of human rights.

16. See UN General Assembly, 44th Session, *Convention on the Rights of the Child*, G.A. res. 44/25, annex, 44 U.N. GAOR Supp. (No. 49) at 167, U.N. Doc. A/44/49 (1989), and UN General Assembly, 34th Session, *Convention on the Elimination of All Forms of Discrimination against Women*, G.A. res. 47/94, 47 U.N. GAOR Supp. (No. 49) at 175, U.N. Doc. A/47/49 (1992). The former, for example, appears to allow parents only doubtful authority to control their children's choice of associates and entertainment. See David M. Smolin, "Will International Human Rights Be Used as a Tool of Cultural Genocide? The Interaction of Human Rights Norms, Religion, Culture and Gender," *Journal of Law and Religion* 12:1 (1996): 143–71, and Patrick F. Fagan, "How U.N. Conventions On Women's and Children's Rights Undermine Family, Religion, and Sovereignty," Heritage Foundation Backgrounder #1407 (February 5, 2001), http://www.heritage.org/Research/InternationalOrganizations/BG1407.cfm (accessed December 6, 2007).

17. For a brief account of how human-rights conventions transfer power upward and away from the people, see Klaus Dieter Wolf, "Die Entrechtung des Souveräns: Internationale Konventionen höhlen die Demokratie aus," *Schweizerzeit*, April 6, 2001.

18. David K. Shipler, *A Country of Strangers: Black and White in America* (New York: Vintage Books, 1998), 491.

19. The required terminology changes: "crippled" becomes "handicapped" and then "disabled" or even "differently abled," while a "negro" born in 1935 has by stages found himself transformed into a "Negro," a "black," and now an "African American."

20. See, e.g., Stephan Thernstrom and Abigail Thernstrom, *America in Black and White: One Nation, Indivisible* (New York: Simon & Schuster, 1997), 498–99; Dinesh D'Souza, *The End of Racism: Principles for a Multiracial Society* (New York: Free Press, 1995), 490.

21. *The Oxford English Dictionary*, 2nd ed. (New York: Oxford University Press, 1989).

22. Eric Pace, "George Dunne, 92, Priest and Ecumenist, Dies," *New York Times*, July 14, 1998.

23. John Jay, *The Federalist*, No. 2, in Alexander Hamilton, John Jay, and James Madison, *The Federalist*, 9.

24. Opposition to bigotry often seems specifically aimed at sexually normal white men. In their case, it is thought to include any distrust of others, any special concern or preference for their own, and any recognition of people like themselves as a particular kind of people with particular qualities, some of them good. In contrast, women praise women and complain about men quite freely in public, and public statements by blacks can be hateful without consequence. See, e.g., *End of Racism*, 400 ff.

It seems paradoxical to suggest that an animus against majority white men could have influence when it is mostly majority white men who run things, but our ruling elites value themselves for education, ideology, and social position rather than for their traditional identities. Their claim to rule is based on their superiority to such identities, and they can demonstrate their superiority while currying minority support by making targets of rank-and-file white men. In the case of affirmative action, governing elites routinely override lopsided popular majorities that would protect whites, and to some degree men, from adverse treatment.

At bottom, however, such tendencies have a largely principled explanation. The movement against bigotry naturally favors whatever weakens the ability of traditional distinctions to function, and encouraging minority group feeling and assertiveness sets ethnic and sexual ties and distinctions against each other and so makes them less functional as principles of social order. What looks like a double standard serves the stated overall goal of the movement.

25. See chapters 1 and 11 of Andreas Kinneging, *Aristocracy, Antiquity and History* (New Brunswick NJ: Transaction Publishers, 1997), on the contrasting ontologies of classicism and modernity, the former featuring a real world of essences and natural ends known by reason and the latter a purely technological outlook.

26. Cf. Gottfried, *After Liberalism*, 137.

27. The tendency can be seen in the Address of Pope Paul VI during the Last General Meeting of the Second Vatican Council on December 7, 1965: "The religion of the God who became man has met the religion (for such it is) of man who makes himself God. And what happened? Was there a clash, a battle, a condemnation? There could have been, but there was none. . . . A feeling of boundless sympathy has permeated the whole of it. The attention of our council has been absorbed by the discovery of human needs (and these needs grow in proportion to the greatness which the son of the earth claims for himself). . . . A wave of affection and admiration flowed from the council over the modern world of humanity. . . . The modern world's values were not only respected but honored, its efforts approved, its aspirations purified and blessed." http://www.vatican.va/holy_father/paul_vi/speeches/1965/documents/hf_p-vi_spe_19651207_epilogo-concilio_en.html (accessed December 6, 2007). For Paul VI, such sentiments had to do with a pastoral approach balanced by other more fundamental concerns, but others within the church have been less restrained.

Chapter Four: Through the Looking Glass

1. Rawls proposes a conception of "reasonableness"—a taste for cooperation as an equal to bring about one's own goals—to serve as a motive for people to come together and support his "political liberalism." John Rawls, *Political Liberalism* (New York: Columbia University Press, 1993). He does not say why everyone should have that motive and no other—for example, a taste for cooperation that accepts hierarchy as necessary in various ways for virtue, community, and transcendent goods.

2. Anthony Lewis, "Abroad at Home: Right To Life," *New York Times*, March 12, 1993. It is alarming to consider what Mr. Lewis might have said were he not so devoted to nonideological tolerance and compromise. Similarly, Arthur M. Schlesinger Jr. tells us that "most of the killing taking place around the world has been caused by religious conflict," predicts that "unrebuked and unchecked,

fundamentalists of all faiths will continue to believe that they are serving God by mayhem and murder," and worries that "more than a third of American adults claim that God speaks to them directly. Am I alone in finding this a scary statistic?" Arthur M. Schlesinger Jr., "The Worst Corruption," *Wall Street Journal*, Eastern ed., November 22, 1995.

3. For an account of how a combination of political requirements and the need to avoid offending pressure groups affect public school textbooks, see Diane Ravitch, *The Language Police: How Pressure Groups Restrict What Students Learn* (New York: Knopf, 2003), and Diane Ravitch, "Education after the Culture Wars," *Dædalus* 131:3 (Summer 2002): 5–21. Accounts of curricula and classroom presentations, which are less exposed to public scrutiny, are more anecdotal, impressionistic, polemical, and contested, but they suggest that more play is given to the mostly left-wing biases of professional educators. See, e.g., David Horowitz, *Indoctrination U: The Left's War Against Academic Freedom* (New York: Encounter Books, 2007); Ben Shapiro, *Brainwashed: How Universities Indoctrinate America's Youth* (Nashville, TN: Thomas Nelson, 2004).

4. Polling data indicates that a quarter of American whites hate and fear fundamentalists as much as the most anti-Semitic 1 percent hate and fear Jews. Louis Bolce and Gerald De Maio, "Our Secularist Democratic Party," *Public Interest* 149 (Fall 2002): 3–20.

5. A recent example: rational and cautious remarks suggesting some innate basis for the lesser representation of women in the sciences made at a closed academic conference by the president of Harvard University led to an outcry that even a pledge of $50 million to support gender diversity could not still. The controversy contributed to the president's subsequent resignation and to the appointment as his successor of the academic feminist whose committee's report had led to the $50 million pledge. Lawrence H. Summers, "Remarks at NBER Conference on Diversifying the Science & Engineering Workforce," January 14, 2005, http://www.president.harvard.edu/speeches/2005/nber.html (accessed December 6, 2007); Michael Dobbs, "Harvard Chief's Comments on Women Assailed: Academics Critical of Remarks About Lack of Gender Equality," *Washington Post*, January 19, 2005.

6. In Germany, "*Zivilcourage*" is now taken to include persecution by organized left-wing activists of a demonized and powerless Right.

7. Compare *United States v. Eichman*, 496 U.S. 310 (1990), which held that burning a flag is protected "speech," with the cases discussed in "This Wasn't Supposed to Happen Here," *Issues and Views* (April 21, 2003), in which teenagers were sentenced to long prison terms for burning a cross. http://www.issues-views.com/comment.php/article/21059 (accessed December 6, 2007). But see *Virginia v. Black, et. al.*, 538 U.S. 343 (2003), which held that an intent to intimidate must be proven to justify a prosecution for cross burning.

8. Alexander, *Illiberal Europe*, includes examples of criminal prosecutions and convictions for criticizing Islam.

9. Compare *United States v. Playboy Entertainment Group, Inc.*, 529 U.S. 803 (2000) and *Ashcroft v. Free Speech Coalition*, 535 US 234 (2002), which held respectively that sexually explicit cable

TV and virtual child pornography are constitutionally protected, with *McConnell v. Federal Election Commission*, 540 U.S. 93 (2003), which held that "issue ads" by nonparty groups mentioning federal candidates within sixty days of an election are not protected.

10. The Sexual Orientation Regulations recently adopted in Britain under the Equality Act forbid religious schools from teaching the Christian view that homosexual conduct is wrong. In Brazil, it is reported that proposed legislation would impose criminal penalties of up to five years in jail on those who so teach. *Zenit*, March 18, 2007, http://www.zenit.org/english/visualizza.phtml?sid=104735 (accessed December 6, 2007).

11. In The Episcopal Church, for example, the practical content of the faith has apparently become the United Nations Millennium Development Goals. See, e.g., the Investiture Sermon of Presiding Bishop Katharine Jefferts Schori, November 4, 2006, http://www.episcopalchurch.org/3577_79214_ENG_HTM.htm (accessed December 6, 2007). In some Episcopal churches, the traditional Stations of the Cross have been replaced by the Stations of the Millennium Development Goals.

12. For a discussion of the ideological aggressiveness of American foreign policy, see Claes G. Ryn, *America the Virtuous: Crisis of Democracy and the Quest for Empire* (New Brunswick, NJ: Transaction Publishers, 2003). Also see the response of the editors of the *New Republic* to the terrorist attacks of September 11, 2001: "Does anybody doubt that the crusade against globalization is to a significant degree a crusade against the proliferation of American values and American practices around the world? . . . Anybody who hates modernity hates America. Anybody who hates freedom hates America. Anybody who hates privacy hates America. Anybody who hates human rights hates America. Anybody who hates ballots and bookshops and newspapers and televisions and computers and theaters and bars and the sight of a woman smiling at a man hates America. Osama bin Laden and the terrorists of Al Qaeda chose the United States as their target in perfect accordance with their beliefs." "It Happened Here," *New Republic* (September 24, 2001): 10–12, 10–11. Ideological aggression can of course be carried on through international assistance and human-rights conventions as well as through military action.

13. As one critic comments, under liberalism, "life is the joyless quest for joy." Strauss, *Natural Right and History*, 251.

14. For a general summary of social trends, see William J. Bennett, *The Index of Leading Cultural Indicators: American Society at the End of the 20th Century*, rev. and expanded edition (New York: Broadway Books, 1999). For imprisonment among young black men, see Brett V. Brown, Kristin A. Moore, and Sharon Bzostek, "A Statistical Portrait of Well-being in Early Adulthood," *CrossCurrents*. Issue 2, August 2004. http://www.childtrendsdatabank.org/PDF/Young%20Adults%20Brief.pdf (accessed December 6, 2007).

Chapter Five: Are Objections to Liberalism Overstated?

1. For a description of the process and its results, see the Gottfried trilogy: *After Liberalism, Multiculturalism and the Politics of Guilt*, and *The Strange Death of Marxism*.

2. See Rawls, *Political Liberalism*.

3. International human-rights treaties make such pressure a requirement of international law. For example, the Convention on the Elimination of All Forms of Discrimination against Women, Art. 5, states: "States Parties shall take all appropriate measures . . . to modify the social and cultural patterns of conduct of men and women, with a view to achieving the elimination of . . . customary and all other practices which are based on the idea of . . . stereotyped roles for men and women."

4. "We tolerate monomaniacs, it is our habit to do so; but why should we be ruled by them?" Michael Oakeshott, "On Being Conservative," *Rationalism in Politics and Other Essays* (Indianapolis: Liberty Fund, 1991): 407–37, 428.

5. For a discussion of free speech by a prominent academic thinker that suggests the instability of the notion, see Stanley Fish, *There's No Such Thing as Free Speech: And It's a Good Thing, Too* (New York: Oxford University Press, 1994).

6. See *Doe v. University of Michigan*, 721 F. Supp. 852 (E.D. Mich. 1989), in which the court invalidated a school harassment policy under which university authorities had proceeded against a graduate student for expressing the view that homosexuality could be cured by counseling.

7. See, for example, *Lochner v. New York*, 198 U.S. 45 (1905), in which it was held that a New York law establishing a maximum sixty-hour workweek for bakery employees was a violation of freedom of contract.

8. For a very moderate view of the state of legal reasoning in the United States, see Mary Ann Glendon, *A Nation Under Lawyers: How the Crisis in the Legal Profession is Transforming American Society* (New York: Farrar, Straus and Giroux, 1994).

9. See Emily Bazelon, "What Would Zimbabwe Do?" *Atlantic Monthly* (November 2005): 48–52.

10. One study of well-being data for 100,000 randomly chosen Americans and Britons from the early 1970s to the late 1990s found that men's reported happiness has increased over that period but women's has diminished substantially, so much so as to push down overall happiness levels. David Blanchflower and Andrew Oswald, "Well-Being Over Time in Britain and the USA," NBER Working Paper No. 7487 (January 2000). For an account of two not-yet-published papers confirming the trend, see David Leonhardt, "Economic Scene: He's Happier, She's Less So," *New York Times*, September 26, 2007. Also see Bradford Wilcox, *Soft Patriarchs, New Men: How Christianity Shapes Fathers and Husbands* (Chicago: University of Chicago Press, 2004), showing that married men with children active in conservative Protestant churches do less household labor, are more likely than other fathers to use corporal punishment, and affirm the importance of male headship. They are also the most active and emotionally engaged group of fathers and husbands, and therefore, it appears, the group most satisfactory to their wives and children. See W. Bradford Wilcox and Steven L. Nock, "What's Love Got To Do With It? Equality, Equity, Commitment and Women's Marital Quality," *Social Forces*, 84:6 (March 2006): 1321–45, http://www.virginia.edu/sociology/peopleofsociology/wilcoxpapers/Wilcox%20Nock%20marriage.pdf (accessed December 6, 2007), which confirmed that what is most important for women's happiness

in marriage is men's "emotion work"—attentiveness, consideration, and willingness to make an effort—which in turn is tied to commitment to marriage as an institution and acceptance of traditional gender roles.

11. "The basic facts of black economic progress are well known. Since 1940, black wages and occupational status have improved, approaching the higher levels that whites enjoy. Beginning in 1965, the rate of improvement in black relative wages and occupational status accelerated. However, since 1975, relative black economic status has not advanced and may have deteriorated slightly." James J. Heckman and Brook S. Payner, "Determining the Impact of Federal Antidisrimination Policy on the Economic Status of Blacks: A Study of South Carolina," *American Economic Review* 79 (1989): 138–77, 143, quoted in Richard Epstein, *Forbidden Grounds: The Case Against Employment Discrimination Laws* (Cambridge, MA: Harvard University Press, 1992), 243. Figures on the percentages of black and white families in poverty fill out the picture to some degree: in 1966, those percentages were 35.5 and 9.3. By 1974, they had fallen to 26.9 and 6.8, by 1993 they had risen to 31.3 and 9.4, and by 1999 they had fallen again to 21.9 and 7.3. Throughout these periods, black families have been three to four times as likely as white families to live in poverty. *Historical Statistics of the United States*, Millennial Edition, v. 2 (New York: Cambridge University Press, 2006), Table Be283–309.

12. For example, in 1970, 35.8 percent of all prison inmates were black. In 2000, it was 46.3 percent of a much larger number. Andrew Hacker, *Two Nations: Black and White, Separate, Hostile, Unequal* (New York: Scribner, 2003), 224. In 1960, 24.4 percent of black households were headed by women, in 1970, 34.5 percent, and by 2000, 53.5 percent. Ibid., 89. In 1960, 11.5 percent of the women who headed such households had never been married, by 2000 it was 64.8 percent. Ibid., 96.

13. See Ellis Cose, *The Rage of a Privileged Class* (New York: HarperCollins, 1994).

14. The publication *Issues & Views*, formerly a print newsletter and now available online at http://www.issues-views.com (accessed December 6, 2007), explores these issues from a black perspective. The section "When We Were Colored," http://www.issues-views.com/index.php/sect/1000 (accessed December 6, 2007), is especially helpful on the self-sustaining black progress achieved before the sixties.

15. See Ariel Levy, *Female Chauvinist Pigs: Women and the Rise of Raunch Culture* (New York: Free Press, 2006), for an anecdotal account of the hypersexualization of young women by someone who considers herself a liberal and a feminist, and who finds the phenomenon male-centered and mindlessly stereotypical. She believes freedom and power are the highest goods, for women as for men, but notes that acting like a porn star is not the way to get either. Also see Carol Platt Liebau, *Prude: How the Sex-Obsessed Culture Damages Girls (and America, Too!)* (Nashville: Center Street, 2007).

16. See Jean M. Twenge, *Generation Me: Why Today's Young Americans Are More Confident, Assertive, Entitled—and More Miserable Than Ever Before* (New York: Free Press, 2006), for a discussion of the changing attitudes and habits of young people over the generations as revealed by personality tests.

Also see Kay S. Hymowitz, *Liberation's Children: Parents and Kids in a Postmodern Age* (Chicago: Ivan R. Dee, 2003).

17. The abolition of slavery is another reform that is often thought to provide a crushing objection to any traditionalist view. Still, it is not obvious what was specifically traditionalist about a "peculiar institution" found in a small part of Western society that people at the time considered odd and in need of a special explanation, that denied the network of mutual obligation which is the essence of traditional social relations, and that came back in a far more brutal form and on a far larger scale among twentieth-century antitraditional regimes.

18. America is less middle class than it once was. As a result, our time is notable for distinctions of wealth; emphasis on status markers like academic credentials, consumption choices, and ideological posturing; and rancor.

19. For an anecdotal account of what life has become for many people in Britain, see Theodore Dalrymple, *Life at the Bottom: The Worldview that Makes the Underclass* (Chicago: Ivan R. Dee, 2001). The author blames the misery and degradation of the British underclass, and the spread of underclass habits and attitudes to once-respectable layers of society, primarily on liberal elite attitudes propagated through the whole of society. He develops such ideas further in *Our Culture, What's Left of It: The Mandarins and the Masses* (Chicago: Ivan R. Dee, 2005).

20. It is for that reason that liberal society has created its equivalent of the crime of blasphemy in the form of laws against Holocaust revisionism and other crimes of speech and thought. Such actions are crimes in much of the West because they attack common understandings viewed as basic to the established order. As Joschka Fischer has said, "Auschwitz is the founding myth and moral justification of a continued German nation-state." Gottfried, *The Strange Death of Marxism*, 81. For European laws and rulings on the subject, see, e.g., Alexander, *Illiberal Europe*.

21. Raphael Lemkin, *Axis Rule in Occupied Europe* (Washington, DC: Carnegie Endowment for International Peace, 1944), 79.

22. For example, discrimination and the stubbornly ingrained ignorance and malice of ordinary people are the generally accepted explanations for group differences in achievement. Those explanations are wrong, and they have obviously bad political effects (unless the transfer of power from the people to experts and managers is the highest political good), but alternatives cannot be seriously discussed publicly.

Chapter Six: Irrationality and Self-Destruction

1. Particular scientists may try to go beyond such limits, but when they do so—by proposing materialism as a true metaphysical principle, for example—they lose their authority as scientists.

2. Rawls, *A Theory of Justice*.

3. The "Wars of Religion" might also be called the "Wars of the Rise of the Modern State." The Protestant reformers would have gotten nowhere without the backing of ambitious princes who wanted to assert their own independence. The Thirty Years War featured Catholic France in alli-

ance with Lutheran Sweden. For a discussion of the general issue, see William Cavanaugh, "'A Fire Strong Enough to Consume the House': The Wars of Religion and the Rise of the State," *Modern Theology* 11: 4 (October 1995): 397–420.

Chapter Seven: Blind Alleys

1. A parallel case is provided by art, in which a cult of creativity resulting from loss of confidence in goods that transcend the artist began with manifestos and provocations but has ended in art that is boring, imitative, empty of content, obsessed with technique, and dominated by the same forces that dominate liberal society—money, success, bureaucratic maneuvering, and the politics of mindless aggression and rebellion.

2. Roger Scruton, "Decencies for Skeptics," *City Journal* (Spring 1996): 43–49.

3. It is not clear why, if piety and tradition end up in possession, they would not reorder human belief in favor of some transcendent object of faith understood as objectively absolute. Is skepticism even possible except as a rhetorical maneuver or as academic theory?

4. *Zorach v. Clauson*, 343 US 306, 313 (1952).

5. The quotation appears in a number of forms, and I have been unable to find its source. Buckley did not appear to deny saying it.

6. See David Kuo, *Tempting Faith: An Inside Story of Political Seduction* (New York: Free Press, 2006), for a recent insider's account of the manipulative attitude of Republican politicians toward Christian voters and the seduction of politically active Christians by partisan politics.

7. Examples include the effect of media treatment of the 1964 Goldwater campaign and of Patrick Buchanan after his surprise victory in the 1996 New Hampshire primary.

8. 539 US 306 (2003).

9. 539 US 558 (2003).

10. 505 U.S. 833 (1992). *Gonzales v. Carhart*, 127 S. Ct. 1610 (2007), upheld a congressional ban on partial-birth abortion, in which the victim is almost entirely born before being killed. This indicates a possible boundary for abortion rights. It was a 5–4 decision, however, and Justice Kennedy's concurring opinion indicated that little would be necessary to make him go the other way on similar issues.

11. Gottfried so argues in *After Liberalism* and *Multiculturalism and the Politics of Guilt*. He includes accounts of populist movements on which I draw for my own discussion.

12. A symposium on "The End of Democracy? The Judicial Usurpation of Politics," published in the November 1996 issue of *First Things* (a predominantly Catholic publication) with the participation of such respected figures as Robert H. Bork, Russell Hittinger, Hadley Arkes, and Robert P. George, was thought to raise the spectre of violent social disorder and theocracy and led to the resignation of Gertrude Himmelfarb, Peter Berger, and Walter Berns from the editorial board. The apparent objection was that participants in the symposium treated their loyalty to the political order actually established in the United States, as that order might exist from time to time, as subordinate to other loyalties and therefore contingent.

13. See Russell Kirk, *The Conservative Mind, from Burke to Santayana* (Chicago: Henry Regnery Company, 1953).

14. See Twelve Southerners, *I'll Take my Stand: The South and the Agrarian Tradition* (New York: Harper & Brothers, 1930).

15. See David Gelernter, "Americanism—and Its Enemies," *Commentary* (January 2005): 41–48.

Chapter Eight: Putting It Back Together

1. Scientists are not always aware of their situation. When they venture beyond their narrow specialties into larger practical and theoretical issues, as when they talk about politics or religion, what they say is often ill-advised and overconfident. The habit of striving for impersonality leads them to exclude too much for well-founded decisions to be possible. In their area of specialization the density of expertise provides a corrective. In the absence of that corrective they often become quite uncritical when they feel called upon to say something.

2. Among mathematicians, the latter relationship is formalized as one's Erdős number. Someone who coauthored a paper with the late Hungarian mathematician Paul Erdős has an Erdős number of 1, someone who coauthored a paper with someone with an Erdős number of 1 has an Erdős number of 2, and so on.

3. See Confucius (e.g., *Analects*, Bk. v, ch. 18) and Plato (the myth of the cave, *Republic*, Bk. vii) on the Good, the *Tao Te Ching*, and Paul's "through a glass darkly" (I Corinthians 13:12). Arthur Waley, trans., *The Analects of Confucius* (New York: Vintage Books, 1989), 111–112; Allan Bloom, trans., *The Republic of Plato* (New York: Basic Books, 1968), 193 ff.; Lao Tzu, *Tao Te Ching*, trans. D. C. Lau, (London: Penguin Books, 1963).

4. My definition is more favorable than others that have been offered, for example Jaroslav Pelikan's "Tradition is the living faith of the dead; traditionalism is the dead faith of the living." Jaroslav Pelikan, *The Christian Tradition: A History of the Development of Doctrine* (Chicago: University of Chicago Press, 1989), 9. In response to Pelikan, it is worth noting that a faith adequate to reality and worth living by is a faith we fall short of and do not fully possess. It is therefore one that (for us) is partly dead. We need traditionalism to keep what we lack present and available.

5. Blaise Pascal, *Pensees* (London: Penguin Books, 1995), 181–83.

6. John Henry Newman, *An Essay in Aid of a Grammar of Assent*, ch. ix (New York: The Catholic Publication Society, 1870): 330–72.

7. The principle is applied somewhat opportunistically, since the rightness of sexual attraction to those of the same sex is routinely supported by claims that those who experience and habitually act on such an attraction have a different essential identity than other people.

8. What immediately follows will concentrate on freedom rather than reason, but similar points apply to reason, and will be touched on in the next chapter on faith and authority.

9. Cf. Article 29 (3) of the Universal Declaration of Human Rights: "These rights and freedoms may in no case be exercised contrary to the purposes and principles of the United Nations." UN

General Assembly, Third Session, *Universal Declaration of Human Rights*, G.A. res. 217A (III), U.N. Doc A/810 at 71 (1948).

10. In the EU, human-rights principles require that a man who identifies himself as a woman and has been subjected to surgery and drugs that give him superficially feminine characteristics have the right to have his birth certificate changed to reflect the sex he claims to have chosen.

11. That seems to be happening. Robert D. Putnam's recent research shows that diversity means less trust and less social capital. His solution to the problem is the managed reconstruction of individual and social identity. Robert D. Putnam, "E Pluribus Unum: Diversity and Community in the Twenty-first Century," *Scandinavian Political Studies* 30:2 (June 2007). 137–74. Also see Peter Berger, "On the Obsolescence of Honor," *European Journal of Sociology* 11 (1970): 339–47; reprinted in Peter Berger, Brigette Berger, and Hansfried Kellner, *The Homeless Mind: Modernization and Consciousness* (New York: Vintage, 1974).

12. Some harbor such an aspiration. The young Karl Marx foresaw the day when alienation would be abolished "in communist society, where nobody has one exclusive sphere of activity but each can become accomplished in any branch he wishes, society regulates the general production and thus makes it possible for me to do one thing today and another tomorrow, to hunt in the morning, fish in the afternoon, rear cattle in the evening, criticise after dinner, just as I have a mind, without ever becoming hunter, fisherman, herdsman or critic." Karl Marx, *The German Ideology: Part I* (1846), in Robert C. Tucker, ed., *The Marx-Engels Reader* (New York: W. W. Norton, 1972): 110–64, 124.

13. Cartoon by Peter Steiner, *New Yorker* (July 5, 1993), 61.

14. Indeed, it is rather difficult to show that antidiscrimination laws have benefited blacks on the whole except to the extent that their initial application helped get rid of a system of state-mandated discrimination formerly found in some places but now no longer existent. Epstein, *Forbidden Grounds*, chapter 12.

15. For a discussion of the consequences of depriving young people of such traditions, see Kay S. Hymowitz, *Liberation's Children: Parents and Kids in a Postmodern Age* (Chicago: Ivan R. Dee, 2003).

Chapter Nine: Faith and Authority

1. Hebrews 11:1.

2. Compare Rawls's point in *Political Liberalism* that pluralism is the natural result of free democratic institutions. It is hard to understand, taking Rawls's view, how a liberal could reasonably accept even his own beliefs. Other beliefs are no less reasonable, and there is no objective way to decide among them, so all particular belief becomes arbitrary. To view one's own belief as arbitrary, however, is to reject it as belief. Why not go beyond Rawls to Samuel Beckett? Can self-satisfaction—I believe it because it is *my* belief—really be an adequate epistemology?

3. I should point out that my use of arguments for certain religious positions that are based on the social function rather than the truth of those positions reflects a desire to maintain the focus and

limit the scope of this book. It does not reflect a belief that the positions are not true or that those are rationally the best arguments available.

4. Cf. David Cosandey, *Le Secret de l'Occident* (Paris: Arléa, 1997).

5. For a reflective survey of cultural accomplishment that touches on the need for cultural coherence and transcendent goods, see Charles Murray, *Human Accomplishment: The Pursuit of Excellence in the Arts and Sciences, 800 B.C. to 1950* (New York: HarperCollins, 2003).

Chapter Ten: Bringing It All Back Home

1. Recent war monuments have to do with suffering or presence at an event rather than with a heroism that no longer makes public sense.

2. That is true even in the case of professed conservatives: "Burke brought home to me that our most necessary beliefs may be both unjustified and unjustifiable from our own perspective, and that the attempt to justify them will lead merely to their loss. . . . The real justification for a prejudice is the one which justifies it as a prejudice, rather than as a rational conclusion of an argument. In other words it is a justification that cannot be conducted from our own perspective, but only from outside, as it were, as an anthropologist might justify the customs and rituals of an alien tribe." Roger Scruton, "Why I Became a Conservative," *New Criterion* (February 2003): 4–12, 9.

3. Even the titles of publications betray a recognition that fear lies at the basis of liberalism. See Shklar, "The Liberalism of Fear," and Jacob T. Levy, *The Multiculturalism of Fear* (New York: Oxford University Press, 2000).

4. "What matters at this stage is the construction of local forms of community within which civility and the intellectual and moral life can be sustained through the new dark ages which are already upon us. And if the tradition of the virtues was able to survive the horrors of the last dark ages, we are not entirely without grounds for hope. This time however the barbarians are not waiting beyond the frontiers; they have already been governing us for quite some time. And it is our lack of consciousness of this that constitutes part of our predicament. We are waiting not for a Godot, but for another—doubtless very different—St. Benedict." Alasdair MacIntyre, *After Virtue*, 2nd ed. (Notre Dame, Indiana: University of Notre Dame Press, 1984), 263.

5. Compulsory celebration of diversity that includes sexual diversity would be an example.

6. There could be no guarantee of ultimate equality among them, however, a circumstance that would limit the degree to which they could pursue a common cause. While federalism, limited government, and a principle of moderation and prudence would allow for a great deal of diversity, an attempt to give all traditions guaranteed equal standing in a single political society would make diversity an absolute and re-create bureaucratic multiculturalism.

7. For a discussion of the effects of redefining marriage as a personal relationship between two adults rather than as a multigenerational social institution, see Kay S. Hymowitz, *Marriage and Caste in America: Separate and Unequal Families in a Post-Marital Age* (Chicago: Ivan R. Dee, 2006).

8. See Thomas Byrne Edsall, "Blue Movie: The 'Morality Gap' Is Becoming the Key Variable in American Politics," *Atlantic Monthly* (January 2003): 36–37.

9. Dennis Cauchon, "Marriage Gap Could Sway Elections," *USA Today*, September 27, 2006, http://www.usatoday.com/news/washington/2006-09-26-marriage-gap_x.htm (accessed December 6, 2007).

10. Republicans, whose liberalism is generally less advanced, report substantially more happiness and better mental health than Democrats. Lydia Saad, "A Nation of Happy People," *Gallup*, January 5, 2004, http://www.gallup.com/poll/10090/Nation-Happy-People.aspx (accessed December 13, 2007); Frank Newport, "Republicans Report Much Better Mental Health Than Others: Relationship Persists Even When Controlling for Other Variables," *Gallup*, http://www.gallup.com/poll/102943/Republicans-Report-Much-Better-Mental-Health-Than-Others.aspx (accessed November 30, 2007).

11. See John Stuart Mill, *On Liberty* (Millis, MA: Agora Publications, 2003), 68, 99.

12. Such a conversation will of course require talking points. The need for snappy arguments is especially acute for those who are supported by neither institutional expertise nor a grand theory like libertarianism that answers all questions immediately. Here are some initial talking points for traditionalist use against liberalism:

- If liberalism is tolerant, why all the propaganda and reeducation programs?
- If it is based on consent, why the emphasis on judges, experts, bureaucrats, and theorists?
- If it is skeptical and empirical, why the demand for radical transformation of all social arrangements everywhere?
- If liberalism emphasizes the individual and unleashes creativity, why does it make everyone and everything the same?
- If liberalism lets people choose their own values, how can it prescribe their opinions of others' values?
- If choosing my own values is good, why does it become bad if I choose cultural cohesion and traditional sex roles?
- How can "diversity" (respecting differences) and "inclusiveness" (destroying the effect of differences) be the same?
- Equal celebration of cultures means that every particular cultural standard must be driven out of social life, since otherwise one culture will dominate others. How is that situation different from the abolition of culture?
- What is the difference between saying someone has to treat all beliefs about God and morality as equally worthy, and saying he has to treat his own beliefs as personal tastes and thus not beliefs about God or morality at all?
- How can government be based on discussion as opposed to force when the point of government is that discussion sometimes does not work and force is needed?

- What can freedom in private life amount to if government claims the right to insist on the radical reform of family life and reeducation of children? If the freedom of private life does not include the closest human relationships, what good is it?

- Liberals say that the public celebration of diversity does not violate conscience because in private people can still think what they like. Would it equally respect conscience if the pope ran things and insisted on the public celebration of Catholicism while permitting private free thought?

- People value different things in themselves and others. Some value the ability to form and carry through personal life projects, others participation in group goals, others the pursuit of human excellence, others the love of God. When those views come into conflict, why is it neutral if the first view always wins?

Chapter Eleven: Looking Forward

1. See Gottfried, *After Liberalism*, 126–28.

2. See Phillip Longman, "The Global Baby Bust," *Foreign Affairs* 83:3 (May/June 2004): 64–79, 76–77: "Does this mean that the future belongs to those who believe they are (or who are in fact) commanded by a higher power to procreate? Based on current trends, the answer appears to be yes."

Index

abortion, 37, 303n10
Adorno, Theodor, 52
affirmative action, 19–20, 49, 67, 297n24
alienation, 305n12
American compromise, 164–67
American conservatism, 163–69, 185–87. See also conservatism
American Dream, 165
American identity, 70
American Revolution, 16, 164
Anselm, Saint, 233
anti-abortionists, 88–89
anti-bigotry, 68–75
anti-discrimination efforts and laws: black Americans and, 305n13; liberalism and, 63–68; purpose and consequences of, 229–30; restricting, 273

anti-racism, 69–70
art, 303n1
Ashcroft v. Free Speech Coalition, 298–99n9
authority: liberalism and, 93–94; religion and the church, 244–45, 250; in a traditionalist society, 273; tradition and, 211–12, 256–57

bigotry, 68–75, 296–97n24
black Americans: antidiscrimination laws and, 305n13; civil-rights revolution and, 122–23; economic progress, 301n11; incarceration figures, 301n12; liberalism and, 125; stereotypes and, 224, 225–26
Blair, Tony, 292n6

Kirk, Russell, 185
knowledge: faith and, 234–36; moral,
139–40; naturalized, 234–36

language: inclusive, 67–68; tradition
and, 237
Lawrence v. Texas, 171
Left, 154–55, 158–59
leftism, 154–55
legal principles, 78
Lewis, Anthony, 88–89, 297n2
liberal guilt, 21
liberal identity, 100–102
liberal institutions: abolition of politics
and, 46; characteristic ones, 45; democracy and, 46–51; global capitalism,
57–60; hierarchy of, 46; human rights,
60–62; role and purpose of, 45–46;
scientism and tolerance, 51–53; tolerance and social control, 53–56
liberalism: anti-bigotry position, 68–75;
belief in the end of history, 13; censor-
ship as freedom, 90–92; church-state
separation and, 252–53; classic compromise with conservatism, 164–67;
comparison with other regimes, 75–81;
compulsory conformity and, 78; conservative response to, 184–85; constitutionalism and, 170–71; continuities
of principle, 23; critique of, 3–12; cultural coherence and, 295n11; denial
of human nature, 132; discrimination
and, 63–68; disestablishment of, 269–
70; dissidence and, 79–80; the end of,
285–89; equal freedom and, 14–15,
21–23; erosion and self-demolition

of, 142–50; force and, 76–77; forced
consent and, 87–90; free speech and,
116–19; fundamental contradictions,
102–3; goals of, 18–20, 127; the good
and, 39–40, 137–38; hedonism and,
138–42; historical development, 16–
18; implications of, 126–32; individualism and, 97–102; insufficiency of,
133–42; intellectual life and, 78–79;
irrationalism and, 40–44, 155–56;
justice and, 157–59; leftism and, 154–
55; libertarianism and, 177–81; as
limited, 110–19; managerial, 23–24;
meaning of, 14–15; moral progress
and, 119–20; moral rationality and
goodness, 39–40; neoconservatism
and, 172–77; neutrality and, 84–87,
134; persecution and, 96–97; phases
of, 105–6; populism and, 181–82;
power and, 24–29, 80; proceduralism
and, 75; promotion of social goods,
75–76; radicalization, 114–16; rationality and reason, 30–40, 189–96;
religious conservatism and, 182–84;
restraining principles, 116–19; scientism and, 135–37; as secularized
and rationalized Christianity, 40; as
secular theocracy, 92–97; significance
of understanding conceptually, 106–
10; simple conservatism and, 159–63;
the sixties and, 166; social justice and,
120–23; subjectivism and, 35–39;
supposed benefits of, 119–23; talking
points against, 307–8n12; tolerance
and, 123–26, 134; tradition and, 161;
transformations within, 20–24; transparency and, 77; tyranny and, 128–31,

About the Author

James Kalb, who holds degrees from Dartmouth College and Yale University, is a lawyer and independent scholar whose reviews and essays on political thought have appeared in various journals in the United States and Europe, including *Modern Age* and *Telos*. He lives and works in Brooklyn, New York.